Palgrave Studies of Entrepreneurship and Social Challenges in Developing Economies

Series Editor
Rajagopal, EGADE Business School, Tecnológico de Monterrey, Mexico City, Mexico

This series explores the role of entrepreneurship in managing social challenges comprising poverty, gender inequality, sustainability and climate change, income disparity, social healthcare, community housing and homelessness, and clean food and water supplies across Asia, Africa, and Latin America.

Entrepreneurship in developing countries has an economic motivation and it is taken up as a survival occupation. The books in this series discuss various attributes of social enterprises, innovation, technology, and the role of leadership in meeting the recurring social challenges. The discussion on entrepreneurship in this book series is central to social entrepreneurship, family enterprises, entrepreneurial business models, disruptive innovation, consumer behavior, marketing-mix, branding, profit and performance, market expansion, new product development, operations and supply chain, manufacturing, and servitization. In addition, the volumes in this book series also address the PESTEL (political, economic, social, technological, environmental, and legal) perspectives that support socio-economic development.

Arturo Molina · Rajagopal

Challenge-Based Learning, Research, and Innovation

Leveraging Industry, Government, and Society

palgrave
macmillan

Arturo Molina
Institute of Advanced Materials for Sustainable Manufacturing
Tecnologico de Monterrey
Monterrey, Mexico

Rajagopal
EGADE Business School,
Tecnologico de Monterrey
Mexico City, Mexico

ISSN 2731-6874 ISSN 2731-6882 (electronic)
Palgrave Studies of Entrepreneurship and Social Challenges in Developing Economies
ISBN 978-3-031-29155-5 ISBN 978-3-031-29156-2 (eBook)
https://doi.org/10.1007/978-3-031-29156-2

Cover illustration: Maram_shutterstock.com

This Palgrave Macmillan imprint is published by the registered company Springer Nature Switzerland AG
The registered company address is: Gewerbestrasse 11, 6330 Cham, Switzerland

To my wife Silvia, daughter Monse, and son Julio
—Arturo Molina

To my wife Arati and grandchildren Akhilesh and Niharika
—Rajagopal

Preface

Challenge-based research is used in product innovation and design of equipment. The higher education on engineering and technology has significantly contributed to providing basic and managerial education to stakeholders which helps in exploring right opportunities. While coevolving with academics and stakeholders, firms can identify appropriate technologies, carry out innovations, and prepare for effective technology transfer through training programs on face-to-face and digital platforms. Such integrated efforts leverage the social and industrial consciousness for developing new products in renewable energy, sustainability, and meeting the social challenges like poverty alleviation, housing, and community health. The technological revolution has driven the digital transformation as firms are engaged in co-creating value in industrial markets. Among the many forms of technology development, digital technologies have encouraged artificial intelligence which has the strongest pervasive impact.[1] Challenge-based research is a systematic journey to explore solutions for social and industrial problems. The futuristic outlook of the industry in the context of society and sustainability may be towards achieving net-zero carbon economy in a net-zero industry with net-zero products, services, processes, and production systems. To achieve these goals, the challenges at the foreground include obtaining solutions to green energy,

[1] Robertson, D. and Hjuler, P. (2009). Innovating a Turnaround at LEGO. *Harvard Business Review*, 87(9), 20–21.

water conservation, zero-emission, waste reduction to zero level, and managing cradle-to-cradle approach in product designing and resource utilization. The cradle-to-cradle philosophy addresses positive ecological impacts in the built environment.[2]

In the context of above discussion, most developing nations have promulgated comprehensive public policies to streamline corporate governance on implementation of sustainability-driven business model in all industries. Public policies are focusing on macro-economic disruption due to sustainability issues in developing economies.[3] Therefore, large companies are developing alliances with local governments on public-private partnerships (PPP) in implementing sustainability norms and enhancing social value. The PPP initiatives in various geo-demographic sectors have generated social awareness among people and inculcated environmentally conscious consumption in society. Environmentally conscious consumption is one of the key concerns in modern society, and it is increasingly affecting urban consumers. Most research studies on environmentally conscious consumption suggest that the purchase intention is driven by intrinsic factors such as demographics comprising income, education and social status, consumer cognition, and personality attributes.[4] In addition, external factors and social influences also affect an individual's environmental consumption behavior.[5]

This book has been divided into three parts and spread across nine chapters. The Part-I of the book on Social Perspectives includes three chapters on social challenges in developing economies focusing on convergence of research and industry (Chapter 1), discussing the triple bottom line in the context of people, planet, and profit (Chapter 2), and sensitizing entrepreneurship by managing growth touchpoints (Chapter 3). Part-I of the book presents thematic convergence as it addresses multilayered themes on social challenges, the triple bottom line,

[2] Ankrah, N. A., Manu, E., & Booth, C. (2015). Cradle to Cradle Implementation in Business Sites and the Perspectives of Tenant Stakeholders. *Energy Procedia*, 83, 31–40.

[3] Béal, V. (2015). Selective public policies: sustainability and neoliberal urban restructuring. *Environment and Urbanization*, 27(1), 303–316.

[4] Tsarenko, Y., Ferraro, C., Sands, S., and McLeod, C. (2013). Environmentally conscious consumption: The role of retailers and peers as external influences. *Journal of Retailing and Consumer Services*, 20 (3), 302–310.

[5] Rajagopal (2020). Sustainable Businesses in Developing Economies - Socio-Economic and Governance Perspectives. New York: Palgrave Macmillan.

and entrepreneurship as a driver for research, learning, and innovation. The challenge-based research that constitutes the Part-II of the book integrates thematic discussion on foundations, functionality, and future perspectives of challenge-based research (Chapter 4), rising arguments on the social well-being by linking research output with the business (Chapter 5), and ways to foster institutional roles, relationship, and responsiveness in diffusing innovation and technology (Chapter 6). The chapters in this part of the book put forth arguments on blending research with social and industrial development in emerging markets; in addition, thematic discussions on economics, transferability, and consumerism in the context of research-based innovation (Chapter 7). The discussion on design, development, and diffusion of technology (Chapter 8) constitutes Part-III of this book. The synthesis of discussion on social challenges, applied research, institutional role, innovation, and technology as offered in the different parts of the book is summed up in Chapter 9 by bridging concepts and practices leading to shaping the future of society and industry. The interrelationship between the topical discussion across chapters reveals that all key topics of the book as discussed above are aligned linearly to facilitate reading without logical and cognitive interruptions. Agility in business has evolved as a built-in concept among the customer-centric companies, which tend to better understand consumer behavior including neurobehavioral perspectives (in-store and online shopping practices) to develop approaches to stay customized, applied, and transformative in the market.[6]

One of the major concerns with challenge-based research is to effectively manage the transfer of technology to industry and end users of innovation. Transferring the product and processes technology in accordance with the market demand and inculcating user experiences are complex. Knowledge transfer on innovation and technology explored through the challenge-based research is largely based on the exchange of individuals' experiences and work-related knowledge of the research team.[7] This book categorically reviews the theories on business agility,

[6] Morgan, R.E. & Page, K. (2008), Managing business transformation to deliver strategic agility. *Strategic Change*, 17, 155–168.

[7] Ibidunni, A. S., Kolawole, A. I., Olokundun, M. A., & Ogbari, M. E. (2020). Knowledge transfer and innovation performance of small and medium enterprises (SMEs): An informal economy analysis. *Heliyon*, 6 (8), (in press). https://doi.org/10.1016/j.heliyon.2020.e04740

consumer behavior, social intervention, collective intelligence, decision-making, and stakeholder values. It also examines previous research and analyzes the strategic and tactical stewardship of firms in managing neurobehavioral responses of consumers and designing agile business models. The book discusses new strategies suitable to co-create agile business models in association with the market players and consumers for the companies in emerging markets. This book significantly contributes to the existing literature and serves as a learning post and a think tank for students, researchers, and business managers.

Some of our research contributions on challenge-based research, sustainability, and entrepreneurship in the emerging markets have been published in the international refereed outlets, which have driven new insights on the subject. Refining some concepts and management practices from our previous research experience has been presented in the book with applied illustrations and updated literature review on social entrepreneurship, innovation, technology, and socio-economic development. The principal audience of this book are working managers, and students of undergraduate and graduate management studies, research scholars, and academics in different entrepreneurship, sustainability, and ecological engineering disciplines with focus on social development. This book has been developed also to serve as a research reference to the undergraduate and graduate students who are pursuing studies in managing people, agile marketing, brand socialization, corporate governance, and new generation development studies. Besides serving as principal reading in undergraduate and graduate programs, this book would also inspire working managers, social analysts, and development consultants to explore various socio-economic and developmental solutions at the grassroots.

Mexico City, Mexico
January 2023

Arturo Molina
Rajagopal

Acknowledgements

Challenge-based research is a growing discipline and evolving from its nascent state. This subject has enveloped various faculties from engineering and sustainability to business and social well-being. The involvement of Tecnologico de Monterrey a largest private university system in Mexico and North America has been divulged in an in-house seminar by Arturo Molina, which triggered the idea to exhibit the concept and applications of challenge-based research in developing economies. Rajagopal has been teaching innovation management at the department of administrative sciences at Metropolitan College in Boston University since 2013, has driven me to connect to the obscure areas of challenge-based research and explore the social and sustainable innovations, which constituted the core discussions in this book.

The emerging storyboards on challenge-based research at the niche and macro-economic levels, have given many insights to me, which stayed central to this book. Rajagopal has also benefitted from the discussions of my colleagues within and outside the EGADE Business School and Boston University. He is thankful to Dr. Tanya Zlateva, Dean, Metropolitan College of Boston University, for giving him an opportunity to teach related subjects, which enabled him to apply the research output on sustainability-based business modeling in the classes. Discussions with Dr. Vladimir Zlatev, Associate Professor of Practice at Administrative Sciences Department, Metropolitan College, Boston University, have also benefitted the horizon of knowledge on the subject immensely. He has also benefitted by the thematic interactions of students and faculty of India campus of the University of the Fraser Valley, Canada. Rajagopal would like to acknowledge the support of Dr. Osmar Zavaleta, Interim Dean, EGADE Business School, and Dr. Claudia Quintanilla, Director, Marketing and Business Intelligence Department of EGADE Business School, who have always encouraged me to take up new challenges in teaching graduate courses, develop new insights, and contribute to the existing literature prolifically.

Arturo Molina wants to offer his sincerest gratitude to the team of the Vice-presidency of Research and Technology Transfer (Vicerrectoría de Investigación y Transferencia Tecnológica) of Tec de Monterrey for all these years supporting our activities of research, innovation, and technology transfer, especially all ideas that are included in this book. The team constituted with Paty Mora, Berenice Ramírez, Miguel Angel Romero, and Neil Hernández and Jorge Avendaño, who have been of great support. Also, Arturo Molina wants to express his sincere thanks to the researchers and students of the Tecnologico de Monterrey without whom all the projects and cases presented here would not have been successful.

Contents

About the Authors

Dr. Arturo Molina is currently Professor and Director of the Institute of Advanced Materials for Sustainable Manufacturing at Tecnologico de Monterrey, Mexico. He was Vice-Rector for Research and Technology Transfer, full Professor, Researcher, and Leader of the Strategic research group on Product Innovation. Dr. Molina received a Ph.D. in Manufacturing Engineering from the Loughborough University of Technology and a University Doctorate in Mechanical Engineering from the Technical University of Budapest. He received a Master of Science with specialization in Computer Science degree and Bachelor's degree in Computer Systems Engineer from Tec de Monterrey. He is the co-author of more than 150 scientific articles in journals, editor, and author of 14 books, inventor of three patents granted in Mexico and five patent applications in the process (four in Mexico and one in the USA). He is member of the National Researchers System of Mexico (SNI-Level III), Mexican Academy of Sciences, Mexican Engineering Academy, Mexican Academy of Computation. He also participates in international research networks, co-Chair in the Global Universities Network's Climate Change Global Challenge (WUN), Chair of Researcher Leader Group Engagement of Universitas 21 (U21), as Chair of the international federation for Information Processing (IFIP) WG 5.12 Architectures for Enterprise Integration. He is the founder and co-owner of a technology-based company: IECOS—Integration Engineering and Construction Systems (http://www.iecos.com/).

Dr. Rajagopal is Professor of Marketing at EGADE Business School of Tecnologico de Monterrey (ITESM), at Mexico City Campus and Fellow of the Royal Society for Encouragement of Arts, Manufacture and Commerce, London. He is also fellow of the Chartered Management Institute, and Fellow of Institute of Operations Management, United Kingdom. He is Visiting Professor at Boston University, Boston, Massachusetts since 2013. Dr. Rajagopal is also visiting professor since August 2020 at the UFV India Global Education of the University of the Fraser Valley, Canada, and teaches marketing related courses. He has been listed with biography in various international directories.

Dr. Rajagopal holds post-graduate and doctoral degrees in Economics and Marketing respectively from Pandit Ravishankar Shukla University in India. His specialization is in the field of Marketing Management. He has to his credit 71 books on marketing management and rural development themes and over 400 research contributions that include published research papers in national and international refereed journals. He is Editor-in-Chief of International Journal of Leisure and Tourism Marketing and International Journal of Business Competition and Growth. Dr. Rajagopal was Associate Editor of Emerald Emerging Markets Case Studies (2012–2019), published by Emerald Publishers, United Kingdom. He is on the editorial board of various journals of international repute. His research contributions have been recognized by the National Council of Science and Technology (CONACYT), Government of Mexico by awarding him the highest level of National Researcher-SNI Level III in 2013. He has been conferred the honor of Distinguished Professor by the EGADE Business School, Mexico in 2020.

Dr. Rajagopal has been conferred with the highest civilian award of Government of India in the field of Education in January 2023. The award is given to the citizens of India working at overseas destinations.

List of Figures

PART I

Social Perspectives

CHAPTER 1

Social Challenges in Developing Economies: Converging Research and Industrial Needs

Social entrepreneurial initiatives have been widely targeted towards meeting the social challenges. Government policies and enterprises of different sizes and competence have become a key area of interest exploring solutions to the social problems. Studies conducted in developed countries have shown that the crucial determinants in social development involve the contribution of explorative research mediated by industrial interventions, moral obligation, social-efficacy, and perceived social support.[1] This chapter discusses social ecosystem and the attributes of sectoral challenges in food production, poverty, housing, energy, water management, health, sustainability, digitalization, and other vulnerable problems. The possible research-based solutions to these problems in context of the changing needs and lifestyle of people have been discussed in this chapter links the contributions of industry and government. Discussions on public policies, governance, and corporate social responsibilities are also central to this chapter. Social behavior involves many processes including cognitive functions and collective decisions.

[1] Sousa-Filho, J. M., Matos, S. Trajano, S. S., & Lessa, B. S. (2020). Determinants of social entrepreneurial intentions in a developing country context. *Journal of Business Venturing Insights, 14*, Art. E00207 (in press). https://doi.org/10.1016/j.jbvi.2020.e00207.

A. Molina and Rajagopal, *Challenge-Based Learning, Research, and Innovation*, Palgrave Studies of Entrepreneurship and Social Challenges in Developing Economies,
https://doi.org/10.1007/978-3-031-29156-2_1

Poor social environment affects development and maturation of cognitive functions that are important for social cognition, possibly introducing social stress and vulnerability to stress. The socio-economic disruptions in economic recession and the current COVID-19 pandemic cause incidental social challenges and need systematic research to support social innovations for business continuity. Amidst the manufacturing and supply chain disruptions alongside widespread shutdowns, the consumer markets have been significantly affected. The demand for products has been bigger due to health emergency and business shutdowns during the current pandemic, which has significantly reduced the consumer spending and business investment.[2] Therefore, this chapter addresses the rationale, strategy, and benefit to connect research with industry contributions to find effective solutions for the social problems.[3]

Socio-demographic features in developing economies pose complex challenges for economic, social, and sustainable development. Growth in population and depletion in resources have mounting effects on the social and economic development, which demands institutional efforts to explore the socially embedded problems, needs, and solutions through the systematic challenge-based research process. Social challenges are driven by the changing needs in the farm- and non-farm sectors, transforming social requirements to maintain the quality of life, and contextual values. Social innovations often address social challenges in various development sectors such as public health, housing, natural resources management, farming activity, and domestic energy. Social organizations and government develop sustainable development models by critically examining the inputs of innovation subsystem and socio-economic resources. Innovation subsystem largely evolves within the geo-demographic niche and uses initially cost-effective local resources; and it later transforms to commercial propositions in alliance with large organization.[4]

[2] Sharma, P., Leung, T. Y., Kingshott, R. P. J., Davcik, N. S., & Cardinali, S. (2020). Managing uncertainty during a global pandemic: An international business perspective. *Journal of Business Research, 116*, 188–192.

[3] Sakurai, T. (2021). Social processes and social environment during development. *Seminars in Cell & Developmental Biology* (in press). https://doi.org/10.1016/j.semcdb.2021.09.016.

[4] Dionisio, M., & Raupp de Vargas, E. (2020). Corporate social innovation: A systematic literature review. *International Business Review, 29*(2), 1–10.

Social Challenges

Increasing urban expansion has contributed significantly to the depletion of natural resources, ecosystems, and the sustainability required to the human societies concerning the land use, water, and energy consumption. The productivity in the farm sector is largely affected using conventional management practices due to lack of accessibility to the technology and improved production and delivery of services. To meet the social challenges by controlling and minimizing such negative impacts of urbanization, best practices for sustainable urban development must be identified, supported, and reinforced. Collaborative efforts by academics, urban planners, and other relevant actors in this context also help in managing social challenges through challenge-based research. However, such efforts across the institutions require to design and implement relevant methods and tools for testing and projecting scenarios of social-ecological system behavior, changes, and feedbacks, in support of sustainable development of social diaspora across urban, semi-urban, and rural geo-economic systems.[5] There are several challenges towards meeting needs for sustainable housing, transport infrastructure, and other urban services. Handling and minimizing negative impacts on the environment and health (e.g., by air, water, soil pollution) are also affected due to budgetary constraints.[6]

Continuous growth in technology has stimulated digital innovations in the social, sustainable, and industrial business sectors. As digital innovations expand, many small and medium businesses tend to seek partnerships with technology companies to maintain competitiveness among innovative products and services within the digital sphere. But some companies find greater success through an adaptive ecosystem model, by stimulating business collaborators to develop innovations linked business projects, instead of a business-to-business partnership. Such strategy

[5] Kalantari, Z., Ferreira, C. S. S., Page, J., Goldenberg, R., Olsson, J., & Destouni, G. (2019). Meeting sustainable development challenges in growing cities: Coupled social-ecological systems modeling of land use and water changes. *Journal of Environmental Management, 245*, 471–480.

[6] Keivani, R. (2010). A review of the main challenges to urban sustainability. *International Journal of Urban Sustainable Development, 1*(1–2), 5–16.

requires collective intelligence, flexibility, and collaboration of stakeholders and firms in the innovation process.[7] Emerging companies design and implement sustainability programs as pragmatism, while the large and long-standing companies implement sustainability programs out of idealism. These companies have consistently generated significant growth rates and profit margins with the sustainability programs irrespective of their size and destination. Companies with sustainability objectives take a futuristic view and invest in social operating methods that lead to lower costs and higher yields. Companies tend to make local adjustments in sustainable social programs to generate savings in cost, which then identify local administrators for managing these projects.

Sustainability projects are sometime co-funded by the companies and local governments to support operations with advanced technologies and to coevolve business models. Collectively, these companies with socially responsive organizations demonstrate trade-off between sustainability and financial performance. The pursuit of sustainability, therefore, has emerged as a powerful path to grow business enterprises with social values.[8] The concept of systems thinking, in which the business operates as a system in contrast with the linear approach, is commonly used in business and other disciplines to manage the business operations in a systematic way. This approach explains what might cause an action or reaction but ignores any feedback effect between the subsequent action and its cause.[9] Innovating the sustainable business model is about creating superior customer- and firm value by involving stakeholders and market players such as supply chain and packaging partners. Sustainable business model of a company addresses societal and environmental needs through integrated business operations. Ecosystems of different business models are specific to the purpose and the corporate goals of the companies. Some companies that grow with social innovation objectives have a greater number of qualitative designs encompassing social needs, stakeholder education, user value generation, and bridging the corporate social responsibilities. Social sustainability manifests itself in corporate culture,

[7] Furr, N. R., & Shipilov, A. (2018). Building the right ecosystem for innovation. *MIT Sloan Management Review, 59*(4), 59–64.

[8] Haanaes, K., Michael, D., Jurgens, J., & Rangan, S. (2013). Making sustainability profitable. *Harvard Business Review, 91*(3), 110–115.

[9] Sun, J., Wu, S., & Yang, K. (2018). An eco-systemic framework for business sustainability. *Business Horizons, 61*(1), 59–72.

organizational behavior, and functional practices of companies. Sustainable business models are spread longitudinally; so, they are bound to face unforeseen risks which need to be managed in association with the stakeholders. However, companies must engage in mapping the performance of pilot business-experimentation models.[10]

A new commercial reality in today's global marketplace is the rapid shift in consumer behavior due to the emergence of dynamic disruption of innovation and technology in consumer products on a previously unimagined scale of magnitude. Environmental sustainability and consumption of green products has driven the world towards converging openness, transparency, and commonality. Sustainable business models are proactive to the systematic patterns of regulatory, social, or voluntary practices that tend to generate social and commercial value on the business investments. Sustainable business models of textiles, energy, and telecommunication industries have played transformational role within and outside their industries (Schaltegger et al., 2016). Business ecosystems involve multiple players of different types and sizes in a market, industry, or region to create value, develop economies of scale in manufacturing, and serve the markets with maximum capacity. Such business ecosystem has diverse objectives and operations. Their collective ability to learn, adapt, innovate, and coevolve businesses within socio-economic subsystems constitutes the key determinant of their longer-term success. Ecosystem exhibits important intervening variables in business, which influence creating new value chain in the society and among market players. The value perceptions in social business ecosystems are driven by shared interests, goals, and values. Companies collaborate with local companies to meet the increasing customer demands in niche and to invest in the long-term sustainability projects like eco-conservation, public health, and housing, which can derive mutual benefit. Business ecosystems based on social and public economic goals are dynamic, which coevolve with communities of diverse actors who serve to the social responsibilities and create and capture new value through increasingly public–private partnership models.[11] Companies like Nestle (Organic coffee cultivation in

[10] Rajagopal. (2020b). Barriers and benefits towards sustainability driven business models. In S. Hashmi & I. A. Choudhury (Eds.), *Encyclopedia of renewable and sustainable materials* (Vol. 5, pp. 318–327). New York: Elsevier.

[11] Kelly, E. (2015). *Business ecosystems come of age*. The Business Trend Series. New York: Deloitte University Press.

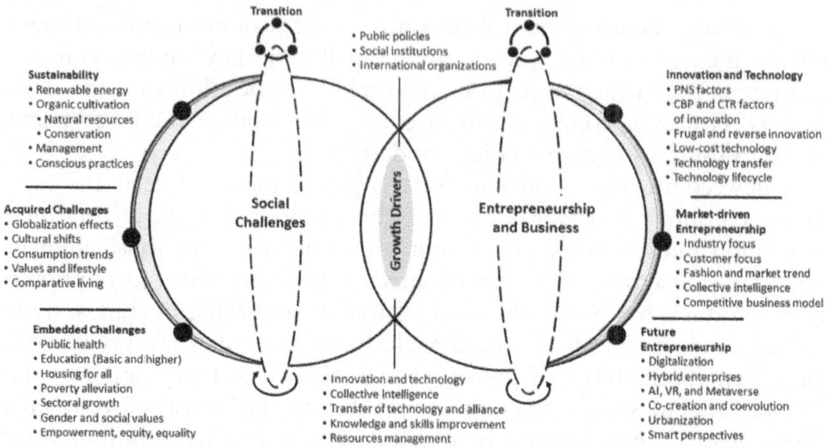

Fig. 1.1 Social challenges and attributes of entrepreneurship (*Source* Author [Rajagopal])

Columbia) and Unilever (empowering rural women in India) could lead the market competition in specific consumer products segments in the regional markets. Nestle continued to be the market leader until 2016 in Latin America, and Unilever is projected to be the market leader in consumer products segment until 2020. Successful companies develop transactional alliances and legal business partnerships with local partners. These companies also invest in developing community buy-ins and in long-term personal relationships based on mutual trust. Companies that create high corporate value through social embeddedness by implementing co-designed corporate social responsibility projects, make them competitive to lead in the market for long term.[12] There are growing social challenges and entrepreneurship is stimulated by both the market forces and public policies to analyze the social problems and needs to offer cost-effective solution. The Fig. 1.1 exhibited the embedded and acquired social challenges and entrepreneurial drivers responding to such questions.

[12] Rajagopal. (2020a). *Transgenerational marketing: Evolution, expansion, and experience*. New York: Palgrave Macmillan.

Entrepreneurship with active business modeling helps to meet several social challenges in the agricultural and agribusiness, public health, housing, sustainability, non-farm income-generating activities and public education. There are many prominent attributes of social challenges and entrepreneurship, which serve as drivers in improving social and economic growth. The Fig. 1.1 illustrates these attributes and explains the possible convergence of entrepreneurship with business to overcome the social challenges. Besides public health, education, and housing for all challenges at the bottom-of-the-pyramid socio-demographic segment, poverty alleviation requires an integrated entrepreneurial approach within the social and economic ecosystem. The parallel growth of farm- and non-farm sectors with innovative entrepreneurship helps in generating household income and empowers people to overcome the incidence of poverty in developing economies. There are many such social challenges that emerge locally; however, global support is made available through government programs. The acquired challenges that include globalization effects, cultural shifts, changing consumption trends, value and lifestyle, and comparative living styles often disrupt promoting local enterprises.

The social challenges are dynamic and changing continuously over time from rural to urban and across the markets. The current challenges in entrepreneurship are broadly associated with sustainability, manufacturing, and marketing. Broadly, the sustainability in enterprises is associated with renewable energy, organic cultivation, and management of conscious practices among the farming communities. Management of natural resources and their conservation has been one of the major challenges besides public health education, and housing. Such transition and social challenges often change the priorities of entrepreneurship, which affects entrepreneurship and business across the geo-demographic consumer segments and markets. Transforming social challenges must be understood from the perspectives of PNS factors comprising embedded problems, needs, and solutions within the society in the context of cost–benefit-profit and cost-time-risk factors associated with innovation and technology. To meet the social challenges at the grassroots, entrepreneurs adapt to frugal innovations while large companies tend to explore opportunities to commercialize innovation that have been developed and experimented successfully at the bottom of the pyramid entrepreneurial segment. The reverse innovation process can be explained as connecting global markets with innovation at the niche level. Low-cost technology is preferred by the entrepreneurs at the niche level to develop high value utilitarian products and attract large industries to explore opportunities to commercialize the innovation lying at the bottom of the pyramid. Consequently, large companies are engaged in transferring technology to small enterprises and develop entrepreneurial consortiums by industry and by region to improve their quality and performance of the product. Such streamlining of entrepreneurial products between upstream and downstream markets facilitates quick movement of products and services at macro level. However micro and small enterprises are critical at adapting to low-cost technology and long technology life cycle in manufacturing products.

Increasing innovation and advancement of technology has leveraged conventional entrepreneurship to enhance its market outreach with industry and customer focus as illustrated in Fig. 1.2. Large industries in various sectors such as consumer electronics are developing consortiums of micro, small, and medium-sized enterprises to serve as original equipment manufacturers (OEM) and supply components for manufacturing. Large industries commonly serve as value added resellers (VAR) for both industrial and consumer goods. Consequently, most OEMs operate in an umbrella of respective mother companies. The product design, manufacturing process, quality control, marketing strategy, and value creation activities are supported by the mother companies, which operate as VAR. These companies keep abreast the consortium enterprises of contemporary fashion trends and operate with the contemporary business model. Nonetheless, the social media and collective intelligence help the OEMs and the mother company to learn about the shifts in consumer preference, market trends, and the changing PNS factor (problems, needs, and expected solutions) of consumers and stakeholders. Manufacturing at the micro, small, and medium enterprises has gradually transformed over the years by reducing the marketing responsibilities and serving as a feeder channel for the mother companies. Consequently, these firms have laid more emphasis on improving their core competencies to serve as feeder channel for mother companies or contracting firms.[13] The trend of channelizing micro, small, and medium industries to serve as feeder sources for mother companies in a consortium system has built the reputation as reliable manufacturers. Many of these firms have entered the market

[13] Wang, Y., Niu, B., & Guo, P. (2014). The comparison of two vertical outsourcing structures under push and pull contracts. *Production and Operations Management, 23*(4), 610–625.

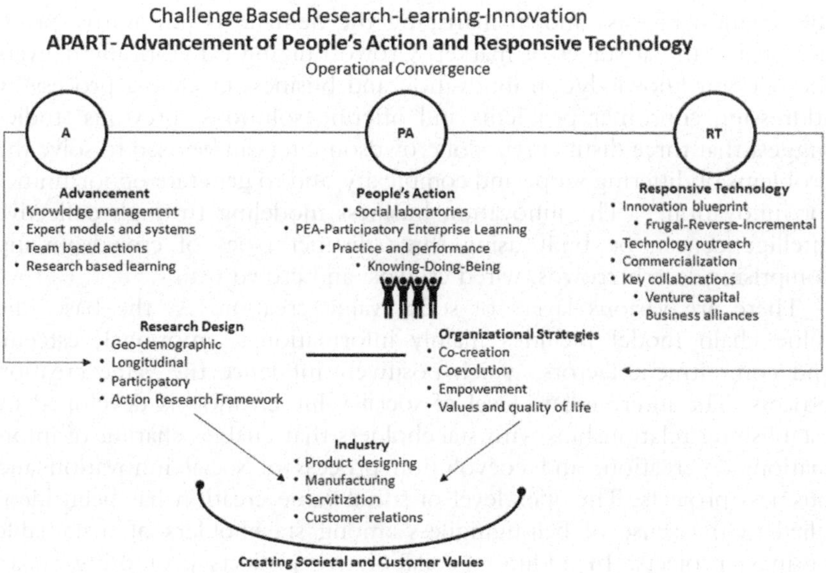

Fig. 1.2 Functional convergence in challenge-based research (*Source* Author [Rajagopal])

successfully with their niche brands alongside operating directly with the contracting firms.

Social innovations emerge as the product of social entrepreneurs driven by the knowledge-intensive social needs and contextual services. Social innovations are often addressed to the non-profit sector such as social health, natural resources management, farming activity, and domestic energy, which are sometimes referred to as social policies and economy. Companies develop sustainable business models by critically examining the inputs of innovation subsystem and socio-economic resources. Innovation subsystem largely evolves within the geo-demographic niche and uses initially cost-effective local resources, and it later transforms to commercial propositions in alliance with large organization.[14] Firms consider collaborative innovations as the most effective source of business modeling today. Collective intelligence plays a significant role in

[14] Dionisio, M., & Raupp de Vargas, E. (2020). Corporate social innovation: A systematic literature review. *International Business Review, 29*(2), 1–10.

the ideation process and in managing the demand of innovative products in the initial stages of market. Crowdsourcing categorically delivers the relevant knowledge in innovation and business modeling process by addressing consumer problems and offering solutions. Previous studies suggest that three distinct types of crowdsourcing can be used to solve the problems of differing scope and complexity, and to generate opportunities for innovation.[15] The innovation business modeling through collective intelligence can be built using three distinct types of crowdsourcing comprising search crowds, wired crowds, and crowd teams.

There are various layers of social value creation. At the base, the value chain model includes mainly informational, emotional, esteem, and commitment factors, which positively influence the value creation process. The intermediate level of social value creation is developed by establishing relationships with stakeholders that enables sharing of information, co-creation, and coevolution process of social innovation and business projects. The apex level of social value creation has been identified as the sense of belongingness among stakeholders of sustainable business projects. In addition, collaborative projects promoting stakeholder engagements in managing sustainable projects, innovations, and technologies contribute to the social value creation. The value chain management, and deliveries of sustainable business projects show effective results when organizations follow collaborative work culture with autonomy and employee engagement. The corporate social responsibility projects of most multinational companies are implemented as a pilot to test the sustainability-based business model. Broad macro factors include ecology and environment, needs that are contextual to principal social sector (health, housing, agriculture, energy, natural resources, and local industries), and relevant public policies. The macro factors are affected by various micro elements in the implementation of sustainable business projects due to improper prioritization across the geo-demographic segment, which represents misleading social values and lifestyle. In a broad context, social entrepreneurship tends to co-create social innovations while implementing the sustainability projects in the region and coevolve with the collaborating organizations. Collective intelligence (crowdsourcing) helps to enhance the ideation process on socially sustainable business projects and leads to frugal or low-cost innovations. Frugal

[15] Williams, A., Seidel, V. P., & Woolley, A. (2020). Make your crowd smart. *MIT Sloan Management Review, 61*(2), 1–6.

innovation is often associated with sustainability (ecological and social) as it is developed with an objective to minimizing the use of resources (raw material, production resources, energy, fuel, water, waste, financial resources) and maximize the output within the given space, time, and application limitations. Frugal innovations are affordable and easily accessible as compared to conventional innovations.[16]

The RISE Paradigm

The bottom line of social and industrial development is shifting rapidly since the mid-twentieth century with the advancement of technology, challenge-based research, and the changing society-business relationship.[17] The bottom line of socially responsible industries has moved over time from aggressive manufacturing to socially conscious manufacturing and marketing. The growing complexities in market competition due to disruptive technologies have led to research-based business models, which address both the social- and business-related problems, needs, and solutions.[18] The complex process of transfer of technology through research and practice in both manufacturing and services industries has shown high interdependencies between the research and industries demand.

A series of relationships between the stages of processing of raw materials and the customer also affect the manufacturing process holistically.[19] The concept of Advancement of People's Action and Responsive Technologies (APART) is being practiced in many developing countries including India. With the extensive usage of research in the context of social and industrial challenges, low-cost innovation affordable to the end users has become a popular development process. Deriving from social and industrial research output, people and companies have

[16] Weyrauch, T., & Herstatt, C. (2016). What is frugal innovation? Three defining criteria. *Journal of Frugal Innovation, 2*(1), 1–17.

[17] Guillet de Monthoux, P. (2015). Art, philosophy, and business: Turns to speculative realism in European management scholarship. *European Management Journal, 33*(3), 161–167.

[18] Von Delft, S., & Zhao, Y. (2021). Business models in process industries: Emerging trends and future research. *Technovation, 105*, Art102195 (in press). https://doi.org/10.1016/j.technovation.2020.102195.

[19] Hullova, D., Trott, P., & Simms, C. D. (2016). Uncovering the reciprocal complementarity between product and process innovation. *Research Policy, 45*(5), 929–940.

learned to follow a new pace in business led by the voice of crowd and collective intelligence.[20] The RISE paradigm integrates people's participation in the context of Research (challenge-based), Innovation (low-cost and incremental), Sustainability (energy, emission, environment), and Entrepreneurship (micro, small, and medium enterprises) to create and enhance social value. The theory of social change and values suggest co-creating innovations for social entrepreneurs looking to address culturally rooted and entrenched societal problems.[21]

Challenge-based research suggests transforming the existing businesses to profitable ventures through co-creation and coevolution. The research output stimulates firms to design and implement agile business models.[22] The challenge-based research supports innovations for social development ranging from sustainable farming to cleaner and affordable energy to the people across geo-demographic segments.[23] Collaborative research between universities, firms, and customer in biotechnology sector is contributing to improved food production,[24] while technology-led mobile learning tends to improve the reading skills and enhance rationale in solving mathematical theorems and riddles.[25] In addition, telemedicine practices are reducing the incidence of maternal and neonatal mortality in indigenous communities in developing economies. The collaborating research has also addressed the challenges associated with potable rainwater harvesting and sustainable housing in these countries.

[20] Dong, W. X. (2016). Crowd intelligence: Analyzing online product reviews for preference measurement. *Information & Management, 53*, 169–182.

[21] Stephan, U., Patterson, M., Kelly, C., & Mair, J. (2016). Organizations driving positive social change: A review and an integrative framework of change processes. *Journal of Management, 42*(5), 1250–1281.

[22] Rajagopal. (2019). *Contemporary marketing strategy: Analyzing consumer behavior to drive managerial decision making*. New York: Palgrave Macmillan.

[23] Laurett, R., Paço, A., & Mainardes, E. W. (2021). Sustainable development in agriculture and its antecedents, barriers and consequences—An exploratory study. *Sustainable Production and Consumption, 27*, 298–311.

[24] Chen, K. J., Marsh, T. L., Tozer, P. R., &. Galinato, S. P. (2019). Biotechnology to sustainability: Consumer preferences for food products grown on biodegradable mulches. *Food Research International, 16*, 200–210.

[25] Cai, P. (2021). Thinking skills development in mobile learning: The case of elementary school students studying environmental studies. *Thinking Skills and Creativity, 42*, Art. 100922 (in press). https://doi.org/10.1016/j.tsc.2021.100922.

Philosophically, the crowd dynamics can be explained as collective intelligence, which reveals that no one knows everything while everyone knows something.[26] Contemporary marketing has evolved alongside the customer-centric perspectives as a cognitive science and has spanned across advanced marketing-mix comprising twenty-seven elements.[27] Therefore, customer value has become central to business modeling. Most companies develop marketing strategies (a principal constituent of business model) on assumptions of customer values, which might be a misfit while implementing a business model. Collective intelligence provides the real perceptions of customers and the rationale for new products and services.[28]

Systems Thinking in Social Entrepreneurship and Innovation

Challenge-based research helps in enabling intelligent manufacturing systems. The Industry 4.0 revolution has significantly encouraged the explorative research to learn from the consumers and stakeholders about the existing and latent problems and needs and developing possible solutions. The research outputs derived from customers and stakeholders' perceptions, besides conceptualizing the engineering design, can serve as key design input in manufacturing and sensing smart sustainable designs. Systems thinking has been used as a powerful tool to develop innovative product designs and complement Industry 4.0 operations applying the growing concepts of Industrial Internet of Things (IIOT). Research supported systems thinking explains a holistic approach to examine how

[26] Lévy, P. (1997). *Collective intelligence: Mankind's emerging world in cyberspace.* New York: Plenum Trade.

[27] The advanced marketing-mix consists of 11 Ps as core elements and 16 Ps as peripheral elements. The 11 Ps include product, price, place, promotion, packaging, pace, people, performance, psychodynamics, posture, and proliferations. The peripheral elements have been discussed in the text referred to this footnote. The attributes of advanced marketing-mix are discussed comprehensively in the following footnote (Rajagopal, 2019).

[28] Rajagopal. (2019). *Contemporary marketing strategy: Analyzing consumer behavior to drive managerial decision making*, Chapter 5 (pp. 121–149). New York: Palgrave Macmillan.

different functions are interrelated and work within the predefined manufacturing and operations model.[29] Systems thinking approach in product designing and manufacturing advocates that firms should create shared value. Systems thinking in industries adds value propositions simultaneously to the firm and society during the design and manufacturing process.[30] Systems thinking is a comprehensive tool, which can be applied to understand problems at a systemic level in a generally non-quantitative manner. It can be used in the construction of causal loop diagrams and can be beneficial for building insight into complex systems. The systems thinking approach helps to explain why it is often so difficult to get companies to adopt corporate social innovation.[31] The systems thinking in challenge-based research reduces the proximity to connect society with industry. Some earlier contributions of Peter Senge argue how systems thinking, continuous learning, and research are interconnected to enhance innovation, organizational design, and performance of companies. People in organizations are learning today to adapt to collective learning, research, and co-creation. Continuous learning through collective efforts develops interconnections and long-term effects to make appropriate decisions on innovation and technology in the context of social and industrial needs.[32] Systems thinking for social innovations backed by challenge-based research motivates researchers and managers to develop synchronized efforts in co-creating innovations with stakeholders and customers. Since organizational and industry learning processes are likely to be stemmed out of research and social interactions, they present

[29] Molina A., Ponce P., Miranda J., & Cortés D. (2021). Integrated product, process and manufacturing system development reference model framework. In *Enabling systems for intelligent manufacturing in Industry 4.0*. Cham: Springer.

[30] Herrera, M. E. B. (2015). Creating competitive advantage by institutionalizing corporate social innovation. *Journal of Business Research, 68*(7), 1468–1474.

[31] Maltz, E., & Pierson, K. (2022). Maximizing corporate social innovation to enhance social and shareholder value: A systems thinking model of industry transformation. *Journal of Business Research, 138*, 12–25.

[32] Senge, P., & Sterman, J. D. (1992). Systems thinking and organizational learning: Acting locally and thinking globally in the organization of the future. *European Journal of Operational Research, 59*(1), 137–150.

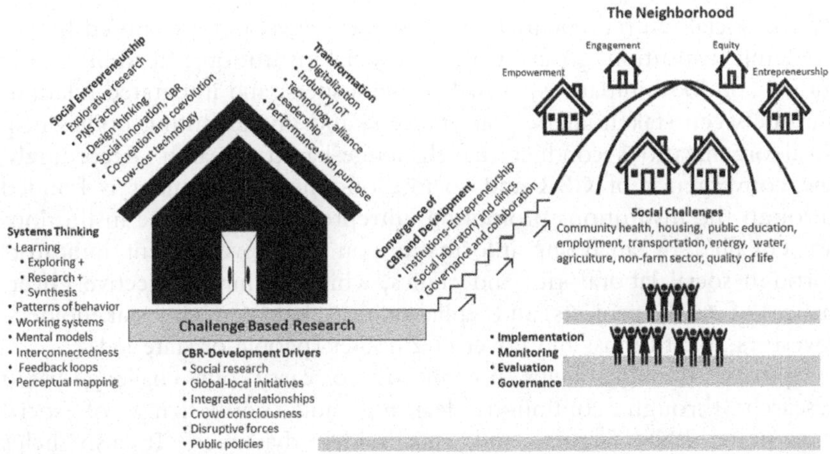

Fig. 1.3 Research-based challenges and social development (*Source* Author [Rajagopal])

challenges in manufacturing, marketing, and services within the industrial ecosystem.[33]

Companies tend to get closer to the customers by engaging them in co-creating new products, carrying out incremental innovations, improving packaging, and developing attractive promotions and competitive business strategies. Firms aim to attract emotional customers, so that the bonds between the customers, stakeholders, and firms grow deeper. Over time, firms can share emotional experiences with potential customers and motivate their engagement.[34] The transfer of outcomes of challenge-based research for social development and growth is exhibited in Fig. 1.3.

Challenge-based research (CBR), aimed at meeting various social and economic challenges, is broadly supported by the three principal domains comprising systems thinking, social entrepreneurship, and transformation process as illustrated in Fig. 1.3. Challenge-based research is driven

[33] Gupta, S., & Polonsky, M. (2014). Inter-firm learning and knowledge-sharing in multinational networks: An outsourced organization's perspective. *Journal of Business Research, 67*(4), 615–622.

[34] Das, G., Agarwal, J., Malhotra, N. K., & Varshneya, G. (2019). Does brand experience translate into brand commitment? A mediated-moderation model of brand passion and perceived brand ethicality. *Journal of Business Research, 95*, 479–490.

by the social, entrepreneurial, and innovative research promoted by the academic institution, government, and social institutions. In addition, the global and local initiatives, crowd consciousness, and integrated relationship between stakeholders, policymakers, and implementing bodies help local organizations conduct the challenge-based research. Accordingly, the convergence of CBR and socio-economic development is bonded through the institutions promoting entrepreneurship. These institutions are engaged by analyzing information on key development indicators through social laboratories and clinics, which requires collective governance of CBR projects and collaboration between the stakeholders, investors, institutions, and governing bodies (people or state-led).

Systems thinking helps institutions to carry out challenge-based research through continuous learning and synthesizing of social ecosystem, PNS factors, and stakeholder dynamics. It also helps researchers in mapping the patterns of stakeholder behavior and mental models across the changing development trends. The interconnectedness and different workplace systems like participatory research appraisal, crowd platforms for pooling knowledge, and collective decision-making also contribute to the systems thinking process. PNS challenges are evolved in a society and businesses are built within the society. Convergence of such relationship between society and business constructs the consumer behavior. Consequently, collectivism influences consumerism and consumer groups (including individuals), which tend to share consumer experiences on innovations, products, values, and market developments generate awareness among the society. The collective opinions influence the buyers and the society for meeting their needs. Knowledge of consumers' conditions, factors, and behavioral reasons ensures competitiveness in businesses.[35]

Spatial and temporal explorative research with focus on PNS factors and business opportunities motivates social entrepreneurship and social innovations to carry out through collective design thinking process. Entrepreneurs with social objectives are engaged in adapting to the low-cost innovation and technology through co-creation and coevolution process, which helps these enterprises in transformation of benefits and values to the stakeholders. The entrepreneurial transformation in the era

[35] Sirgy, M. J. (2018). Self-congruity theory in consumer behavior: A little history. *Journal of Global Scholars of Marketing Science, 28*(2), 197–207.

of the Internet is largely driven by the need for digitalization of manufacturing processes and services as most industries have adapted to the Internet of Things practices. The changing conventional leadership style to transformative approach has leveraged entrepreneurs to explore technology alliances with the large companies within the industry to enhance their performance. The reforms of public administration and democratic approach to social enterprises have led to a decentralization of power and a redistribution of responsibilities to the lowest possible level of administrators. Therefore, social governance has become closer to the citizens and stakeholders to make appropriate decisions locally.[36]

Social Institutions and Markets

Various social institutions engaged in encouraging research and innovation to ensure economic growth contribute to disseminating new ideas and serve as a pool of collective intelligence. However, the review of previous literature suggests that the overall effect of crowdsourcing on business modeling has not been thoroughly investigated. Social institutions help in integrating the customer and stakeholder ideation in developing behavioral business models to achieve *performance with purpose*. Drawing on the resource-based view, discussion on how social challenges can be linked with industrial value chain through collaborative research, knowledge sharing, and transfer of technology to deliver value, needs significant social and academic contributions. Converging society and industry is essential for the business ecosystem to stay competitive in the marketplace.[37] Socialization of business is a process where people build trust through interpersonal interaction, learn market trends, co-create products and services, and inculcate value-based organizational culture. The collective intelligence has evolved over time through experiential interactions on social media channels. Socialization of businesses encourages people from different segments, socio-cultural backgrounds, and

[36] Benites-Lazaro, L. L., & Mello-Théry, N. A. (2019). Empowering communities? Local stakeholders' participation in the clean development mechanism in Latin America. *World Development, 114*, 254–266.

[37] Rajagopal. (2021). *Crowd-based business models—Using collective intelligence for market competitiveness*. New York: Palgrave Macmillan (in press).

ethnicity to co-create innovative business ideas. The socialization process of business helps firms grow agile and customer-centric.[38]

With the advancement of technology and convenience-led marketing, elderly consumers are feeling out of place in the market today as they are unable to cope with the technology-driven marketing approaches, applications, and self-service platforms. Consequently, reverse socialization is gearing up in the families as elderly consumers are being influenced by the young consumers. Reverse socialization is a process, which allows adolescents' influence on their parents' knowledge, skills, and attitudes related to consumption. Such behavior is driven by emotions, changing perceptions on products and services, and restructured cognitive ergonomics.[39] The applied concepts on converging research and technology with the industry requirements meet the persistent social challenges like poverty, community health, housing, energy, food production and quality, and education. The triple bottom-line[40] strategies integrate people (society), planet (sustainability), and profit (industry and business) as an integrate construct for socio-economic and regional development. Arguments converging systems thinking and social entrepreneurship focus on building resilience in societal development by connecting people with industry. Cognition on social development and relative changes contributes to the social self-concept, which determines the buying decisions and the relative degree of influence.[41]

The William's Syndrome of social phenotype is associated with a strong drive to approach strangers and sociable personalities, social commitments, and developing social engagements. These attributes affect neurobehavioral status of people and instill positive or negative emotions with the firms, brands, and product portfolios in general. The growing research on the social phenotype and neurobiological evidence indicate

[38] Fayard, A. L., Weeks, J., & Khan, M. (2021). *Designing the Hybrid Office*. Harvard Business Review Digital Article. Boston: Harvard Business School Publication.

[39] Gentina, E., & Muratore, I. (2012). Environmentalism at home: The process of ecological resocialization by teenagers. *Journal of Consumer Behaviour, 11*(2), 162–169.

[40] Aguiñaga, E., Henriques, I., Scheel, C., & Scheel, A. (2018). Building resilience: A self-sustainable community approach to the triple bottom line. *Journal of Cleaner Production, 173*, 186–196.

[41] Singh, P., Sahadev, S., Oates, C. J., & Alevizou, P. (2020). Pro-environmental behavior in families: A reverse socialization perspective. *Journal of Business Research, 115*, 110–121.

alterations in structure, function, and connectivity of the social brain. The social phenotype attributes to empathic, friendly, and emotional personality among consumers, which affects the neurobehavioral outcomes and entrepreneurship.[42]

Innovation and Technology

There is a growing interest in the role of universities in promoting social and industrial innovations. With the changing social and business scenarios, the participation of academics in research has faced complexities and perspective challenges over time. Consequently, connecting research with the social and industrial problems has emerged as one of the keyways to manage innovation and technology systematically.[43] Public universities actively engage in problems that confound social innovation researchers and industries. Governments usually provide voice support for this vision, as they fund public universities. The private universities largely depend on outsourcing funds from the industries to boost innovation and technology research, modeling, and implementation. Within the given resources, the private university tends to connect researchers and practitioners to form a robust transformative innovation and technology ecosystems.[44] The rising prominence of social innovation in manifesting the voice of stakeholders has become the guiding phenomenon for the firms in building and reinforcing customer relations. Social research provides a powerful relationship management tool to companies that enables them to interact, engage, and provide customized value of innovations.[45] Such trend in the developing economies today has warned firms to be prepared for low-cost and disruptive trends in innovation and focuses on developing agile

[42] Järvinen-Pasley, A., Bellugi, U., Reilly, J., Mills, D. L., Galaburda, A., Reiss, A. L., & Korenberg, J. R. (2008). Defining the social phenotype if Williams Syndrome: A model of linking gene, the brain, and cognition. *Development and Psychopathology, 20*(1), 1–35.

[43] Tjörnbo, O., & McGowan, K. (2022). A complex-systems perspective on the role of universities in social innovation. *Technological Forecasting and Social Change, 174*, Art. 121247 (in press). https://doi.org/10.1016/j.techfore.2021.121247.

[44] Avelino, F., Wittmayer, J., Pel, B., Weaver, P., Dumitru, A., Haxeltine, A., & Kemp, R. (2019). Transformative social innovation and (dis)empowerment. *Technology Forecasting and Social Change, 145*, 195–206.

[45] Clark, M., & Melancon, J. P. (2013). The influence of social media investment on relational outcomes: A relationship marketing perspective. *Journal of International Marketing Studies, 5*(4), 132–142.

marketing strategies. Social innovations are the attempts to solve persistent social challenges through a variety of initiatives.[46] The recent trends of innovation include co-creation involving users and stakeholders from various social perspectives. The collective intelligence, and collaborative problem-based research and learning trends have significantly encouraged the need for open social and industrial innovations.[47] The competition among the firms to gain advantage of new innovative and technology products raises the pertinent questions on 4As comprising awareness, attributes, affordability, and adaptability.[48] However, the collaborations among researchers, innovators, policymakers, and industries typically center on the solution and often equate any innovation primarily with the solution. Therefore, systematic research on identified and predefined problems makes a higher contribution in innovation and technology among industries than an absolute managerial ideation.[49] By recognizing social needs and market gaps, it is possible for marketers to explore innovative products and gain valuable insight into the competitive marketplace. Consequently, it is critical for the firms to establish a congruence between the user perceptions and the innovations to develop a meaningful relationship. Accordingly, firms develop social business portfolios that will continually evolve with incremental innovations and changing technology.[50]

The major challenge with the closed innovation and technology is the effective transfer to users. It is important in innovation and technology developments to project clearly their lifetime value and develop alliances

[46] Edwards-Schachter, M., & Wallace, M. L. (2017). Shaken, but not stirred: Sixty years of defining social innovation. *Technological Forecasting and Social Change, 119*, 64–79.

[47] Ramus, T., La Cara, B., Vaccaro, A., & Brusoni, S. (2018). Social or commercial? Innovation strategies in social enterprises at times of turbulence. *Business Ethics Quarterly, 28*(4), 463–492.

[48] Rajagopal. (2019). *Contemporary marketing strategy: Analyzing consumer behavior to drive managerial decision making*. New York: Palgrave Macmillan.

[49] Chandra, Y., Shang, L., & Mair, J. (2021). Drivers of success in social innovation: Insights into competition in open social innovation contests. *Journal of Business Venturing Insights, 16* (in press). https://doi.org/10.1016/j.jbvi.2021.e00257.

[50] Biswas, D. (2019). Sensory aspects of retailing: Theoretical and practical implications. *Journal of Retailing, 95*(4), 111–115.

for global–local initiatives.[51] Upon critically examining the technology-led customer relationship management practices, there is a need to redefine the customer relationship processes through database creation and analysis of relationship portfolios, customer selection and targeting, relationship marketing models, privacy issues, and suggests new metrics necessary to evaluate the efficacy of customer relations.[52] Consumer behavior is a set of socio-psychological indicators that cultivate a cognitive process in human beings. It refers to the range of personality attributes exhibited by people, which are influenced by societal values, culture, attitudes, emotions, values, ethics, power, relationships, and persuasion. Behavior in humans grows as a learned, acquired, or shared process over the spatial and temporal factors. Consumer-centric companies periodically map behavioral patterns of consumers by understanding major perceptional and attitudinal patterns and interpret them to develop appropriate marketing strategies. However, consumer behavior is sensitive to the social dominance, self-esteem and self-actualization, hedonic values, and vogue in the marketplace.[53]

Contextual marketing helps firms stay agile in the market by developing marketing strategies congruent with the customer personality, social values and lifestyle, social equity in consumption, and social motivations. Most customer-centric firms lack in delivering enough value to induce customers to encourage repeat buying behavior and grow profitable. These factors significantly affect the neurobehavioral dimensions of customers and instill social and crowd consciousness. Previous studies have identified consumer attitudes as constructs, which analyze how consumers think about (cognition), feel about (affect), and act towards (conation) developing consumption and buying preferences.[54] Such approaches would help firms to understand real-time technology effects

[51] Farazi, M. S., Gopalakrishnan, S., & Perez-Luño, A. (2019). Depth and breadth of knowledge and the governance of technology alliances. *Journal of Engineering and Technology Management, 54*, 28–40.

[52] Winer, R. S. (2001). Framework for customer relationship management. *California Management Review, 43*(4), 89–105.

[53] Carter, T. J., & Gilovich, T. (2010). The relative relativity of experiential and material purchases. *Journal of Personality and Social Psychology, 98*(1), 146–159.

[54] Vakratsas, D., & Ambler, T. (1999). How advertising works: What do we really know? *Journal of Marketing, 63*(1), 26–43.

and improve the marketing capabilities of the firm accordingly.[55] In the digital marketplace today, consumers invest enormous time and effort on information analytics to support their decision towards the purchase of a product or service. Consumer's collect the decision-support information from the corporate communications, advertisements, customer-generated contents, and referrals. However, fuzzy consumer decision often leads to an irrational focus of firms on implementing marketing strategies causing low satisfaction and customer value.[56] Consequently, large firms tend to invest in customer-centric innovation and technologies to drive positive social effects on business and consumption practices. It is argued that to compete in an aggressively interactive environment, companies must shift their focus from transactional strategies to maximizing customer lifetime value. Such shift in the corporate ideology delineates that products and brands must be made subservient to customer relationships.[57]

The convergence of technology with customer value provides a higher competitive advantage and interacts frequently with the complex market players and customers in streamlining the business activities. The convergence marketing is woven around five Cs comprising customization, community, channels, competitive value, and choice that drive "fusion" in the corporate marketing strategies.[58] The social utility of trust considers that firms selling "fair trade," "organic," or other socially beneficial products must be congruent to the neurobehavior of consumers based on the social stimuli. The cooperative and network marketing practices have witnessed such effects of social motivation on the neurobehavior of consumers.[59] Refurbishing business with collective intelligence, social values, and neurobehavioral analytics helps companies increase their business performance by introducing strategic engagement of stakeholders

[55] Nemet, G. F. (2009). Demand-pull, technology-push, and government-led incentives for non-incremental technical change. *Research Policy, 38*(5), 700–709.

[56] Lala, V., & Chakraborty, G. (2015). Impact of consumers' effort investments on buying decisions. *Journal of Consumer Marketing, 32*(2), 61–70.

[57] Rust, R. T., Moorman, C., & Bhalla, G. (2010). Rethinking marketing. *Harvard Business Review, 88*(1), 94–101.

[58] Wind, Y., & Mahajan, V. (2001). *Convergence marketing: Strategies for reaching the new hybrid consumer*. New York: Free Press.

[59] Lee, N., Broderick, A. J., & Chamberlain, L. (2007). What is 'neuromarketing'? A discussion and agenda for future research. *International Journal of Psychophysiology, 63*(2), 199–204.

with the manufacturing and operational processes.[60] Disruptive forces like e-commerce, low-cost technology products, and tactical marketing strategies have driven behavioral uncertainties and rapid shifts in innovation, technology, and consumer experiences in the twenty-first century. Consequently, a robust thematic discussion on inclusive business practices and delivering innovation and technology suitable to the social and consumer behavior calls for the immediate attention.[61]

Business Modeling in Economic Turbulence

Doing business in political and economic disruptions has been challenging which has been evident in the business shutdown during the COVID-19 pandemic occurred since early 2020. The challenge-based research focuses on evaluating the production and business alternatives through digitalization and network channels. Businesses have diversified their manufacturing and marketing activities through consortium strategies and social media channels. The paradigm shift in the business model during the turbulent socio-economic situations has focused fragmented markets encouraging customized services to customers, low-cost manufacturing, and connecting business functions (backward and forward linkages) with the local firms. The reverse business modeling during the turbulent economic situations focuses on developing scenario-based damage management strategies to handle alike pandemic-led consequences. Such business models implement the scenario drivers on both economic and social facets of businesses.[62] In the COVID-19 pandemic, business shutdown across regions have given a new impetus among business to reorient on e-commerce using social networks to stimulate social behavior towards adapting to the alternate ways of business. Firms of all sizes have analyzed the social behavior on social networks to improve e-business accordingly. Social networking has been extensively

[60] Hawkins, G. (2001). Plastic bags: living with rubbish. *International Journal of Cultural Studies, 4*(1), 5–23.

[61] Van Westen, A., Mangnus, E., Wangu, J., & Worku, S. G. (2019). Inclusive agribusiness models in the Global South: The impact on local food security. *Current Opinion in Environmental Sustainability, 41*, 64–68.

[62] Hajipour, V., Aminian, M., Gharaei, A., & Jalali, S. (2021). A business retrieval model using scenario planning and analytics for life during and after the pandemic crisis. *Healthcare Analytics, 1* (in press). https://doi.org/10.1016/j.health.2021.100004.

used not only for promoting products and services through digital advertisement, webinars, and experience sharing on micro-blogs but also in selling products through the social media channels. The mobile applications have also been contributed extensively in propagating the use of online platforms to manage the business-to-consumer and business-to-business activities during the COVID-19 pandemic situation. The social e-commerce customers' purchasing behavior game model integrates different e-commerce social networks, calculates the internal interaction between web and customer exchange, and estimates the buying rate in various social e-commerce networks.[63]

The change in the product designs with value enhancements has also affected the conventional businesses during the economic turbulence as observed using the COVID-19 pandemic. Due to incidental unemployment and diminishing household income, most companies have switched to low-cost production to provide products at the low price to customers. Consequently, the scope of frugal innovation (FI) has gained significant importance during the turbulent trade and economy situations. The use of FI has emerged as a novel way to serve low-income consumers in developing countries and encouraged niche businesses models. The FI-led products significantly support the consumers of lower purchasing power and their distinct buying preferences. Consequently, the use of FIs has become a new frontier for multinational companies.[64] However, many local enterprises find it difficult to adopt existing technological platforms that best serve their needs, as their needs differ from already established firms in the marketplace. Hence, the need to find and adopt new technological platforms designed to offer strategic services arises for the start-up enterprises in emerging markets.[65]

[63] Lv, J., Wang, T., Wang, H., Yu, J., & Wang, Y. (2020). A SECPG model for purchase behavior analysis in social e-commerce environment. *International Journal of Communication System,* 33:e4149. https://doi.org/10.1002/dac.4149.

[64] Hossain, M. (2021). Frugal innovation and sustainable business models. *Technology in Society, 64* (in press). https://doi.org/10.1016/j.techsoc.2020.101508.

[65] Ferneley, E., & Bell, F. (2006). Using bricolage to integrate business and information technology innovation in SMEs. *Technovation, 26*(2), 232–241.

Public Policies and Governance

The expansion of ecological innovation has been accompanied by the philosophy of in-home solutions with low-cost technologies and high-utilitarian values. Considering the growing global environmental concerns, such as green energy and the increasing scarcity of resources, the manufacturing industries have shown more interest in sustainable production with the social business models. These models present the low-end econoscape for the consumers and are jointly implemented through the public–private partnership as corporate social responsibility (CSR) initiatives. However, the social awareness and effective implementation of public policies have improved the efficiency of sustainable consumption and growth of the emerging markets. Reduction in the emission of greenhouse gases has been considered as a priority among the governments of developing countries, and many have adopted strategic frameworks. Interestingly, the economic leverage to enterprises engaged in manufacturing green products and providing eco-conservation services developing countries have raised social consciousness from the environmental protection programs to achieve sustainable goals. In developing countries, the green recovery public policy has attracted public investment in environmental technologies and encouraged the implementation of collaborative sustainability projects. Green recovery projects are targeted towards regenerating ecological conservation that have been affected by the community ignorance in urban-rural geo-demographic segments (Rajagopal, 2021). The green recovery concept has geared up over time as a core part of economic stimulus measures at global–local levels.

The shared economy has also significantly affected the business ecosystem today and the inclusivity concept in business has outgrown over time from the shared economy practices. The shared economy concept broadly refers to social innovation activities that improve the collective efficiency through crowd-based platforms and service integration approaches such as manpower management, machines, space, services, knowledge or information, and consumable resources. Such integration is carried out by creating a pool of common resources on digital platforms in the sharing economy. The combination of sharing economy and social innovation has a great potential to deliver the corporate social responsibility (CSR), as it shares the common goal of the triple bottom line by way of involving people (inclusivity), reducing environmental impacts, focusing on the principles of reusing (sustainability), generating profit with purpose, and working closely with the business philosophy of recycling and sharing. The shared economy and inclusive business supported by crowd behavior and collective intelligence help in co-creating and coevolving corporate social responsibility. Such a business ecosystem founded on stakeholders, community leaders, public policy support, and corporate involvement drive business opportunity and community assets to align with delivering economic interests, corporate commitments, stakeholder values. The growing popularity of inclusive business models has been admired for encouraging stakeholder engagement in business planning, implementation, monitoring, and evaluation. The concept of inclusivity in business promotes liberal businesses across developing economies. However, differences exist in social governance of businesses and public policies, which affect the processes for making public policy decisions, delivering values to the stakeholders, and generating profit with purpose.[66] Business ecosystems are more complex and work differently in the context of markets, social attributes, stakeholder culture, governance model, public policy support, and possible corporate collaboration. Complexity stems from the diversity of relationships among the key partners, key activities, and key resources, which affects the planning and implementation of business strategies in the target markets. Furthermore, many of these relationships are systemic, with companies having to influence each other indirectly. Such complexity in relationships inside the ecosystem leads to the formation of diverse structures and patterns that determine the functioning of the system within a socio-economic sub-domain.[67]

The relationships between stakeholders and organizations largely depend on the stakeholders' needs and personal attitudes of managers, which form the corporate behavior demonstrating the social, economic, and financial health of the firms. The co-created and coevolved stakeholder relationship with the firms contributes towards mutual benefits in the long run. However, agile relationships between firms and stakeholders (customers and investors) raise individual optimism and the

[66] Keim, G. D., & Hillman, A. J. (2008). Political environments and business strategy: Implications for managers. *Business Horizons, 51*(1), 47–53.

[67] Visnjic, I., Neely, A., Cennamo, C., & Visnjic, N. (2016). Governing the city: Unleashing value from the business ecosystem. *California Management Review, 59*(1), 109–140.

degree of risk in governance and leadership over time. Such behavior jeopardizes the inclusivity in business and fragments the role of stakeholder engagement in the governance of the firm.[68] Although organizational culture is an important factor that influences corporate decisions-making efforts and ensuing corporate behavior, the inclusivity in business helps in the convergence of social values and governance. Such corporate philosophy in developing countries is meaningful and makes significant differences in motivating stakeholder investment and governance in inclusive businesses. The inclusivity in business needs strong relations between the degree of personal attitude of managers, stakeholder engagement, and relative public–private investment in developing countries.[69] Previous studies have emphasized that belief, emotion, and trust are critical to organizational effectiveness in customer-centric firms. Personal beliefs, emotional attachment with the organization, and trustworthiness strengthen the role and operational involvement of stakeholders in a firm. Accordingly, the inclusivity of stakeholders in business ensures consistency, clear communication, and a democratic philosophy as the business driver among the social enterprises. The major reasons of a diminishing organizational performance are low trust, inconsistent flow of decisions from top management, variability in operational standards, tolerance to incompetence or bad behavior, dishonest feedback, and functionality, and downplaying the stakeholders' suggestions to improve business operation.[70] Reliability serves as a bridge between the company and stakeholders, which helps in inclusive decision-making to serve the mutual interest keeping atop the performance of goals of the organization. Hence, the attributes of trust, beliefs, and emotions significantly affect the roles of stakeholders and managers in organizational governance and decision-making. The corporate loyalty programs contribute

[68] Rajagopal. (2022). *Agile marketing strategies: New approaches to engaging consumer behavior*. Cham, Switzerland: Palgrave Macmillan.

[69] Graham, J. R., Harvey, C. R., & Puri M. (2013). Managerial attitudes and corporate actions. *Journal of Financial Economics, 109*, 103–121.

[70] Galford, R., & Drapeau, A. S. (2003). Enemies of trust. *Harvard Business Review, 81*(2), 88–95.

significantly to the corporate reputation and performance and attract stakeholder participation in the governance and decision-making.[71]

The collective intelligence embeds social emotions and strong psycho-dynamics that have the potential to disrupt the demand of existing brands in the competitive marketplace. Crowd-based ideation supports companies in co-creation and coevolution process with stakeholders through social interaction, social innovations, and social governance. The stakeholders in social enterprises tend to lead collective challenges and streamline transformational leadership regardless of the outside-in effect on the entrepreneurial ecosystem. Reverse accountability and social governance have congruent philosophy, which can drive collective strategies to generate new lines of business with stakeholder involvement to resolve problems and promote social practices in business. Reverse accountability helps in streamlining leadership traits, improving democratic skills in organizations, and retaining social values. The paradox of reverse accountability lies in vertical decision-making practices and leader-oriented organizational integration. The success of reverse accountability has been evidenced in self-help groups and social organizations that exhibit collective values and social control of organization. This has big implications in streamlining leadership, abridging gaps between diverse groups of employees, and networking human values within social framework.[72] People-led governance in businesses explains how the social vigilance in business organizations helps in controlling unethical moves of the firms for profit at the cost of customers and stakeholders. People's involvement in business also benefits the multi-stake business model and strengthens multi-stakeholder mechanism in business governance by co-designing the organizational structures, processes, and principles. People's participation and social governance have grown over time in promising forms of sharing and leveraging its benefits, while circumventing its pitfalls

[71] Yan, Y., Huang, C., Wang, Q., & Hu, B. (2020). Data mining of customer choice behavior in internet of things within relationship network. *International Journal of Information Management, 50*, 566–574.

[72] Rajagopal & Rajagopal, A. (2023). Reverse accountability and leadership in social enterprises: Analysis of social control and openness for pragmatic organizational design. *International Journal of Business Excellence* (in press). https://doi.org/10.1504/IJBEX.2021.10041966.

is becoming increasingly important in economic recoveries caused due to the current pandemic.[73]

The core elements constitute stakeholders, society, innovation and technology, macroeconomic factors, sustainability, and corporate governance. Crowdsourcing or collective intelligence has emerged as a dynamic tool in the business ecosystem today, which is supported by the stakeholders. They support companies in co-creation and coevolution process with stakeholders through social interaction, social innovations, and social governance. Business ecosystems linked with sustainability goals drive public–private entrepreneurship (collaborations) to meet the sustainable development goals through social- and frugal innovations. Taxonomy of leadership and employee engagement largely drive the corporate governance practices as central to the business ecosystem. Among various subsystems associated with the core business ecosystems, stakeholders are influenced by the cognitive subsystem comprising perceptions, emotions, and social interactivities. Social and innovation subsystems include social values, entrepreneurship education, and utilitarian innovations. Management of resources and factors of production, procurement and transactions of public goods constitute some significant factors of macroeconomic subsystem.[74]

The taxonomy of governance of social and entrepreneurial development projects has four broad categories comprising open system, social system, corporate system, and mixed system. The open system business governance is common in crowd-based businesses, which encourages proportional representation of customers, stakeholders, long-term investors, and crowd leaders in the collective governance process through a formal board set-up. As most crowdfunded projects are initiated in the social businesses or social innovation projects, the social leaders engaged in the non-commercial (social value creation), transformational (driving social tasks from conventional wisdom to digital and automated technologies), and inspirational (spiritual and art of life) leadership practices contribute to the social businesses. Crowdfunded social businesses are encouraged to have total or partial community governance backed by the

[73] Di Pietro, F., Prencipe, A., & Majchrzak A. (2018). Crowd equity investors: an underutilized asset for open innovation in startups. *California Management Review, 60*(2), 43–70.

[74] Rajagopal. (2020). *Sustainable businesses in developing economies—Socio-economic and governance perspectives*. Cham, Switzerland: Palgrave Macmillan.

non-governmental organizations or progressive youth leaders. Both the open and social business governance systems are influenced by the social value system. In these forms of business governance, social benefits of the business have higher priority as compared to revenue generation and profitability. The corporate governance system of crowdfunded business firms tends to follow bottom-up governance model by accommodating the customers, investors, and employees in managing the firm. In the bottom-up governance system, corporate decisions are initiated, processed, and endorsed by the governing body comprising the stakeholders, customers, alliance partners, and employees. Grameen Bank model of Bangladesh, dairy farmers' cooperatives in Japan and India, and microfinance institutions in Mexico are good examples of the bottom-up governance. However, the boards of public enterprises, which constitute public equities and government capital resources, are headed by the social and political representatives or civil servants.[75]

The recent shift in the business philosophy has influenced the companies operating on public and private resources to develop business models to integrate the governance system based on design-to-market, design-to-society, and design-to-value. However, there also exists mixed-governance system in many regional and international companies which combines the representation of stakeholders, customers, employees, society, and government entities in the formal board. Hybrid governance model is an emerging phenomenon in the corporate world. In this model, a large number of representations from various groups (stakeholders, customers, technology experts, government, financial institutions, and social platforms) occupy the middle ground in the state-owned, public-sector enterprises, and fully privatized companies operating in emerging markets. As sizable government stakes in leading industries in the form of ownership, management, subsidies, or other preferential forms is common in the public companies. Such shifts are both market-driven and regulatory; and they lead to hybrid governance with a blend of human resources, technology, and regulatory framework. The hybrid governance helps firms in multi-stakeholder management, crowdfunded business projects, and publicly financed corporations that compete in the local and global

[75] Rajagopal. (2021). *Crowd-based business models—Using collective intelligence for market competitiveness*. Cham, Switzerland: Palgrave Macmillan.

marketplaces. The hybrid governance encourages also public–private partnership in businesses, induces crowd cognition, and collective controls (commons), which operate with strategic goals and operational plans.[76]

[76] Khanna, P. (2012). *The rise of hybrid governance*. New York: McKinsey & Company.

CHAPTER 2

People, Planet, and Profit: Crossing the Triple Bottom Line

The triple bottom line (TBL) comprises people, planet, and profit, which encourages sustainable innovations, technology, and manufacturing. The three components of the TBL encourage collaboration among society, academics, and industry. The TBL goals embrace social equity, economy, and environment. The words people, planet, and profit are often used to denote TBL and the desired goals of related business within the sustainability framework. This chapter discusses people's perspectives on sustainable innovation and technology complying with the concept of TBL. Participatory social development in co-creating innovations through reserve accountability and sustainable business modeling benefits consumers and stakeholders at the grassroots. In addition, this chapter discusses collective development design through challenge-based research and engaging industries with design-to-society and design-to-value goals. The corporate citizenship behavior has also been discussed in this chapter. This chapter contributes to providing a critical analysis of sustainable development of micro-manufacturing sectors and corporate citizenship behavior within the TBL concept.

A. Molina and Rajagopal, *Challenge-Based Learning, Research, and Innovation*, Palgrave Studies of Entrepreneurship and Social Challenges in Developing Economies,
https://doi.org/10.1007/978-3-031-29156-2_2

Putting the People First

Most companies that are currently engaged in building inclusiveness in business aim at earning profit with people, purpose, and sustainability (Triple bottom line), while some companies tend to complement the inclusive business approaches with people, reverse accountability, organizational control (social), and transformational initiatives (Quadruple bottom line). The success of inclusive businesses in the context of innovation, technology, and new product development motivates people-led companies to adapt to agile business modeling and drive co-creation and coevolution initiatives. The contemporary philosophy of development economics focuses on social and entrepreneurial production, employment, and income to equalize the gap between centralized and decentralized manufacturing and marketing systems. Sustainable entrepreneurship is, therefore, moved with the triple bottom line by recognition, evaluation, and exploitation of opportunities by stakeholders and entrepreneurs who create future products and services and deliver economic, social, and ecological gains.[1] Most customer-centric companies such as Unilever, Nestlé, and agribusiness division of Indian Tobacco Company tend to serve the society by engaging stakeholders, investors, customers, employees, and communities. However, to induce real change companies need to empower stakeholders and develop the ability to control valued resources, such as executive hiring, compensation, and list its priorities for growing business with the stakeholders. To coevolve firms must be revamp organizational culture by empowering employees and stakeholders in exercising collective decision-making and inculcate reverse accountability not only for their financial performance but also for their social and environmental impacts.[2]

In view of the global pressure on environmental protection and role of companies on managing social responsibility, corporate sustainability is often considered as a top strategic priority. Companies, however, struggle to link the social responsibility projects with the profitability goals and often fail to gain the stakeholder value. The sustainability-based view of companies suggests that decisions on sustainability projects should

[1] Patzelt, H., & Shepherd, D. A. (2011). Recognizing opportunities for sustainable development. *Entrepreneurship Theory and Practice, 35*(4), 631–652.

[2] Battilana, J., & Casciaro, T. (2021). *Power sharing can change corporations for the better*. Harvard Business Review Digital Article. Cambridge: Harvard Business Review.

be managed through a pyramidal paradigm with interrelated objectives comprising sustainability on the top, and social equity and profitability connected at the bottom of the pyramid in a linear path. Critically, the triple bottom line comprising planet, people, and profit is congruent with the pyramidal paradigm. Accordingly, the sustainability complements the traditional triple bottom approach through social consciousness and motivation to achieve relevant and timely competitive and societal impact.[3] The reverse accountability and shared accountability are largely considered as similar in organizational control process. However, elements of the formal control structure, in particular budgetary controls, are centralized in large companies while the accountability is shared in social enterprises and crowd-based companies. These companies are built with cybernetics, stakeholder accountability, and management-by-exceptions, which help the company to monitor dynamic operations and controls. Consequently, managers attempt to pursue their strategic forcing roles become involved in interdependencies with stakeholders and teams in working at the bottom-line responsibilities and accountabilities.[4]

One of the major challenges in the conventional social and cultural environment is the empowerment of entrepreneurs that builds confidence among the innovators to inculcate pro-innovation cognitive drive. Entrepreneurs need to scrutinize enormous personal and professional information of the interested people to induct into the innovation project and constitute appropriate teams. Besides driving the innovation project through the challenges of managing the resources efficiently, handling operational risk, marketability, and cost and time overrun, entrepreneurs often face market failures and piling-up of sunk cost due to radical and experimental innovation approach. Such endeavors cause risk roll-outs throughout the project leading to abort the innovation untimely, which develops serious cognitive dissonances among entrepreneurs.[5]

[3] Schneider, A. (2015). Reflexivity in sustainability accounting and management: Transcending the economic focus of corporate sustainability. *Journal of Business Ethics, 127*(3), 525–536.

[4] Frow, N., Marginson, D., & Ogden, S. (2005). Encouraging strategic behavior while maintaining management control: Multi-functional project teams, budgets, and the negotiation of shared accountabilities in contemporary enterprises. *Management Accounting Research, 16*(3), 269–292.

[5] Rajagopal. (2016). *Innovative business projects: Breaking complexities, building performance (Vol. 1)—Fundamentals and project environment*. New York: Business Expert Press.

Empowering stakeholders and employees help in exploring creativity and attraction towards new technologies, which boosts market competitiveness, business performance, and power economic growth. Successful firms empower these people and entrust them the creative lead, innovation, and business growth. However, accommodating the complex and chaotic nature of the competition with creativity and innovation is a complex phenomenon, while increasing efficiency, improving quality, and raising productivity largely depend on the organizational work-culture and employee relationship. Managing creativity with stakeholders and employees in an organization rests on triadic practices within the organization, which suggests keeping them intellectually engaged with no distractions. It is also necessary to fix accountability among employees and stakeholders to drive creativity, and it fits to business growth perspectives meticulously. In addition to engaging stakeholders and employees, engaging customers as creative partners could improve the design, development, and delivery of products. Embedding these triadic practices, firms can foster interaction among the crowd, stakeholders, employees, and society and stay competitive.[6]

Consumerism is co-constructed with social media and digital technology today. The cross-cultural attributes of consumerism have led lifestyle beyond community and enabled people to have their voice, views, validity, and value heard with liberal ethos. The diffusion of culture on social media is sometimes vehement that damages the brand image and it is not content-neutral. The collective intelligence in consumerism reflects and reinforces the dynamic consumption culture.[7] Most people at this stage seek social validation and reward for their decision to stay with the sustainable products and tend to lead environmental advocacy and green leadership at niche and regional levels of society. However, as social consciousness grows, self-actualization on sustainability commitments increases. Further, the political ideologies, government support, and stakeholder engagement contribute to the definitive green behavior of people on sustainable products and services. Social consciousness in entrepreneurship has emerged as a tool for collective problem-solving,

[6] Florida, R., & Goodnight, J. (2005). Managing for creativity. *Harvard Business Review*.

[7] Ali, M., Azab, N., Sorour, K., & Dora, M. (2019). Integration vs polarization among social media users: Perspectives through social capital theory on the recent Egyptian political landscape. *Technological Forecasting and Social Change, 145*(3), 461–473.

which typically addresses the PNS factors comprising problems, needs, and solutions. The optimal design for communication networks within organizations enables inflow of information and voice of stakeholders. The social networks govern problem-solving ideation process, and the wisdom of the crowd helps in collective judgment riding over the individual decision-making. Recent computational and experimental studies have also endorsed the network effects on collective problem-solving using the wisdom of the crowd.[8]

Corporate behavior is an outcome of organizational culture, relationships with stakeholders and employees, and organizational performance. The relationships between stakeholders and organizations largely depend on the stakeholders' needs and personal attitudes of managers, which form the corporate behavior demonstrating the social, economic, and financial health of the firms. The co-created and coevolved stakeholder relationship with the firms contributes towards mutual benefits in the long run. However, agile relationships between firms and stakeholders (customers and investors) raise individual optimism and the degree of risk in governance and leadership over time. Such behavior jeopardizes the inclusivity in business and fragments the role of stakeholder engagement in the governance of the firm. The innovative and risk-taking behavior of corporate executives and stakeholders affects the firm's actions towards investment in innovation and technology, value creation, and delivering social responsibilities. The corporate involvement in financial, marketing, and strategic decisions is a familiar concept in conventional practices. However, the business philosophy is transforming today, with a focus on inclusivity (stakeholder engagement) and optimism (social responsiveness and value creation) to stand competitive at the triple bottom line comprising people (stakeholders), planet (sustainability in business), and profit (profit-with-purpose). Optimism in firms of various sizes and performance has evolved today as a social perspective. However, there are geo-demographic differences, which reflect the extent to which people are accountable in social growth of business and can nurture expectancies for their future. The optimism and social design of the companies link to the core processes that form both corporate and social behavior. Based on the psychosocial behavior of the firms, the synergy of coevolution is driven by most business-to-consumer and business-to-business firms. These firms

[8] Centola, D. (2022). The network science of collective intelligence. *Trends in Cognitive Sciences*. https://doi.org/10.1016/j.tics.2022.08.009.

develop an energetic and task-focused approach, which is reinforced as corporate goals and connects with the socioeconomic leverages.[9]

The long subscribed corporate philosophy to earn profit with solo performance in business has been carried away with the changing trends of most corporations to transform the business philosophy to the profit with purpose by focusing on sustainability and society in general. The social business model of large firms restrains maximizing short-term profits and returns to shareholders overlooking the social and sustainability goals. Consequently, institutional logic drives the most high-performing and sustainable companies. These companies believe that they are not only the business leaders but also serve as a vehicle for advancing societal goals by delivering both social returns and enduring institutions. The institutional logic of large firms evolves alongside the economic logic in research, analysis, and managerial decision-making. The determinants of institutional logic of the firms include a common growth purpose, a long-term business focus, stakeholders and employee engagement, social partnering, frugal innovation, and profit with purpose. Firms with the above determinants drive social leadership in the firms and alter corporate behavior to gain sustainable competitive advantage.[10]

For example, Council for Advancement of Peoples' Action and Rural Technology (CAPART) is an autonomous federal government organization in India, which reviews the social and sustainable development proposals submitted by non-governmental organizations (NGOs) and self-help groups and decides whether to fund or lend financial or technological support. Over the years, CAPART has evolved into a networking hub for NGOs by promoting the exchange of ideas and exploring collaborations on delivering appropriate technology for social development and sustainability projects. CAPART has also teamed up with the Confederation of Indian Industries (CII) to tap into the Corporate Social Responsibility (CSR) programs of its member industries and The Energy and Resources Institute (TERI) to align its activities with the government's concerns against climate change and sustainability. The

[9] Ikeda, N., Inoue, K., & Sugitani, S. (2021). Managerial optimism and corporate investment behavior. *Journal of Behavioral and Experimental Finance, 30* (in press). https://doi.org/10.1016/j.jbef.2021.100492.

[10] Kanter, R. M. (2011). How great companies think differently. *Harvard Business Review*.

business ecosystem standpoint has evolved with the increasing technologies, administering experimental business models such as agile, inclusive, and crowd-based business models. Such transitions in business modeling suggest that firms focus on acquiring survival skills within expanding networks of stakeholders and grow on the triple bottom line comprising people (stakeholders), planet (sustainability), and profit (driving profit with purpose). The business model of any type is primarily aimed at achieving competitive advantages in a networked context, and firms tend to leverage value creation through a wider network of the key partners as well.[11] In the process of business innovation, firms have also faced transition across the market segments across upstream, big-middle, and bottom of the pyramid. The business philosophy of the firms has also changed over time from competitive business focus to inclusivity in business. In addition, the triple bottom has reinforced the concept of inclusivity, stakeholder accountability, and transformation. Such stakeholder inclusiveness would lead firms to experience changes in organizational behavior and encourage practices to comply with the triple bottom-line philosophy and PACT approach to coevolve business. The inclusivity approach in business largely promotes team-based work culture and transformational leadership. The social dynamics demand firms to develop businesses by reorienting their philosophy towards design-to-society and design-to-value and develop strategic partnership and corporate alliance with the local bodies to coevolve business. The need for putting people first in challenge-based research to support social and economic development is illustrated in Fig. 2.1 with various critical variables.

While putting the people first, it is important to understand and explore social needs by analyzing the existing problems, needs, and probable solutions based on the collective intelligence as exhibited in Fig. 2.1. The development needs and the public elements associated with the process to offer solutions to these challenges serve as drivers to manage the challenge-based research with focus on the triple bottom line comprising people (stakeholders), planet (sustainable solutions), and sharing profit by driving social enterprises. The stakeholder engagement contributes significantly in research-based development on various social challenges such as farm and non-farm sector economic activities, housing,

[11] Park, J., Lee, J. N., Lee, O. K. D., & Koo, Y. (2017). Alignment between internal and external IT governance and its effects on distinctive firm performance: An extended resource-based view. *IEEE Transactions on Engineering Management, 64*(3), 351–364.

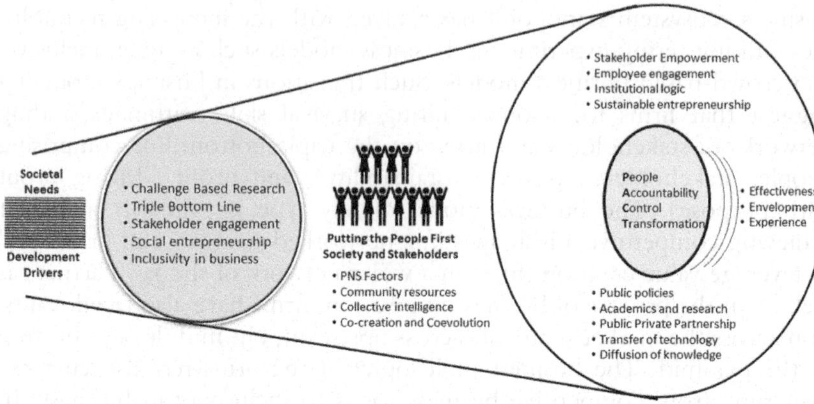

Fig. 2.1 Stakeholder engagement and socio-economic development concerns (*Source* Author [Rajagopal])

social health, education, and the like. The inclusivity and diversity in development will have a value addition in transferring the delivering the outputs and creating social consciousness. Consequently, putting the people first needs to integrate social leadership, stakeholders, and public policies to ensure the delivery of challenge-based research outcomes. The community resources and collective intelligence stimulate co-creation and coevolution of development perspectives in both social enterprises and development institutions. The linear process of social development based on challenge-based research and PNS factors must be managed through the people, accountability, collective control, and cross-sectional cascading of the transformational outcomes. This process over time grows as a systems thinking across the social strata and development institutions, which reveal the need for stakeholder empowerment, employee engagement, forward institutional logic, and encouragement of the sustainable entrepreneurship. These touchpoints must be supported by the public policies, academic research, public–private partnership, process of transfer of technology, and diffusion of knowledge to expand the outreach of challenge-based research to drive social and economic development.

The challenge-based research helps in exploring the PNS factors within society and engages community in various developmental perspectives. Community engagement in developing countries has shown significant contribution and effects in management of biodiversity, sustainability, and social entrepreneurship. Plausibly, poverty alleviation has often been focused on exploiting biodiversity through natural resource-based activities, which are initiated by the social enterprises under the support of public policies in developing economies. Value-added natural and organic products are often manufactured and marketed as raw or processed products with their commercial attributes by the local enterprises. They provide a regular or seasonal income to the entrepreneurs and contribute to the "sustainable development" movement.[12]

Among developing economies, the green energy program for rural population applied by the Government of India can be cited as a popular people's program. This program and the implementing organization have been named *Urjagram* (Energy Village) aimed at providing renewable energy for domestic and agricultural purposes. This organization focuses on distribution of solar energy in the entire village ecosystem with zero greenhouse gas emissions, which can be harnessed using a variety of devices. With recent developments, under government community programs solar energy systems are made available for agricultural and domestic use with the added advantage of minimum maintenance. Use of solar energy is promoted as a financially viable option with government tax incentives and rebates. The current architectural designs make provision for photovoltaic cells and necessary circuitry while making building plans. The National Solar Mission is a major initiative of the Government of India and the State Governments to promote ecologically sustainable growth while addressing India's energy security challenge. It will also constitute a major contribution to the global effort by India to meet the challenges of climate change. *Urjagram* focuses on bringing affordable solar lighting to people across India. Solar lights rental models, self-help group (SHG) rental models, and setting up solar charging stations providing solar lights on a rental basis create livelihood opportunities for the entire villages.[13] With the intensive involvement of SHGs, transformational consumerism in the green energy segment has been successful within the total target population. The *Urjagram* process includes following linear process involving SHGs as a change agent:

[12] Gorman, J., & Ennis, G. (2022). Community engagement in aboriginal enterprise development—Kakadu plum as a case analysis. *Journal of Rural Studies, 92*, 109–119.

[13] Neudoerffer, R. C., Malhotra, P., & Venkata Ramana, P. (2001). Participatory rural energy planning in India—A policy context. *Energy Policy, 29*(5), 371–438.

- Briefing about the solar products and its benefits.
- SHGs are engaged in setting up solar-based livelihood projects.
- SHGs propose energy projects for funding to the bank to process. The bank loans are aimed at buying the Solar LED lights or setting up small solar grids for predetermined domestic connections in the village.
- Bank processes the loan for Setting up of Village Solar Centre.
- SHGs provide lights to the villagers on rental basis.

In the background, *Urjagram* in association with SHGs delivers education to farmers through designed curriculum to enhance farm productivity, increase farm income by value addition, and promote conservation of resources. In addition, the *Urjagram* initiative also focuses in empowering women and educating them to improve their economic condition by organizing them into SHGs and arranging for skill development to facilitate income generation in the village. The "Energy Village" program of Government of India is a vital example of power autonomy at the grassroots of the society. Excessive dependence on traditional energy sources is becoming complex today, while increasing dependency on renewable energy and fossil fuels is a zero-sum competition that demands initial business investment to lower the recurring consumption costs on energy. The impact of greenhouse gases is serious to the environment and adversely affects the neighborhood ecosystem, productivity, social reputation of the companies. By decentralizing power generation through renewable energy and biomass fuel technology, the power distribution design will lead to integrating the power autonomy. This would reduce the risks of power generation, distribution, and generation by categorically developing energy portfolios of rural, urban, and industrial energy markets. However, impending regulatory restrictions on renewable energy would help in creating more appealing products for customers that induce cost-effective consumption.[14]

The sustainability-based view of companies suggests that decisions on sustainability projects should be managed through a pyramidal paradigm with interrelated objectives comprising sustainability on the top, and social equity and profitability connected at the bottom of the pyramid

[14] Unruh, G. C. (2010). *Power autonomy: Using the biosphere's rules to renew your company with renewable energy*. Boston, MA: Harvard Business School Press.

in a linear path. Critically, the triple bottom line comprising planet, people, and profit is congruent with the pyramidal paradigm. Accordingly, the corporate sustainability complements the traditional triple bottom approach through social consciousness and motivation to achieve relevant and timely competitive and societal impact.[15] Consequently, the social and business environment nurtures the triple bottom line by integrating people (stakeholders), planet (sustainability), and profit (business performance). The organizational and business ecosystem focuses on the design-to-society and design-to-value strategies through transformational leadership and stakeholder management. Accordingly, the social enterprise business modeling encourages inclusivity in business, agility and collectivism in decision-making process, and towards implementing the corporate social responsibility. Broadly, the social consciousness is also driven by the stakeholder and corporate engagements, community participation, and various personality dimensions such as emotions and cognition, culture, values, self-reference, and responsiveness towards society and business.

Reverse Accountability

The concept of inclusive business has been explained in context of the various ecosystems that affect the business orientation and functionality of firms. Consequently, business, social, crowd, and behavioral ecosystems significantly contribute to the attributes of business inclusiveness. These ecosystems are built on triple and quadruple bottom lines as explained in the above Figure. Most companies that are currently engaged in building inclusiveness in business aim at earning profit with people, purpose, and sustainability (Triple bottom line), while some companies tend to complement the inclusive business approaches with people, reverse accountability, organizational control (social), and transformational initiatives[16] (Quadruple bottom line). Reverse accountability in monitoring performance in people-led business firms supplements the leadership perspectives on inclusive business. Such governance system creates competitive

[15] Schneider, A. (2015). Reflexivity in sustainability accounting and management: Transcending the economic focus of corporate sustainability. *Journal of Business Ethics, 127*(3), 525–536.

[16] Rajagopal. (2022). *Evolving with inclusive business in emerging markets: Managing the new bottom-line*. New York: Business Expert Press.

advantage through higher customer value and contributes to business growth of the company and society.[17] The frequent shift in business models has attracted considerable scholarly attention and managerial efforts towards increasing a firm's competitive advantages.[18] Continuous transition of business models of the firms over time in emerging markets has significantly moved the locus of value creation and value capture to the changing business ecosystems. Accordingly, the stakeholders (e.g., customers, competitors, suppliers, social organizations, and other institutions) and the key partners play an important role in determining (co-creating), implementing (coevolution), and monitoring (reverse accountability) the performance of businesses. Firms strengthen the relationships among all stakeholders associated with the business organizations as they increasingly rely on stakeholders within the business ecosystem to co-create and capture value by redesigning inclusive and crowd-based business models.[19]

Social enterprises have several push and pull factors that influence organizational behavior. These enterprises undertake necessity-based manufacturing and services operations for upstream growth by managing financial resources through social institutions and aiding through public programs. Social enterprises largely invest in knowledge management and engage stakeholders in creating and sharing ideas and transforming conventional business models. The organizational behavior of these enterprises is influenced by the transformational leadership, stakeholder participation, and employee engagement to co-create innovations and coevolve business. The push and pull factors drive organizations to adapt to the existing social trends and develop *profit with purpose* business goals. One of the salient features of social enterprises is the reverse accountability, which emphasizes organizational governance by the stakeholders. With the advancement of technology and convenience-led marketing, elderly

[17] Bocken, N. M. P., Short, S. W., Rana, P., & Evans, S. (2014). A literature and practice review to develop sustainable business model archetypes. *Journal of Cleaner Production, 65*(1), 42–56.

[18] Yi, Y., Chen, Y., & Li, D. (2022). Stakeholder ties, organizational learning, and business model innovation: A business ecosystem perspective. *Technovation, 114* (in press). https://doi.org/10.1016/j.technovation.2021.102445.

[19] Wei, Z., Song, X., & Wang, D. (2017). Manufacturing flexibility, business model design, and firm performance. *International Journal of Production and Economics, 193*(1), 87–97.

consumers are feeling out of place in the market today as they are unable to cope with the technology-driven marketing approaches, applications, and self-service platforms. Consequently, *reverse socialization* is gearing up in the families as elderly consumers are being influenced by the young consumers. Reverse socialization is a process which allows adolescents to influence their parents' knowledge, skills, and attitudes related to consumption. Such behavior is driven by emotions, the changing perceptions on products and services, and restructured cognitive ergonomics[20] (Gentina & Muratore, 2012).

People's involvement in business has proved effective in social institutions, which attained commercial significance over time. For example, *Gramin Bank* (Rural bank) in Bangladesh has emerged as a social institution, which is built by the people as a self-help group and attained the status of a national commercial bank over time. Similarly, dairy farmers' cooperatives in the state of Gujarat in India have evolved in the mid-twentieth century as people's organization for mutual benefits and grown as a largest commercial organization with the corporate brand AMUL (Anand Milk Union Limited). In these organizations, the stakeholders (members of the institution) have exercised social control and reverse accountability to manage the business with commitment. In view of the above and several such examples, it is evident that the PACT philosophy is embedded in the customer-centric and social business organizations. This book discusses the attributes of PACT philosophy in business and critically examines its role in enhancing the business performance from the crowd perspective.[21]

The increasingly crowded Mexican microfinance market has deep penetration within the niche population and microentrepreneurs face complexities in business and their income contribution has the lowest two quintiles. Consequently, the business pressure is mounting on new players who desire to reach a healthy portfolio size and achieve long-term sustainability in both entrepreneurship and business. In view of the changing scenario, microfinance institutions (MFIs) have made great efforts to overcome traditional geographic and operational barriers and expanded their outreach to cover over 90% of the 2,500 municipalities in

[20] Gentina, E., & Muratore, I. (2012). Environmentalism at home: The process of ecological resocialization by teenagers. *Journal of Consumer Behaviour, 11*(2), 162–169.

[21] Prpić, J., Shukla, P. P., Kietzmann, J. H., & McCarthy, I. P. (2015). How to work a crowd: Developing crowd capital through crowdsourcing. *Business Horizons, 58*(1), 77–85.

the country. The growth in the sector has primarily focused on rural areas as there is a high concentration of competitors in urban and semi-urban areas. It is therefore not a coincidence that of the five Mexican states with the highest rural populations, four have the highest number of operating MFIs in the country (Chiapas, Veracruz, Estado de México, and Oaxaca). Three of these states also have the lowest Human Development Index scores in Mexico (Oaxaca, Veracruz and Chiapas). PRONAFIM is a program managed by the Finance Ministry (Sectretaría de Economía) that provides funding for microfinance institutions. The Smart Campaign has worked closely with PRONAFIM to support client protection in the market for over a year. This tool will help PRONAFIM to evaluate these MFIs against minimum industry standards in areas like transparency, prevention of over indebtedness, and responsible pricing practices to identify, stakeholder empowerment, and reform client protection practices across the MFIs.[22] The specific attributes of agile marketing are inclusivity and reverse accountability (customer engagement and role in agile governance), which help companies encourage agile teams to participate in co-creation of products, services, brands, and marketing strategies along with the customers and stakeholders. The co-creation will be meaningful for the companies if the problems, needs, and probable solutions are meticulously explored by the agile teams, customers, and stakeholders.

Reverse accountability emphasizes the me-too concern in business management through participation in decision-making and performance evaluation activities of a firm. The underlying principles of reverse accountability are towards protecting stakeholder interest, customer values, and obtaining secured business growth. Engaging customers and stakeholders in business processes not only allows collaboration in organizational growth but also in recognizing their psychological sensitivity in people-led business organizations. However, firms constantly face ideological differences and conflicting goals while involving people in business operations under unstructured or semi-structured business modeling process. It is difficult for people's evaluation in short-term business goals due to lack of sensitivity to the dynamics of business ecosystem elements. Nonetheless, reverse accountability serves as a potential instrument for integrating social and customer values, and strategic

[22] Kleynjans, L., & Hudon, M. (2016). A study of codes of ethics for Mexican microfinance institutions. *Journal of Business Ethics, 134*(3), 397–412.

revenue goals. Reverse accountability has grown out of social organizational structure, which demonstrates community practices and social governance in radically managing the organizational performance and collective leadership.[23] The stakeholders in social enterprises tend to lead collective challenges and streamline transformational leadership regardless of the outside-in effect on the entrepreneurial ecosystem. Reverse accountability and social governance have congruent philosophy, which can drive collective strategies to generate new lines of business with stakeholder involvement to resolve problems and promote social practices in business. Reverse accountability helps in streamlining leadership traits, improving democratic skills in organizations, and retaining social values. The paradox of reverse accountability lies in vertical decision-making practices and leader-oriented organizational integration. The success of reverse accountability has been evidenced in self-help groups and social organizations that exhibit collective values and social control of organization. This has big implications in streamlining leadership, abridging gaps between diverse groups of employees, and networking human values within social framework.[24]

Sustainable Business Modeling

The growing concerns of circular economy and circular business have reoriented companies towards developing sustainable business models with effective social value chain management. Circular economy encourages sharing of ideas, processes, and outcomes that are widely connected with sustainability projects. Sharing the economy of consumers, stakeholders, and society related to the consumer products companies encourages them to develop sustainable business model. Most companies are engaged in building and implementing sustainable business models in the social interest that helps in value chain creation and acquiring new customers. While sharing socio-cultural attributes of geo-demographic

[23] Di Pietro, F., Prencipe, A., & Majchrzak A. (2018). Crowd equity investors: An underutilized asset for open innovation in startups. *California Management Review, 60*(2), 43–70.

[24] Rajagopal, & Rajagopal, A. (2023). Reverse accountability and leadership in social enterprises: Analysis of social control and openness for pragmatic organizational design. *International Journal of Business Excellence* (in press). https://doi.org/10.1504/IJBEX.2021.10041966.

segments has been a long-standing practice in society, the sharing economy is used as an umbrella concept to exhibit broad range of disparate consumption practices and organizational models.[25] The value proposition of both customers and social communities contributes significantly to the sustainable business modeling process. Value proposition describes the attributes of product/service offering, the customer segments, and their relationship in the social deliveries, while value creation and delivery describe how value is provided to customers (the channel efficiency and value delivery process), including the structure and activities in the value chain.[26]

The success-driven social sustainability dimensions of corporate culture include sustainability-strategy and leadership, mission, communication and learning, social care and work life, and loyalty and identification. In addition to other indicators related to measurement of the business performance of a company, the indicators mentioned above are taken into consideration for a company to be classified as financially successful. Collaborative and longitudinal approaches over phased project timeline work better to create and measure the impact of sustainable business models on environment, society, economy, and other key stakeholders. Hence, a systemic form of sustainable business model can be developed to ensure clarity in propositions and constructs and make geo-demographic expansion possible. Sustainable business models are spread longitudinally, so they are bound to face unforeseen risks which need to be managed in association with the stakeholders. Creating Shared Value (CSV) serves as the fundamental guiding principle for consumer-centric companies. Sustainable development can be easily integrated into business activities by creating shared values. Such business models with focus on sustainability are increasingly attracting long-term investors and involving unrelenting stakeholder participation. CSV brings business and society together by generating values for the local livelihood economy, global economic concerns, and value for society.[27]

[25] Habibi, M. R., Davidson, A., & Laroche, M. (2017). What managers should know about the sharing economy. *Business Horizon, 60*(1), 113–112.

[26] Osterwalder, A., & Pigneur, Y. (2010). *Business model generation: A handbook for visionaries, game changers, and challengers*. Hoboken, NJ: Wiley.

[27] Rajagopal. (2020b). *Barriers and benefits towards sustainability driven business models*. In S. Hashmi & I. A. Choudhury (Eds.), *Encyclopedia of renewable and sustainable materials* (Vol. 5, pp. 318–327). New York: Elsevier.

Sustainability-driven companies make sustainable choices on prioritizing social and environmental elements in developing business models and make them visible to the consumer as product- or service attributes. Such marketing strategies are embedded in the business models as part of the value proposition. Marketing strategies that are backed by social choices converge key partners, activities, and resources in the business model. The social products are marketed to customer with value propositions, which deliver utilitarian values upon purchasing the products or services. Consequently, customers develop perceived value consistently, which later develops loyalty for brands. The sustainability linked business modeling, therefore, relies significantly on the value proposition.[28] Social sustainability is manifested in corporate culture, organizational behavior, and functional practices of the companies. To create and measure the impact of sustainable business models on environment, society, economy, and other key stakeholders, collaborative and longitudinal approaches over phased time span work better. Successful businesses in manufacturing and service sectors tend to understand the challenges and opportunities linked to business transition towards sustainability in a society today. They create considerable awareness on the environment and green consumption practices in the society.[29]

Consumer-centric companies are engaged in sustainable agriculture, developing green by-products emerging from ecological conservation projects. Stakeholders contribute significantly in developing sustainability projects with the companies, and in carrying out the implementation of projects at the field level. Accordingly, stakeholders collaborate, co-create, and co-manage sustainability projects. Value perceptions of sustainability projects integrated into business model innovations are closely associated with the development needs, economic growth, and quality-of life improvement of society in general and stakeholders of the company in particular. Sustainable social development projects have spanned over a long time and their measurable impact is longitudinal. Companies look for return on investment made in sustainable social development projects

[28] Pal, R., & Gander, J. (2018). Modelling environmental value: An examination of sustainable business models within the fashion industry. *Journal of Cleaner Production, 184*(2), 251–263.

[29] Rajagopal. (2020b). *Barriers and benefits towards sustainability driven business models*. In S. Hashmi & I. A. Choudhury (Eds.), *Encyclopedia of renewable and sustainable materials* (Vol. 5, pp. 318–327). New York: Elsevier.

sooner or later. Therefore, integrating sustainable social development projects into business model(s) is the only option for the companies. Among the elements of canvass, measuring cost-time-risk (CTR factors), key partners, possible shared resources, predetermined revenue stream and its management, social value generation, investment on social innovation, and analyzing market trends make significant contributions.

Sustainability-based business models are developed and implemented by most companies at the corporate level by applying uniform strategies across their subsidiaries with marginal field-level adjustments. However, multi-domestic companies operating with the subsidiaries in different destinations with a definite focus on manufacturing and marketing tend to develop homogeneity in the business models for implementation. For example, Nestlé has uniform social sustainability business models towards organic coffee cultivation, green curing of coffee, and dairy farming practices in Latin American, African, and Asian destinations. The boundary spanning sustainability-based business models have different types of organizational boundary changes between the subsidiaries and their external stakeholders as these business models seek exploring, negotiating, disrupting, and realigning organizational boundaries. The complexity for alignment can be seen through different ways of perceiving the stakeholder and societal values, serving to diverging sustainability interests, risks and responsibilities, and connective efficiently with the existing processes and activities. Openness for strategic alignment of business models with stakeholder needs, culture, and societal values significantly affect the implementation of sustainable business models.[30]

As the business environment is changing rapidly, the performance of sustainability-based business models is becoming complex. Seamless implementation of business projects has taken a long time to gain social value as its stakeholders initially found it difficult to adapt to the change from conventional to digital or self-service technologies. However, a well-implemented business model allows a company to gain economic value by providing social and environmental benefits over time.[31] Managing

[30] Velter, M. G. E., Bitzer, V., Bocken, N. M. P., & Kemp, R. (2020). Sustainable business model innovation: The role of boundary work for multi-stakeholder alignment. *Journal of Cleaner Production, 247*. https://doi.org/10.1016/j.jclepro.2019.119497.

[31] Schaltegger, S., Lüdeke-Freund, F., & Hansen, E. G. (2016). Business models for sustainability: A co-evolutionary analysis of sustainable entrepreneurship, innovation, and transformation. *Organization and Environment, 29*(3), 264–289.

sustainability-linked business models refers to the approaches dealing with social, environmental, and economic issues in an integrated manner to transform businesses that create social values and equity of brands of the company. Such business models contribute to sustainable development of the economy and society within the ecosystem. Accordingly, a sustainability-based business model describes the design, delivery, and captures mechanisms to create social value. It emphasizes stakeholder and customer needs and defines ways through which companies deliver value to them, invests in value creation, and co-creates resources through the proper design and operation of the various elements of the value chain.[32]

Implementation and governance of sustainability-based business models are shared through public–private partnerships. In addition, stakeholder-driven governance forms such as cooperatives, public private partnerships, or social businesses help companies transcend narrow profit-maximizing models. The business models are analyzed from a sustainability perspective to overcome the economic, social, and technological bias of sustainability approaches. Accordingly, entrepreneurial approaches are designed in improving social sector, and operate through a typology of "isolated" and "interactive" business models categorically in geo-demographic market segments (Sánchez & Ricart, 2010). The practice of developing sustainability-linked business model has dyadic leverage for companies and society and listed below:

- It stimulates new approaches in the corporate sustainability management and sustainable entrepreneurship.
- Its conventional experience strengthens the business paradigm of social value creation.

The value proposition embedded in these business models provides ecological, social, and economic values through sustainable products and services, while business infrastructure enables the sustainable supply chain management to operate with public–private partnership and involving stakeholders and corporate resources. The customer interface during the implementation of business models enables direct relationships with stake holders, key partners, and public systems, and share responsibility of

[32] Rajagopal. (2021). *Sustainable businesses in developing economies—Socio-economic and governance perspectives*. New York: Palgrave Macmillan.

production, services, and consumption systems.[33] The emerging and existing companies are engaged in working with innovative business models respecting society and environment to stay competitive in the marketplace. Trends like circular economy, business waste control (manufacturing, packaging, logistics, and inventory wastes), value-oriented recycling under growing consciousness of circular business, and the sharing economy are some of the many sustainable entrepreneurial approaches. The framework of attributes is associated with the sustainable business modeling process. Among others, ***design-to-market***, ***design-to society***, and ***design-to-value*** are the three principal emerging concepts that guide the sustainable business modeling process. Convergence of these concepts is a major challenge in building sustainable business models and ensuring its effective implementation. There are micro-environmental factors that influence sustainable business modeling process which comprises value chain creation and delivery, leadership taxonomy through the sustainable business modeling and implementation process, and public–private partnership and performance. Companies engaged in developing business models embedded with sustainability objectives need to strengthen capital resources and infrastructure to ensure achievable milestones through the right strategies. These companies divide the long-term business plans into rolling plans of shorter duration and operate through collaborative projects by engaging stakeholders.

The business model canvas has two facets, background and foreground, which have many elements from concept development to generation of revenue streams. The principal elements at the background of the canvas consist of concept development, design thinking, industry attractiveness, market research, cost-structure, and management of revenue streams. The foreground of the canvas has elements contextual to the operations of the business model. These elements include organizational design, key partners, key activities, key resources, marketing channels, sales, customer relations management, and value propositions of the business model in the context of circular economy (CE) concepts. The CE epoch is associated with open innovation and encourages crowdsourcing in developing circular business and recycling concepts and setting up transforming ideas into the industrial economic and business frameworks.

[33] Boons, F., & Lüdeke-Freund, F. (2013). Business models for sustainable innovation: State of the art and steps towards a research agenda. *Journal of Cleaner Production, 45*(1), 9–19.

Accordingly, companies set goals, objectives, and CE mission complementing the global sustainability development goals. While developing sustainable product concepts, firms also conduct extensive research to understand consumer behavior, moderate values, and locate markets.

Design thinking is central to innovations of sustainable products through cyclical generations in the CE environment, which emerges out of the clear identification of social needs and consumption patterns in society. Accordingly, the design thinking process identifies the right innovation and technology to co-create the second-generation products from the industrial waste, maps product attractiveness, value spread, and determine its shelf-life and end of the cycle product state. Companies categorize CE product development projects and develop project charter by measuring the anticipated cost, time, and risk factors in an operations matrix. Industry attractiveness has always been a prerequisite for developing business models. The industry attractiveness comprising new entrants, growth of substitutes, bargaining power of consumers and suppliers, and competition within the industry dominate the concerns of companies on developing appropriate marketing strategy and customer value. In an industry with fast growing competition, consumers face complexities in developing sustainable perceptions and attitude to inculcate behavior. Rapidly emerging new brands (CE led philosophy) from unfamiliar companies attract consumers with low prices. Although most consumers tend to experiment with low priced products and substitute the products that deliver satisfactory experience, they fail to develop sustainable perceptions and build attitude towards repeat buying. However, industry attractiveness describes competition among traditional pipeline brands, which succeeds by optimizing the activities in their value chains. In addition, as a globalization effect, the platform brands co-created together with the consumers and producers, such as Uber (transport service), Alibaba (e-commerce), and Airbnb (urban housing), are growing in the market by improving the consumer chain and delivering satisfaction.[34] Substitute products in the market affect the industry potential adversely and pose a threat to customer preferences. Bargaining power of buyers refers to the direct or indirect pressure tactics to force the

[34] Van Alstyne, M. W., Parker, G. G., & Choudary, S. P. (2016). *Pipelines, platforms, and the new lines of strategies*. HBR Digital Article. Cambridge: Harvard Business School Press. Retrieved on January 30, 2023, https://hbr.org/2016/04/pipelines-platforms-and-the-new-rules-of-strategy.

industry to reduce prices or increase product features, in view to optimize the customer value. Buyers gain power when they have choices, and when their needs can be met by a substitute product or by the same product offered by another supplier.[35]

Market research is also one of the important factors to be considered in business modeling. Firms engaged in CE business modeling need to explore the market environment for recycled products by analyzing the political, economic, social, technological, and legal factors associated with manufacturing and marketing the predetermined products. Market research also guides the firms to choose the right market, existing or potential, to position their products. However, sometime companies invest in educating consumers on sustainable products and services that support CE business philosophy and attempt to create demand among consumers. Organic cosmetics, textile, and renewable energy products in emerging markets need substantial consumer education to motivate buying decisions. The cost-structure in the context of manufacturing, marketing, human resources, financial overheads, and corporate social responsibility is a sensitive input in developing business models and project the direct, indirect, and future revenue streams associated with the business models. Recycling and customization of products is the growing sustainable business trend for industrial companies. New technologies like additive manufacturing are enablers to advanced technology-based manufacturing and for sustainable production. Companies offering production systems for these technologies are more and more required to embed dynamic cost and risk implications on the manufacturing and marketing process.[36]

Managing Eco-Innovation

Continuing growth in global population, increasing density of urban and rural habitats across countries, and the ecological and sustainability concerns are being overlooked for economic growth by over exploitation of natural resources. This situation demands affordable ecological innovations in some vital economic sectors like energy, transportation and

[35] Rajagopal. (2019). *Contemporary marketing strategy: Analyzing consumer behavior to drive managerial decision making*. New York: Palgrave Macmillan.

[36] Schröder, A., Falk, B., & Schmitt, R. (2015). Evaluation of cost structures of additive manufacturing processes using a new business model. *Procedia CIRP, 30*, 311–316.

logistics, solid and industrial waste management, and reducing particle and gaseous pollutions. The low-cost innovations to improve social and industrial sustainability would help in managing resource scarcity and over-allocation issues that are increasing the pressure on natural resources. In this scenario, ecological governance is positioned as a critical issue not only for large industries but also for the small and medium firms operating in regional markets.[37] Innovation is the critical dimension of economic change in a macro perspective and business growth within the micro perspective. At macro level, economic change revolves around innovation and catalyzes entrepreneurial activities that lead to drive market power. As the market competition is continuously increasing in the global marketplace, the innovation-driven market power could provide better results than the conventional wisdom like price and promotion competition. Alongside product-design and strategy innovation, technological innovation often creates ad hoc monopolies in the market allowing abnormal profits in a short life cycle. Such temporary monopolies are sometimes necessary to provide incentives for firms to develop new products and processes.[38]

Much attention has been paid recently to innovation as a way for industry and policymakers to achieve more radical, systemic improvements in corporate environmental practices and performance. The social-ecological innovation has emerged as an important consideration in environmental governance in addition to the sectoral issues in sustainability. Eco-innovations encouraged in local markets contribute to the resilience of ecosystem services in urban socio-economic and ecological landscapes. Consequently, urban and rural areas need implementation of green recovery programs as a range of important ecosystem services. Urban centers have grown in the recent past with satellite industrial production centers and have observed degradation of environmental standards over the years. These centers have become combined geo-demographic segments with industrial production centers and populous habitats. Crowdsourcing of innovative ideas, collective intelligence to improve the resources utilization, and management of green space in urban social-ecological systems have emerged as effective tools to manage

[37] Molle, F., López-Gunn, E., & van Steenbergen, F. (2018). The local and national politics of groundwater overexploitation. *Water Alternatives, 11*, 445–457.

[38] Pol, E., & Carroll, P. (2006). *An introduction to economics with emphasis on innovation* (2nd ed.). New York: Thomson Learning.

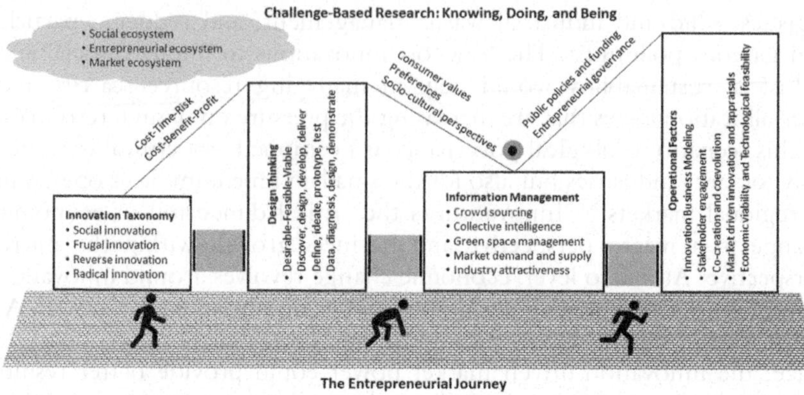

Fig. 2.2 Innovative journey of social entrepreneurs: touchpoints on pathway (*Source* Author [Rajagopal])

sustainability projects. Such practices can drive public–private partnership to develop social-ecological innovation and provide a valuable resource in the production and adaptive management of local ecosystem services with social governance efficacy.[39] The pathway of entrepreneurial journey in managing sustainable and eco-innovations by engaging stakeholders through challenge-based research is exhibited in Fig. 2.2.

The challenge-based research, social entrepreneurship, triple bottom line, and socio-economic development of all stages of growth are linearly aligned with the social, entrepreneurial, and market ecosystems as illustrated in Fig. 2.2. Challenge-based research is an initiative towards different types of innovations including social, frugal, reverse, and radical innovations with a focus on PNS factors. Nonetheless innovation initiative is usually evaluated in the context of cost-time-risk and cost–benefit (values)-profit matrix. Accordingly, design thinking is governed both cognitively and operationally among the entrepreneurs. The design thinking on social innovation is largely based on the review of opportunities with a focus on desirability, feasibility, and viability of the innovation to commercialize and make it adaptable to the social

[39] Dennis, M., & James, P. (2018). Urban social-ecological innovation: Implications for adaptive natural resource management. *Ecological Economics, 150*, 153–164.

and economic development.[40] Economic viability and technological feasibility drive research-based innovations to discover, design, development, and efficiency in delivering the innovation. However, the major challenge in social innovation is to define the needs, ideate solutions, develop prototype based on the inclusive research, and test the products and services at the right target segment. It is necessary to analyze consumer values, preferences, and socio-cultural perspectives while working with the social innovations. Social development projects can be well-conceived by crowdsourcing information, analyzing collective intelligence and market demand to grow innovations within the social green space. However, firms must put enormous efforts to commercialize research-based innovations through collective business models by engaging stakeholders to co-create and coevolve sustainable production in both social and commercial platforms. Such organized efforts require strong public policies, funding support, and entrepreneurial governance. Social innovation, therefore, combined with the concepts of entrepreneurship, inclusion, and co-production; on the other hand, addresses the contemporary rural and urban perspectives.[41] Consequently, the challenge-based research leads to the knowing (exploring), doing (experimenting), and being (living) state of social and economic development.

Many companies have started to use eco-innovation or similar terms to describe their contributions to sustainable development. A few governments are also promoting the concept as a way to meet sustainable development targets while keeping industry and the economy competitive. However, while the promotion of eco-innovation by industry and government involves the pursuit of both economic and environmental sustainability, the scope and application of the concept tend to differ. Impact refers to the effect of eco-innovation on the environment across its life cycle or some other focus area. Potential environmental impacts stem from the target and mechanism of eco-innovation, and their interplay with its socio-technical surroundings. Given a specific target, the potential

[40] Chen, H. C., Knierim, A., & Bock, B. B. (2022). The emergence of social innovation in rural revitalization practices: A comparative case study from Taiwan. *Journal of Rural Studies, 90*, 134–146.

[41] Tricarico, L., De Vidovich, L., & Billi, A. (2022). Entrepreneurship, inclusion or co-production? An attempt to assess territorial elements in social innovation literature. *Cities, 130* (in press). https://doi.org/10.1016/j.cities.2022.103986.

magnitude of the environmental benefit tends to depend on the mechanism of eco-innovation, as more systemic changes such as alternatives and creation generally embody higher potential benefits than modification and re-design.

The community-based natural resources management has been encouraged by the social organizations (self-help groups and non-governmental organizations) on the assumption that the decision-making process in natural resource management is a collective process within the communities and among stakeholders. This community approach has not only fostered knowledge and commitment among the stakeholders, but also stimulated ecological innovation in start-up enterprises at the local level. However, commercialization of frugal and reverse innovations in the green economic and industrial sector is a major challenge. The problem of commercialization of innovation is largely attributed to the interface of top-down (public policies and funding) and bottom-up approaches (social and entrepreneurial governance), which primarily involves the inter-institutional arrangements to diffuse and market the innovations.[42] Ecological innovations have become dispersed as the market is becoming increasingly demanding and the users have formed their niche. Accordingly, innovation has shifted from technology to business models, and is more focused on marketing than the social needs. Many innovations are emerging in the market that are simplified, while some are scaling up in improving the existing products or services and positioning them as innovations. However, managers may align their business strategies with competitive advantages of markets and manage innovation in emerging economies to diffuse and commercialize.[43] Traditionally positioning innovation of products and services makes a company competitive is a myth in the present state of global marketing. Consequently, firms continually reinvent in large and small ways in reference to shift in market demand and changes in the economy and develop competitive marketing strategy in reference to the shifts in the product and market behavior, knowledge of innovative products, and innovation positions. Though the company may develop efficiency about the above strategic positions of

[42] Armitage, D. (2005). Adaptive capacity and community-based natural resource management. *Environment Management, 35*(6), 703–715.

[43] De Meyer, A. (2011, September 15). Diving into the new innovation landscape. *IESE-Insight Magazine*.

product/market, knowledge, and innovation independently, the firms are still risk-averse with the innovation.[44]

Successful innovation leads to customer involvement and profits, which can be achieved through co-creation by aligning consumers and market players in the innovation process. Some multinational companies have invested in sustainability projects by taking advantage of social media to diffuse new ideas and stimulating co-creation of innovative products and services. For example, the role of co-creation has become central to sustainability management in the social initiatives of twenty-first century. Energy market transition, which is enabled by new affordable energy technologies and digitalization, opens novel opportunities for developing innovative energy solutions through collective intelligence and public–private co-creations. The new technologies emerging through co-creation facilitate stakeholders to buy low-cost renewable energy. The process of co-innovation is stretching the ideation process through the extensive use of digital platforms and stakeholder involvement. Co-innovation is an ecosystem-wide activity that involves multiple stakeholders, who collaborate towards a shared social goal and explore niche strategies to commercialize eco-innovations. However, in active societies like Chinese sociological and business culture, the co-innovators simultaneously compete with one another across the geo-demographic segments to market their innovative products and services.[45]

For many companies, developing new products does not occur as a chance or coincidence; innovative products emerge through careful attention to many important criteria. Firms should analyze their innovation practices and capabilities to become more effective in driving innovation as breakthrough and gain the competitive advantage. Innovation and enterprise-integration are two compelling sources of growth in a dynamic competitive marketplace. The ability to coordinate across organizational boundaries largely appears as a critical factor in determining the speed and life cycle of a market-driven innovation. Innovations need to be integrated into the larger operations of the corporation at sufficient level of scale to show a prolific impact on business and sustainability in the marketplace.

[44] McDonough, E. F., Zack, M., Lin, H. E., & Berdrow, I. (2008). Integrating innovation style and knowledge into strategy. *Sloan Management Review, 50*(1), 53–58.

[45] Kotilainen, K., Saari, U. A., Mäkinen, S. J., & Ringle, C. M. (2019). Exploring the microfoundations of end-user interests toward co-creating renewable energy technology innovations. *Journal of Cleaner Production, 229*, 203–212.

Many large businesses spend resources on innovations but fail to capitalize on them. However, some organizations use innovations to optimize local operations than integrating them to create consumer value and corporate image.

Innovations leading to commercialization phase have the major challenge of convincing the customers to adopt them successfully and gain value for money. The diffusion of innovations (DOI) theory suggests that the innovators and the early adopters are generally sensitive to low price and high-quality combinations and are technologically more comfortable. The lead customers are also risk-tolerant, as compared to the later categories of early- and late-majority mass market users. The real commercialization challenges for an eco-innovation (alike other products and services) emerges when it is moved to the mass consumers' market. These features make the innovators and the early adopters more willing to test premature products, whereas the later adopters expect high quality and value for their money. However, co-creation of second-generation innovation with end users can be more prolific to business, which encompasses a range of activities, for example, collecting user feedback, lead user engagement, modified prototype development, product testing, pricing, and distribution strategy, and integrating servitization process.[46]

Frugal innovation is the process of reducing the complexity and cost of products by taking cost-effective measures in manufacturing and following economies of scale. Usually, this refers to removing conspicuous features from products, such as an automobile, to market it in bottom-of-the-pyramid markets and emerging markets. Designing products for such markets may also call for an increase in sustainability of innovative products and selling through modern routes to market. However, profits earned on frugal innovations are much lower than high value-high technology innovative products targeted to the up-front or premier markets. The user-driven innovation conforms to the consumers' needs and would help them realize its value at relatively lower costs. Accordingly, firms can "refresh" innovation policy to embrace user-driven innovation and encouraging user-driven innovation against high cost-complex market

[46] Nambisan, S. (2010). *Virtual customer environments: IT-enabled customer co-innovation and value co-creation*. Information Technology and Product Development—Annals of Information Systems (pp. 109–127). New York: Springer.

innovations.[47] Firms in many industries feel immense pressure to improve their ability to innovate consumer-centric products and services. However, managers know that the best ideas do not always come out of their own research and development laboratory. Hence, a growing number of companies are exploring the idea of open-market innovation, an approach that uses tools such as licensing, joint ventures, and strategic alliances to bring the benefits of free trade to the flow of new ideas.[48] Successful innovation companies should have the following attributes:

- Systematic collection of internal and external (crowdsourced) information could lead to innovation.
- Screening information for economic viability and technological feasibility for developing prototype.
- Analyzing the functionality of eco-innovation and its adaptability.
- Creativity of employees and stakeholders.
- Economics of converting an innovation idea, social values, and expected value for money.
- Co-creation opportunities by within the broad framework of stakeholders, society, and public policies.
- Project-based approach in developing eco-innovations and ability to manage projects with public–private partnership, social or state governance, and entrepreneurial wisdom.
- Cooperation with external experts.
- Ability to take appropriate measures of risk-taking.
- Drive employees' motivation (the employees should be willing to improve the product and the operation of the whole company).
- Ensure the opportunity of continuous learning among employees, stakeholders, and market players.
- Ability to commercialize eco-innovations in the mass markets and industrial market segments.

Open innovation is a model that assumes that firms can and should use external ideas as well as internal ideas, and internal and external

[47] Martin, R., & Milway, J. (2012, September). *User-driven innovation: Putting an end to inventing in the dark* (Working paper). Rotman School of Management.

[48] Rigby, D. K., & Zook, C. (2001). Open-market innovation. *Harvard Business Review, 80*(10), 80–89.

paths to market, with the advancement of technology application in developing innovative products. The concept of open innovation emphasizes that knowledge on new ideas, products, use values, and innovation are widespread in the world and it is not possible for the companies to explore this wealth to their fullest capacity. However, business ideas, concepts, and innovation processes are licensed from other companies. In addition, firms can take internal inventions, not being used in their business, outside the company to get them licensed and earn royalty by selling them to client organizations. Most companies that intend to use open-market innovation apply tools such as licensing, joint ventures, and strategic alliances to bring the benefits of free trade to the flow of new ideas.

Industrialization has been debated for a long time from various perspectives—social, economic, and political. Over time, technological growth has added new dimension to the manufacturing and services industries. The Industry 4.0 movement with digital revolution has further enhanced the scope of economic contribution of industries. However, in the chronological journey of industrial growth, industries have merged as a para-civilization with the concepts of corporate citizenship status. Human society and ecological system have led to steep contradictions between human civilization and nature. Industrial growth, despite economic benefits, have depleted resources and degraded ecological environment endangering social health and quality of life. The basis of sustainable development is modifying the conditions of industrial civilization. The rise of social consciousness would contribute to the environmental consciousness in the industrial sector. Public demonstration projects are used to promote the upgrade of China's green manufacturing technology to accelerate innovation as a catch-up instrument to manage sustainable development and transitions in the industrial concerns on sustainability.[49]

Manufacturing industries are bouncing over the global environmental challenges. However, their future contributions are subject to the rate of adaptation and integration of the eco-innovative approaches best suited to their production patterns. This approach requires a debate on the broad perspective of diffusion of awareness on sustainability of manufacturing and the underlying focus on potential eco-innovative solutions to reduce environmental impacts. In addition, industries must recognize that

[49] Zhao, W., Jeong, J., & Noh, S. D. (2015). Energy simulation framework integrated with green manufacturing-enabled PLM information model. *International Journal of Precision Engineering and Manufacturing Green Technology*, *2*(3), 217–224.

the main features of any innovation are determined early in the innovation process. The benefits are integrated within broad solutions on environmental aspects.[50] However, eco-innovation can be environmentally motivated through social organizations and public policies along with the considerations on reducing production costs. Managing institutional changes in values, knowledge, norms, and administrative actions would attract collaborations with new stakeholders. The impact on technologies for eco-innovation depends on their social adaptation and creation of market demand. Creating demand, therefore, requires identifying a suitable market with sufficient policy support to foster their initial uptake. The mainstream market prefers to adopt new innovative technologies once they are "proven" and endorsed by the consumer.

[50] Reid, A., & Miedzinski, M. (2008). *Eco-innovation* (pp. 2–14). Final Report for Sectoral Innovation. Watch Technopolis Group.

CHAPTER 3

Sensitizing Entrepreneurship: Managing Growth Touchpoints

It has been observed in the developing countries that despite increasingly evolving relationship among government, social institutions, and corporations, the entrepreneurship strategies and economic growth are considerably underexplored and conceptually underdeveloped.[1] Therefore, it is necessary to sensitize entrepreneurship with market-driven skills, innovations, technology, and business models. This chapter addresses the resource management in micro, small, and medium enterprises in the context of raw materials, finance, human capital, skill development, technology, manufacturing, and operations. While integrating innovation and technology to meet the social challenges, the evolution and management of social enterprises are of higher concern in developing entrepreneurship at the bottom of the pyramid than developing them as small business units. Accordingly, this chapter discusses creativity through social collaboration in co-creating innovative ideas, designs, and prototypes for commercialization. Social marketing has emerged as a low-cost and rapid dissemination of innovation led products and services. The use of social networks has been successful in motivating customers at the

[1] Bjørnskov, C., & Foss, N. J. (2016). Institutions, entrepreneurship, and economic growth: What do we know and what do we still need to know? *The Academy of Management Perspectives, 30*(3), 292–315.

A. Molina and Rajagopal, *Challenge-Based Learning, Research, and Innovation*, Palgrave Studies of Entrepreneurship and Social Challenges in Developing Economies,
https://doi.org/10.1007/978-3-031-29156-2_3

downstream markets and towards driving the firms competitive.[2] The discussions in this chapter are also central to the topics on marketing, entrepreneurial training, technology acceptance, empowerment, equality, expansion, and tapping new revenue streams. Sensitizing entrepreneurship is, thus, a necessity for economic development. Entrepreneurship is a channel linking institutions and economic performance, which contributes to the gross domestic product, national income, productivity, employment, and regional economic growth.[3]

Market-Oriented Entrepreneurship

The social value creation and social innovation are vital to the social entrepreneurship phenomenon, which drive social innovation to be conceptualized as an interfacing innovation within the social ecosystem. Most micro, small, and medium enterprises serve as feeder industries and play key roles in the value chain of the large companies. Thus, these enterprises establish industry connections and seek support on entrepreneurship education through an experience-based learning approach. The experience-linked entrepreneurial education drives organizational change with increasing usage of social media.[4] The taxonomy of challenge-based research to encourage social conscious entrepreneurship categorically explains causal and effectuation approaches. The causal approach is related to economic plans and strategies as it focuses on entrepreneurial orientation models that affect business growth and performance. The effectuation approach comprises entrepreneurial experiences that have grown through uncertain business environments. However, in both the approaches of research-led entrepreneurship tend

[2] Borden, D. S., Cohn, S. I., & Gooderham, C. (2018). Transitioning "upward" when "downstream" efforts are insufficient. *Social Marketing Quarterly, 24*, 151–163.

[3] Urbano, D., Aparicio, S., & Audretsch, D. (2019). Twenty-five years of research on institutions, entrepreneurship, and economic growth: What has been learned? *Small Business Economics, 53*(1), 21–49.

[4] Chawinga, W. (2017). Taking social media to a university classroom: Teaching and learning using Twitter and blogs. *International Journal of Education Technology Higher Education, 14*(1), 1–19.

to meet the underlying challenge through systematic diffusion of knowledge on sustainable and crowd-based entrepreneurial models.[5] The entrepreneurial training and skill development programs are designed to deliver mixed knowledge on refining entrepreneurship in tune to Industry 4.0 revolution and develop market-oriented approaches based on practical entrepreneurial needs. Working along the automation trend and following digital marketing practices are the most dominating problems for entrepreneurs for the survival and growth of their businesses.[6] The failure of local entrepreneurial strategies is not only incongruent to their business growth, but also damages the initiatives taken by the governments and private institutions for entrepreneurship development as a socio-economic goal.

The challenge-based research encouraged entrepreneurs to develop design-to-market strategies in view of the lessons learned from social problems, needs, and solutions in relevance to the marketability of products and their experience in managing market strategies beyond the niche. The design-to-market strategies over time become a common practice as entrepreneurial marketing. Accordingly, entrepreneurs follow bottom-up approach by choosing the target market or segment in the beginning, and later explore the needs and demands of their targeted segment through personal relations to serve them efficiently.[7] The entrepreneurial marketing approach involves cost-effective activities by avoiding formal market research or involving mass promotions strategies to promote business. However, entrepreneurs of small and medium business segments significantly depend on their personal networks to collect information about consumers and the market. These entrepreneurs heavily use consumer psychodynamics and interpersonal communication such as word of mouth to promote their products and services.[8] The social facet

[5] Ilonen, S., & Heinonen, J. (2018). Understanding affective learning outcomes in entrepreneurship education. *Industry and Higher Education, 32*(6), 391–401.

[6] Amjad, T., Rani, S. H. B., & Sa'atar, S. B. (2020). Entrepreneurship development and pedagogical gaps in entrepreneurial marketing education. *International Journal of Management Education, 18*(2), 1–7.

[7] Stokes, D. (2000). Putting entrepreneurship into marketing: The process of entrepreneurial marketing. *Journal of Research in Marketing and Entrepreneurship, 2*(1), 1–16.

[8] Copley, P. (2013). The need to deliver higher-order skills in the context of marketing in SMEs. *Industry and Higher Education, 27*(6), 465–476.

of entrepreneurship with market-linked skill development has closer proximity to innovation diffusion and business modeling than the formal teaching pedagogy or regulatory education to entrepreneurs. Though regulatory and social environment resources encourage entrepreneurship to update their business education and skills, they can be can purposely integrated and aligned with the entrepreneurial touchpoints to expand and enhance customers' journeys, customer experience, and marketability of their products or services in the emerging markets.[9] Opportunity-led entrepreneurship grows in the region as entrepreneurs look for alternate work options, but still decide to pursue a government-promoted business opportunity that offers economic benefits such as capital and infrastructure subsidies, and tax advantages. It is a key construct in understanding the entrepreneurial abilities in a country better as compared to the necessity-driven entrepreneurship.[10]

Global marketplace equipped with the application of global communications have become the focus of the global business arena that enables the world markets to remain open and involve in the fair competitive practices. Global marketplace provides scope for opportunity-based entrepreneurship, which contributes to social, economic, and environmental qualities of economic development. The public policies to promote micro, small, and medium enterprises moderate the relationship between opportunity-based entrepreneurship and the quality of socio-economic development. The resource-based view and public governance perspectives augment the scope of market-oriented entrepreneurship development.[11] Efficient multinational companies from the leading countries enter the secured country markets and drain out the regional players from the benefit market segments. Market competition in the global markets has not only entailed the economic process and free markets in relation to developing the local enterprises, but it also envelopes the economic and ecological concerns, corporate power, social rights

[9] Homburg, C., Jozić, D., & Kuehnl, C. (2017). Customer experience management: Toward implementing an evolving marketing concept. *Journal of the Academy of Marketing Science, 45*(3), 377–401.

[10] Acs, Z. J., Desai, S., & Hessels, J. (2008). Entrepreneurship, economic development, and institutions. *Small Business Economics, 31*(3), 219–234.

[11] Dimitratos, P., Johnson, J. E., & Plakoyiannaki, E. (2016). SME internationalization: How does the opportunity-based international entrepreneurial culture matter? *International Business Review, 25*(6), 1211–1222.

and needs, and economic well-being of marginal and small firms. Such complexity also embraces the social, political, and cultural dimensions of doing business beyond boundaries in the globalization process. Thus, entrepreneurship amidst growing market competition has a complex dynamics of business evolution within the social, economic, and technological diffusion on the interpersonal and digital platforms.[12] However, in developing countries the efforts of governments and NGOs have helped entrepreneurs in enriching and expanding business opportunities. Social leadership has also uplifted the low resource creative entrepreneurs from the wealthy and powerful industrial intermediaries. Social entrepreneurs in developing economies are motivated by the government and social institutions to engage stakeholders in helping the unserved and underserved populations that do not have clear PNS (problems, needs, and solutions) diagnosis and have low income to afford products and services they often desperately need.[13]

Sustainable enterprises in the global environment require competitive skills to market their products with niche business models in the initial stages, and to restructure business policies later as the market evolves for the enterprises. Social enterprises including cooperatives often fail to develop an effective customer-centric business model. The phenomenon of the global customer is gaining importance increasingly, and so of the global-customer-centric organization. Going global is not an easy process for social and sustainable development firms. Therefore, both government and industry tend to simulate the impact of sustainable social enterprises in the global market in reference to their resources, target markets, and operational efficiency. Most firms concentrate on product markets considering the customers, who seek benefits or to be served with the same products, services, innovation, and technology regardless of the geo-demographic differences and cognitive behavior. There are several paradoxes in communicating social products in the global markets. It is imperative to enhance market competitiveness of micro, small, and medium enterprises, which requires enabling innovation and technology with adequate finance and institutional structures including human capital. Continuous innovation helps these enterprises

[12] Brinkman, R. L., & Brinkman, J. E. (2002). Corporate power and the globalization process *International Journal of Social Economics, 29*(9), 730–752.

[13] Arogyaswamy, B. (2017). Social entrepreneurship performance measurement: A time-based organizing framework. *Business Horizons, 60*(5), 603–611.

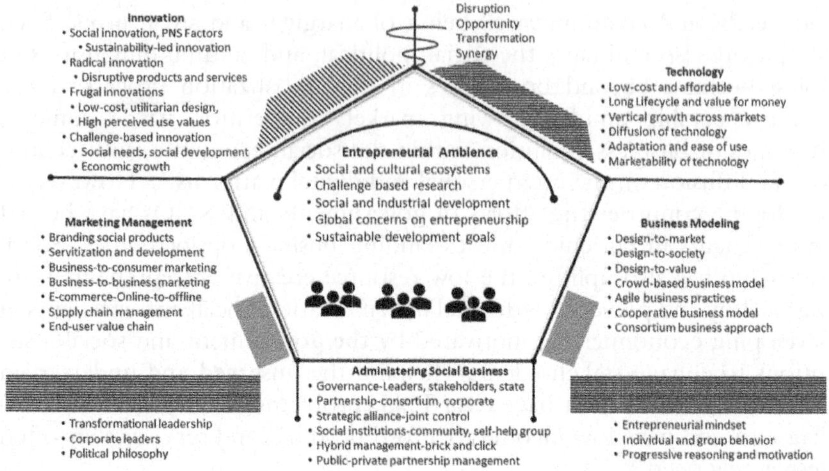

Fig. 3.1 Market orientation and social entrepreneurship (*Source* Author [Rajagopal])

stay competitive and transform into an agent of reverse globalization. Therefore, enterprises at the grassroots must embrace global changes in cultural norms so that they can develop market competitiveness in reference to quality, price, and services to survive and find a place for themselves in the global competitive environment.[14] Attributes influencing market orientation of social entrepreneurship is illustrated in Fig. 3.1.

The challenge-based research to cater to the social and economic developmental needs of stakeholders is largely nurtured within the social and cultural ecosystems, which catalyzes significantly the industrial and consumer marketing practices of local enterprises. In addition, global concerns on entrepreneurship in the context of sustainable development goals motivate both manufacturing and marketing competencies of entrepreneurs as illustrated in Fig. 3.1. Accordingly, the social innovations are driven by the PNS factors and sustainability-led ideation for developing cleaner utilitarian products. Some enterprises with the

[14] Anand, B. (2015). Reverse globalization by internationalization of SME's: Opportunities and challenges ahead. *Procedia—Social and Behavioral Sciences, 195*, 1003–1011.

competencies to manufacture and market radical products, also stimulate demand in the competitive markets, while most enterprises at the bottom of the pyramid are engaged in frugal innovations manufacturing low-cost and utilitarian products, which tend to create high perceived value and demand. Innovations driven by challenge-based research are focused on social needs, social development, and economic growth. The basic motivation for the micro, small, and medium enterprises is to grow competitively by exploring markets opportunities for disruptive products to transform the value chains associated with the existing products in the marketplace. Such an approach of these enterprises helps in developing synergy in business modeling and performance as exhibited in the Fig. 3.1.

Sustainable products with low-cost technology with long life cycle ensures both affordability and inculcating the sense of value for money among consumers. Such strategies of local enterprises encourage vertical growth in upstream or downstream markets and planning the outreach of embedded technologies in the products. Consequently, consumers develop perception on ease of use of products and derive high perceived use value. In a holistic view, these strategies increase the marketability of technology-led sustainable innovative products. In a socially sensitive and technologically advanced enterprise, the business model is architected with design-to-market, design-to-society, and design-to-value perspectives. Many micro and small enterprises have also been benefitted by the crowd-based business modeling, which is significantly supported by collective intelligence. Crowd businesses models are agile and collaborative. Nonetheless, the consortium business models by integrating many micro and small enterprises within the same industry strengthens their bargaining power, negotiation skills, and helps in standardizing the cost, time and technology application by reducing the risk and uncertainty in manufacturing and marketing processes. Consequently, innovative, and sustainable products have to outreach to both business-to-business and business-to-consumer market segments with integrated branding and servitization strategies. During the COVID-19 pandemic (2020–2022), most micro enterprises have also adapted to the e-commerce strategies by combining both the online and offline transactions. However, these firms faced a major challenge in establishing supply chain and value chain benefits in business.

It is yet debatable to determine the governance pattern of social enterprises whether they should be led by the conventional leaders, progressive stakeholders, or the state authorities (government). Alternative reasoning prompts that partnerships such as consortiums and corporate collaborations may also provide strong governance to the agglomeration of enterprises within an industry. Strategic alliances with large firms in production, innovation, technology, marketing, and resource pooling would also help in developing joint governance of local and sponsoring firms. In addition, social institutions such as the community and self-help group, have also emerged as efficient governance. The digital drive in the enterprises has significantly stimulated hybrid management by combining the brick and click marketing strategies. Some social enterprises like housing, health, and energy in the developing countries are successfully managed through public–private partnerships. An appropriate governance system helps entrepreneurs to develop positive mindset and drive both individual and group behavior to inculcate progressive reasoning and entrepreneurial motivation.

The challenge-based research diffused through social institutions has higher outreach among the stakeholders and customers. This has been evidenced during the COVID-19 pandemic in disseminating as the social institutions took the lead in creating awareness about the sanitation regulations and personal and public protection norms. In response to societal grand challenges, professors have unique opportunities to effect change, repurposing their expertise to deploy relevant, timely, practical, and research-backed knowledge for the betterment of communities. Incubation of innovations has emerged as a new model of start-up facilitation in most developing economies. Venture capitalists review the incubators and assess the projected growth and profitability in businesses to invest. The venture capitalists review the incubators to diversify risky investment portfolios, while the prospective entrepreneurs approach the incubators to review the economically viable and technologically feasible support for start-up projects. Entrepreneurial incubators face both challenges and the opportunities to grow competitive enterprises considering the embedded investment and entrepreneurial risks. Broadly, there are five incubator archetypes such as the university incubator, the independent commercial incubator, the regional business incubator, the company-internal incubator, and the virtual incubator.[15] Innovations of local origin are attracted

[15] Carayannis, E. G., & von Zedtwitz, M. (2005). Architecting gloCal (global–local), real-virtual incubator networks (G-RVINs) as catalysts and accelerators of entrepreneurship

to the global companies as they plan to bring back the local innovation, which is largely frugal in nature, to the mass market. Therefore, the relational embeddedness of large companies with external enterprises appears to be essential for the evolution of local innovations to the global scale. The hybrid enterprises working with the social and economic development objectives tend to develop entrepreneurial ideas both through face-to-face interactions and on social media platforms.[16] Turning local innovations into global brands can be identified as innovativeness evoked by the large companies or their subsidiaries at the bottom of the pyramid. However, in this process, transfer of reverse knowledge in the functional areas is a critical perspective.[17] The contemporary research on social entrepreneurship has consistently focused on the benefits and challenges of designing hybrid organizations, which integrate competing institutional reasoning to tackle social problems using market-based methods, especially in developing economies.[18]

The virtual idea blitz among social enterprises is anchored through the collective intelligence focusing on conceptual grounding and framework in the design-sprint methodology popularized at web-based disseminators like Google Ventures.[19] A standard design sprint among the social enterprises is traditionally conducted in a short span to minimize the time required to solve critical business questions and to validate and then implement an idea, exploring the PNS factors. Design sprints are traditionally conducted in person, as they require extensive, uninterrupted collaboration between a team to integrate different skills in the social entrepreneurship. The design-sprint process is evolved around business strategy, innovation, and consumer behavior, with an overarching goal of

in transitioning and developing economies: Lessons learned and best practices from current development and business incubation practices. *Technovation, 25*(2), 95–110.

[16] Bacq, s., Geoghegan, W., Josefy, M., Stevenson, R., & Williams, T. A. (2020). The COVID-19 virtual idea blitz: Marshaling social entrepreneurship to rapidly respond to urgent grand challenges. *Business Horizons, 23*(6), 705–723.

[17] Isaac, V. R., Borini, F. M., Raziq, M. M., & Benito, G. R. G. (2019). From local to global innovation: The role of subsidiaries' external relational embeddedness in an emerging market. *International Business Review, 28*(4), 638–646.

[18] McMullen, J. S., & Bergman, B. J. (2018). The promise and problems of price subsidization in social entrepreneurship. *Business Horizons, 61*(4), 609–621.

[19] Knapp, J., Zeratsky, J., & Kowitz, B. (2016). *Sprint: How to solve big problems and test new ideas in just five days*. New York: Simon and Schuster.

solving big issues quickly. Such cost-time-strategy relationship helps enterprises to avoid steering ideas from the perspectives of economic viability and technological feasibility and reduce risks while bringing an innovative product, service, or feature to the market. Sprints have successfully been applied by organizations including LEGO, Lufthansa, Slack, the United Nations, and Prudential Financial companies.[20]

Most studies reveal that the relationship between innovation efficiency and size of the firm plays a significant role in improving market performance and exploring the prevailing and new market opportunities. Marketing and product innovation strategies are the key contributors to market performance, while the competitiveness has become an indispensable factor for both the social and commercial enterprises to survive the marketplace rivalry.[21] In an open market competition, firms of different types and sizes use upfront marketing strategies and tactics to pull down the competing firms. Such competition forces small firms to struggle for existence against relatively large firms, while large firms strengthen their marketing strategies to sustain the competition and stay fittest in the competitive marketplace. However, large firms at the early maturity stage of their business attempt to consolidate their product line to stay abreast with market competition and develop product portfolios in tune to the market demand. To gain a suitable competitive position in the marketplace, firms pump enormous resources into innovation, technology, advertisement, communication, and sales activities. The low returns on investment builds sunk cost over time.

Social entrepreneurship is rapidly growing organizations in the developing countries that have created models for efficiently catering to basic social needs. Accordingly, socially conscious consumer products are targeted in existing markets and institutions to cater to the social and individual problems, needs, and solutions. Social entrepreneurship combines the resourcefulness of traditional entrepreneurship with a mission to deliver contemporary products and services that are congruent with

[20] Bacq, s., Geoghegan, W., Josefy, M., Stevenson, R., & Williams, T. A. (2020). The COVID-19 virtual idea blitz: Marshaling social entrepreneurship to rapidly respond to urgent grand challenges. *Business Horizons, 23*(6), 705–723.

[21] Blocker, C. P., Flint, D. J., Myers, M. B., & Slater, S. F. (2011). Proactive customer orientation and its role for creating customer value in global markets. *Journal of Academy of Marketing Science, 39*(2), 216–233.

the PNS factors. Social entrepreneurship offers insights, which stimulate ideas for more socially acceptable and sustainable business strategies and organizational forms as it contributes globally recognized sustainable development goals. The social entrepreneurship also encourages established corporations to take on greater social responsibility.[22]

Firms, which simultaneously engage in a high degree of both innovation and efficiency, follow an ambidextrous strategy by adopting both exploitative and explorative strategies in the innovation process. However, few firms can balance between these two emphases despite internal conflicts for resources, and external risks over innovation and its economies of scale. Though the ambidextrous strategy in nurturing the product or service innovation is complex for most of the firms, the turbulent nature and intense competition of today's markets reinforce the need for firms to consider this dual approach for longer-term success.[23] An innovation breakthrough in firms can deliver a strong advantage to the overall posture of the company in the marketplace and drive a major shift in industry leadership. However, not all companies show the ability to foster management innovation due to lack of generating unique ideas. A management innovation creates long-lasting advantage if it is based on a novel principle that challenges the traditional wisdom, is systemic in processes and methods, and is supported by a program of the company to carry out innovation.[24]

The coevolution of small firms with large business organization through developing strategic alliances on production, technology, distribution, or finance can be explained as double helix. Convergence of technology, entrepreneurship education, and public policies including the skill development programs and financial incentive to promote small entrepreneurs are the active elements in the entrepreneurial helix process Exploring new opportunities; right decision-making in business; and developing a design-to-market strategy by building alliances with large companies have been the major focus of double helix approach of the small enterprises. In addition, the enterprises seek the patronage of large

[22] Seelos, C., & Mair, J. (2005). Social entrepreneurship: Creating new business models to serve the poor. *Business Horizons, 48*(3), 241–246.

[23] Sarkees, M., & Hulland, J. S. (2008). Innovation and efficiency: It is possible to have it all. *Business Horizons, 52*(1), 45–55.

[24] Hamel, G. (2006). Why, what, and how of management innovation. *Harvard Business Review, 84*(2), 72–84.

companies to lower the cost-risk ratio and augment profit. The success of double helix approach needs a transformational leadership at both business organizations to help in redesigning organization, creating value chain, developing global standards, investing in business process improvement, and strengthening the backward and forward business linkages. The coevolution of small and big companies enhances investment on innovation, technology, and research and development. Such mergers or acquisitions in the double helix approach help companies strengthen their marketing strategies by developing customer-centric branding and promotion strategies. The convergence of technology, entrepreneurship education, and public policies on entrepreneurship development programs promote hybridization, business performance, and corporate citizenship behavior ambidextrously between small and large enterprises.

Small firms operating in niche markets often face the problems of conventional manufacturing process, obsolete technologies, capital limitation, and lack of updated knowledge. These attributes drive firms to compromise with the product quality and stay non-competitive in the regional or global markets. Such business confinement needs small firms in emerging markets to coevolve with large firms and catch up with them to improve the manufacturing and marketing processes and improve productivity rather than engaging in frugal innovations for niche markets.[25] Small firms in emerging economies often face the challenge of breaking the *glass ceiling* to explore market competitiveness with the frugal innovation strategies and develop tactical marketing approaches to override close business rivals. Entrepreneurs often fail in establishing the regional or global value chains and enhancing their business performance.[26] However, Chinese small and medium enterprises have coevolved as local to global firms over time by establishing mutually beneficial arrangements. These positive outcomes demonstrate the double helix effect in business through carefully orchestrated market reforms. In a large industrial segment of automobile manufacturers of India,

[25] Awate, S., Larsen, M. M., & Mudambi, R. (2015). Accessing vs sourcing knowledge: A comparative study of R&D internationalization between emerging and advanced economy firms. *Journal of International Business Studies, 46*(1), 63–86.

[26] McDermott, G. A., & Corredoira, R. A. (2010). Network composition, collaborative ties, and upgrading in emerging-market firms: Lessons from the Argentine auto parts sector. *Journal of International Business Studies, 41*(2), 308–329.

the double helix effect has been clearly visible. Many domestic auto-manufacturing companies including Tata Motors, Mahindra & Mahindra, TVS Group, and Bharat Forge have developed international strategic alliances with auto manufacturers and survived the transition in their business.[27] Most of these local auto-manufacturing companies have achieved market competitiveness in global markets. Broadly, China and India have survived the transition to open markets and have coevolved as big-emerging markets amidst the business space of many developing markets.

Resources Management

Achieving green growth in Mexico needs more government funding and might require developing more coherent taxation, energy, transport, and agriculture policies at the macro level. While assessing a holistic view of the green growth prospects in the country, it is observed that improving efficiency in state-run electricity and oil industries is the key area that supports the reduction targets of greenhouse gases emissions. The country spends a large sum on energy subsidies and being environmental tax revenues are low contributing indirectly to the gasoline and diesel subsidies in the domestic market. Recently, the gasoline prices are linked to the dynamic market pricing approach; however, Mexico's policy stood a long way on keeping gasoline prices constant in real terms and offering subsidies for household energy. These measures benefitted affluent social groups, whereas direct social transfers have a greater impact on the poor. There has been a prolonged debate on the removal of subsidies that are not economically beneficial to the fiscal and monetary health of the country, and the gross domestic production. Nonetheless, the removal of environmentally harmful subsidies would promote more rational resource allocation across the economy and benefit sustainability projects. A legal framework fostering private investment in environmentally friendly economic sectors also has the merit to help planning and implementation of sustainability projects at various geo-demographic levels in the country. Although the country has a well-developed policy framework for water resource management, policy implementation has

[27] Saranga, H., Schotter, A. P. J., & Mudambi, R. (2019). The double helix effect: Catch-up and local-foreign co-evolution in the Indian and Chinese automotive industries. *International Business Review, 28*(5), 1–18.

been observed in some country studies as uneven, institutional, financing, and governance perspectives. The stakeholder participation in water-management financing and cost recovery for irrigation services needs to be strengthened through strategic financial plans combining public subsidies with endogenous finance raised from users. The integrated approach to water policies can be achieved through better policy coordination between water management agriculture, society, and different levels of government.[28]

There are several approaches to determine social environmental consciousness. However, they are united by their common methodological position that embeds the individual and social consciousness towards the sustainability in multiple social-sectors (agriculture and allied sectors, natural resource management, public health, housing, education, and non-farm industries). There is a wide range of perspectives concerning social sustainability that need to be supported by the preferences of environmental consciousness. With the increasing social consciousness, global markets have entered the new generation management involving stakeholders in developing customer-centric business strategies and growing sustainable in the competitive marketplace. Consumers form perceptions on the viable solutions to the predetermined needs (recognized as problems), which match with their self-congruence, and could offer sustainable value (satisfaction). Social media is an attractive medium where consumers with changing mindsets interact with peers demonstrating their perceptual rationale and validate their feelings and emotions. Their objective in engaging in social media is to learn about recent trends, new development of knowledge, or certain skill sets for further improvement in making buying decisions.[29]

The community-based natural resources management has been encouraged by the social organizations (self-help groups and non-governmental organizations) on the assumption that the decision-making process in natural resource management is a collective process within the communities and among stakeholders. This community approach has not only fostered knowledge and commitment among the stakeholders, but also stimulated ecological innovation in startup enterprises at the local level.

[28] OECD. (2010). *OECD perspectives: Mexico key policies for sustainable development*. Paris: Organization for Economic Cooperation and Development.

[29] Mathur, P., Chun, H. H., & Maheswaran, D. (2016), Consumer mindsets and self-enhancement: Signaling versus learning. *Journal of Consumer Psychology, 26*(1), 142–152.

However, commercialization of frugal and reverse innovations in the green economic and industrial sector is a major challenge. The problem of commercialization of innovation is largely attributed to the interface of top-down (public policies and funding) and bottom-up approaches (social and entrepreneurial governance), which primarily involves the inter-institutional arrangements to diffuse and market the innovations.[30] Ecological innovations have become dispersed as the market is becoming increasingly demanding and the users have formed their niche. Accordingly, innovation has shifted from technology to business models, and is more focused on marketing than the social needs. Many innovations are emerging in the market that are simplified, while some are scaling up in improving the existing products or services and positioning them as innovations. However, managers may align their business strategies with competitive advantages of markets and manage innovation in emerging economies to diffuse and commercialize.[31]

The innovation business projects in most companies follow a boom-bust cycle. As the economy prospers, companies invest substantial resources in developing innovation projects to lead in the competitive markets while they rethink their priorities in view of the cost–benefit ratios when the markets soars. Growing firms are engaged in developing competitive strategies and innovative differentiations in staying sustainable and competitive in the global marketplace. To gain competitive advantages companies, explore innovative business projects to enter the new market segments with first mover advantages. Firms that have higher resources develop better customer relations for boosting customer loyalty as compared to small firms, which have inadequate resources. Large firms cannibalize the market share of small firms also through mergers and acquisition and building strategic alliances with other companies. On the contrary, smaller firms through consortium pose challenge to the large firms by adapting multiple market disruption strategies like low prices, disruptive innovation, mass marketing, and building customer loyalty at the bottom of the pyramid segments.

The technical operating standards and protocols are being widely adapted to synchronize with the global industry standards. The resources

[30] Armitage, D. (2005). Adaptive capacity and community-based natural resource management. *Environment Management, 35*(6), 703–715.

[31] De Meyer, A. (2011, September 15). Diving into the new innovation landscape. *IESE-Insight Magazine*.

are managed externally to a large extent as the best and low-cost materials are procured locally by the multinational companies. The benefits of global sourcing for such companies include low-cost labor, uniform quality, innovative ideas, access to local markets, economies of scale, lower taxes and duties, lower logistics costs, and more consistent supply. However, the low resources companies are still adhering to conventional market infrastructure and are confined within the geo-demographic limits to carry out their innovation business insights.[32] However, large firms at the early maturity stage of their business attempt to consolidate their product line to stay abreast with market competition and develop product portfolio in tune to the market demand. To gain a suitable competitive position in the marketplace, firms pump enormous resources in innovation, technology, advertisement, communication, and sales activities. However, for some firms returns on investment are not encouraging and it builds sunk cost in the long run. For many companies, innovation is a sprawling collection of initiatives, energetic but uncoordinated, and managed with vacillating strategies. Hence, it is necessary for the companies to set up innovative business projects infusing a systematic process. To capitalize on current and future market opportunities, global, regional, and local companies are investing substantial time and resources in developing innovative business projects that could create sustainable competitive differentiation. The chapter discusses entrepreneurial attributes that are basic to develop and implement innovative business projects and guide the process of managing resources and project cost rationally.

Successful innovation leads to customer involvement and profits, which can be achieved through co-creation by aligning consumers and market players in the innovation process. Some multinational companies have invested resources taking advantage of social media to diffuse new ideas and stimulating co-creation of innovative products and services. For many companies, developing innovative products does not occur as a chance or coincidence but through careful attention to many important criteria. Firms should analyze their innovation practices and capabilities to become more effective in driving innovation as breakthrough and gain the competitive advantage. To ensure success in commercializing

[32] Hustin, L., & Sakkab, N. (2006). Connect and develop: Inside Procter & Gamble's new model for innovation. *Harvard Business Review, 84*(3), 58–66.

innovation, companies need to invest substantially in innovative business projects and allocate resources to manage the innovation process at various stages of the project. Lack of resources, or mid-term withdrawals of the innovation projects lead to desertion of the innovation and have low effect on commercialization. Innovation success rates are typically low, and returns are slow if they frequently reverse the innovation at various stages of the innovation path, that also escalates the cost, time, and effect of the commercializing an innovation. This makes innovation initiatives hard to justify when resources are limited, and companies have inadequate competence in carrying out the innovations. The companies that are engaged in commercializing innovations, either acquired from start-up enterprises or co-created, invest enormous resources in exploring markets for launching innovations, carrying out diffusion of innovation, and creating unique values of innovation by exhibiting competitive differentiation and advantages to the consumers. Successful start-up enterprises in emerging markets develop strategic partnership with the sponsors or large companies to launch and manage incremental innovations in the competitive marketplace. Establishing innovative business projects for gaining market competitiveness in the global and emerging markets needs team dynamics at the grassroots, financial and human resources for working with innovation projects, and continuous investment in research and development. However, the risk of commercialization of innovation grows simultaneously as the innovative business projects move ahead.

Good entrepreneurs realistically assess their financial resources, personal and organizational preferences, and goals for the firm. To ensure right utilization of time and money, successful entrepreneurs also optimize the resources use and minimize the occurrence of flaws in production, marketing, and operations process.[33] Entrepreneurs are largely driven by a vision to create value to customers and earn profit through their applied entrepreneurial skills and customer-centric marketing actions. Entrepreneurship and marketing theories share some commonality as both disciplines focus on identifying opportunities and transforming resources into value-creation or co-creation for consumers. Besides driving the innovation project through the challenges of managing the resources efficiently, handling operational risk, marketability, and cost and time overrun, entrepreneurs often face market failures and piling up of

[33] Bhide, A. V. (1994). How entrepreneurs craft strategies that work. *Harvard Business Review, 72*(2), 150–161.

sunk cost due to radical and experimental innovation approach. Such endeavors cause risk rollouts throughout the project leading to abort the innovation untimely, which develops serious cognitive dissonances among entrepreneurs. The major challenge with innovation companies is managing human and capital resources efficiently. The fallacy of most innovative business projects is that more resources and cost involvement in an innovation project would lead to a wider and sustainable outcome. Small innovation projects are set with low human and capital resources that often face the serious disorder of cost overruns in the middle of the project as they are unable to manage the resources efficiently. One of the major tasks in managing human resources is to generate sustainable value from the employees of the company and more specifically within the project team.

Organizational learning is a continuous process, and it involves employees at all levels of management in sharing knowledge and innovative insights that support the business growth of the firm. The learning process is generally embedded in the organizational culture that drives employees to invest resources in creative thinking. Firms also engage the innovation facilities group to explore new developments in the marketplace on the concept, prototypes, or breakthrough of the innovation and impart expert services for in-house initiatives to nurture the innovation within the organization. The innovation assimilation group acts as policy support unit to drive innovation to market. The members of this team provide resources to launch innovation and integrate operations into the business model of the firm. Firms need the above support teams to diffuse innovation and make it more.[34]

Innovation Management

Innovation is the critical dimension of economic change from a macro perspective and business growth within the micro perspective. At macro level, economic change revolves around innovation and catalyzes entrepreneurial activities that lead to drive market power. As the market competition is continuously increasing in the global marketplace, the innovation-driven market power could provide better results than the conventional wisdom like price and promotion competition. Alongside

[34] Cash, J. I., Earl, M. J., & Morison, R. (2008). Teaming up to crack innovation and enterprise integration. *Harvard Business Review, 86*(10), 90–99.

product-design and strategy innovation, technological innovation often creates ad hoc monopolies in the market allowing abnormal profits in a short life cycle. Such temporary monopolies are sometimes necessary to provide incentives for firms to develop new products and processes.[35] The sources of innovation have become dispersed as the market is turning increasingly demanding and the users have formed their niche. Accordingly, innovation has shifted from technology to business models and is more focused on marketing than social needs. Many innovations are emerging in the market that is simplified or is scaling down on improving the existing products or services and positioning them as innovations. However, managers may align their business strategies with competitive advantages of markets and manage innovation in emerging economies to diffuse and commercialize.[36] Traditionally, positioning innovation of products and services makes a company competitive is a myth in the present state of global marketing. Thus, firms continually reinvent in large and small ways in reference to shifts in market demand and changes in the economy and develop competitive marketing strategy in reference to shifts in the product and market behavior, knowledge of innovative products, and innovation positions. Though the firms may develop efficiency about the above strategic positions of product/market, knowledge, and innovation independently, they are still risk-averse with the innovation.[37]

Innovation and enterprise integration are two compelling sources of growth in a dynamic competitive marketplace. The ability to coordinate across organizational boundaries largely appears as a critical factor in determining the speed and life cycle of a market-driven innovation. Innovations need to be integrated into the larger operations of the corporation at sufficient level of scale to show a prolific impact on business and sustainability in the marketplace. Many large businesses spend resources on innovations but fail to capitalize on them. However, some organizations use innovations to optimize local operations than integrating them to create consumer value and corporate image. Large organizations spread

[35] Pol, E., & Carroll, P. (2006). *An introduction to economics with emphasis on innovation* (2nd ed.). New York: Thomson Learning.

[36] De Meyer, A. (2011, September 15). Diving into the new innovation landscape. *IESE-Insight Magazine*.

[37] McDonough, E. F., Zack, M., Lin, H. E., & Berdrow, I. (2008). Integrating innovation style and knowledge into strategy. *MIT Sloan Management Review, 50*(1), 53–58.

the innovation tasks among two groups comprising innovation facilities group (IFG) and an innovation assimilation group. The IFG members provide organizational support on the techniques to carry out innovations and applications for the new technology. Firms also engage the innovation facilities group to explore new developments in the marketplace on the concept, prototypes, or breakthrough of the innovation and impart expert services for in-house initiatives to nurture the innovation within the organization. The innovation assimilation group acts as policy support unit to drive innovation to market. The members of this team provide resources to launch innovation and integrate operations into the business model of the firm. Firms need the above support teams to diffuse innovation and make it more.[38]

The international innovation companies need to segment their markets-upstream and mass that fit into the innovation attributes exhibiting the price, value, for money, perceived value, performance, and product life cycle, Companies may have to deliver high performance of their products in western markets equivalents with high price, while the reverse innovation offers the opportunity for the companies to enter in the emerging markets with the same corporate and extended brand strength. Determining the performance required by a technology as in the case of generic two-wheeler motorbikes engines in reference to emissions reduction and longevity of engine life at the price at which it will be adopted is the critical first step in creating products for emerging markets. The commercialization of reverse innovation often gives a radical push to the product, company, and industry as well. Commercializing reverse innovation is a disruptive leap to hit a product in the target market and it demands to develop organizational insight into how a new product could drive an impact in emerging markets. A product that delivers significantly more performance at a lower price may become the basis for a new product platform, which can have features added or removed to adjust its price and performance to the specific needs of wealthy or poor markets, makes the reverse innovation management a success. GE Healthcare has demonstrated this idea with the customization of its low-cost ultrasound and electrocardiogram machines, which started as emerging market products and then evolved into valuable devices for North America and

[38] Cash, J. I., Earl, M. J., & Morison, R. (2008). Teaming up to crack innovation and enterprise integration. *Harvard Business Review, 86*(10), 90–99.

Europe. Companies can envision the process of engineering reverse innovations before any metal is cut, plastic is molded, or prototypes made. The reverse innovation products move slow in the adaptation process in the non-familiar consumer segments and face price constraints in the market. However, based on the solutions that existing technologies provide, companies can envision the reverse innovation to derive the global product line around a new technology platform by using benchmarks of other products in the marketplace to analyze the possibilities of outwitting, outperforming, and outmaneuvering competitors, while delivering the low-cost and better performing solutions to consumers. By scoping onto the worldwide market opportunities and understanding the probable constraints in marketing the products across market segments and destinations, companies can engineer reverse innovations to mark impact on markets and consumers in the global marketplace.[39]

The reverse innovation can be explained as a process of co-creation and co-designing of innovations at local markets under the aegis of international companies. Reverse innovation offers scope to experience the innovation concept, process, and deliverables in the niche markets and scale them up for a wider market beyond the emerging markets. The start-up enterprises managing innovation need for the relatively smaller geo-demographic segments and at bottom of the pyramid may throw up immense challenges for commercializing the innovations in the international markets. However, it requires a company to follow the institutionalized thinking that guides its actions in the global marketplace. The reverse innovations that are adopted by the sponsor companies need to make design adjustments and fabricate for the mass consumers in the global markets in a radically simpler and cheaper way to serve the customer with high perceived value. Companies can develop new products in emerging markets by using a radical change from below (generic innovation design) combined with smart leadership from top (up-market strategy). The small start-up enterprises may set audacious goals to match with the new organizational structure of sponsors and adopt new design and commercialization methods. However, the start-up enterprises may also nurture the reverse innovation provided they could arrange adequate

[39] Winter, A., & Govindarajan, V. (2015). Engineering reverse innovation. *Harvard Business Review, 93*(7–8), 81–89.

resources to upscale the innovation by shifting the gravity of business beyond emerging markets.[40]

Commercializing Innovations

Large firms operate on economies of scale in the market with low cost and high differentiation of products and services. Such a strategy leads the firms in the mass market and drives them to gain high market share. Many firms operate at the same time in each marketplace and competition among the firms turns fierce. Some firms operate at high cost but also go for high differentiation of products and services. Firms with such attributes locate themselves in the premium market and struggle to achieve high brand equity. On the contrary, firms that have low differentiation of products and services and low cost of marketing, operate in niche by following defensive marketing strategies. In case the firms have low differentiation of products and services at high cost of marketing, the business growth turns slow affecting the brand equity of the firm. If this situation prevails for a long time with such firms, it may cause disaster in the long run. Many small firms that emerge with high cost and low differentiation stay out of market competition and become extinct over a period either by shutting down operations or merging with stronger firms.

Many firms stay in global competition believing that they need to develop innovative products or leading brands before venturing abroad. Some firms become global players in their industries by excelling at old-fashioned capabilities. They skip the risky, expensive strategy of opening their own facilities and extending their reach through acquisitions and alliances. Speed of innovation also appears to be an important factor in the success of newly emerging firms. Faster and appropriate customer-centric business strategies allow the new entrants to pull ahead of competing firms and drive vertical integration. Newly emerging firms with such attributes can get products quickly and cost-effectively to far-flung customers.[41]

[40] Govindarajan, V. (2012). A reverse innovation playbook. *Harvard Business Review, 90*(4), 120–124.

[41] Guillen, M. F., & Garcia-Canal, E. (2010). How to conquer new markets with old skills. *Harvard Business Review, 88*(11), 118–122.

To survive in a competitive marketplace, it is important for the firms to have an obvious sense of advantage and drive the business to achieve its predefined objective. Defining the objective, scope, and advantage requires managing the trade-offs amidst market competition. If a firm pursues growth or size, profitability will be jeopardized, which, in case the firm chooses to serve institutional clients, may ignore retail customers. Hence, trade-offs in the marketplace will bounce if an appropriate decision is not taken by the firms to sustain the market competition. On the contrary, a firm may derive its competitive advantage from scale economies, and it may not be able to accommodate idiosyncratic customer needs. Accordingly, growth of local firms may emerge with high brand equity in niche amidst the threats of large firms while large firms can follow a combination of long-run and short-run strategies to outwit regional firms.

Market competition and growth of innovation and technology have always featured the unpredictable, the surprising, and the unexpected in the global marketplace. However, the increasing deployment of information technology in the firms has developed hyper-connectivity on one hand and complexity in business management on the other. Market competition and growth of technology are now intertwined and interdependent as market need has become the principal driver of innovation and technology. The new products are embryonic to the consumer need and market demand and are grown largely on predicting outcomes. There are too many continuously changing interactive elements in play that create complexities in managing the marketing of technology-led innovative products in different market segments. Managers looking to handle these difficulties need to adopt strategic approaches than tactical for sustainable results, and to overcome conventional wisdom by using the models that simulate the behavior of the market players including consumers to make the technology-led new products sustainable. They should also make sure that their strategies are future-oriented and can manage the market risk. Firms introducing new products rapidly in the marketplace should minimize the need to rely on predictions and work with the user-oriented product design and applications. They can list the complexity factors in a system and build to minimize the consequences of failures in the business system, develop strategic alliances to share the unforeseen risks in the innovation and technologies led products, and enhance organizational capabilities and competencies.[42]

Administrative complexities play a significant role in explaining new technology drive. Process simplification, zero defect products, cost, and profit, and overall governance of new products development have many odds to be either eliminated or managed within the organizational system. Most managers exert in never having considered setting-up business thinking about the odds and complexities or think about them during the process and give up the innovation process. Such behavior is also significantly affected by the perception of administrative complexity.[43] Firms that are engaged in rapid development of new products find the gap between diffusion and adoption. It is expensive for companies to manage over piled inventory of obsolete products unless they can be improved and revert to the active demand. Expensive downtime for production-line changeovers, merchandise languishing on retailers' shelves or in their showrooms also cause serious concerns to the firms engaged in developing new products. For service companies, though, complexity is much harder to spot and root out, largely due to the ease with which new products can be created and marketed.[44]

Large organizations are complex by nature and face new business challenges such as globalization, innovative technologies, and regulations over the period. Market uncertainties and competitive threats add layer upon layer of complexity to corporate structure and management. The technology marketing grid has several factors that pose conflicts and challenges to the innovation and technology development firms during different levels of process. The complexity grid comprises twelve commonly observed points of conflicts, which have independent effects of each point as well as in a matrix form. The conflict points in the grid include ideation, resources management, process management, capabilities and competencies, technology marketing, growth and next generation innovation and technology issues, involvement, organizational policies,

[42] Sargut, G., & McGrath, G. R. (2011). Learning to live with complexity. *Harvard Business Review, 89*(9), 66–76.

[43] van Stel, A., & Stunnenberg, V. (2006). Linking business ownership and perceived administrative complexity. *Journal of Small Business and Enterprise Development, 13*(1), 7-22.

[44] Gottfredson, M., & Schwedel, A. (2008, August 01). Cut complexity and costs. *Harvard Business Publishing Newsletters*.

operational efficiency, competitive decision, business environment, and organizational culture, all of which nurture the innovation and technology development projects in the firm. In the complexity grid ideation process and the extent of involvement of employees, consumers, and market players stage cognitive and organizational conflicts and challenges while management of resources and organizational policies raise various challenging issues during different phases of innovation and technology development. Similarly, the process and operational efficiency commonly drive various issues of concern in reference to capabilities and competencies and work culture of the organization. Firms face many conflicts during the innovation process on marketing of the technology-led products and the existing business environment. Moving innovation and technology to next generation is also not an easy step-up as firms often get snared in the unwise competitive decisions to push the innovation and technology-led products in the marketplace.

Firms operating in niche environment have tried to secure against risks by focusing on potential threats outside the organization like competitors, shifts in the strategic landscape, natural disasters, or geopolitical events. They are generally less skillful at detecting internal vulnerabilities that creep into organizations through various interrelated systems. Indeed, as firms increase the complexity of their systems, they often tend to fail to draw sufficient attention to the introduction of new products and strategies and manage growing system flaws. The possibility of random failure rises as the number of combinations of factors that can go wrong increases, while the opportunity for competitors to counter strategies also goes up. Firms should meticulously assess the risks in technology marketing and stay aware of market information to guard against market uncertainties and make appropriate decisions. It is also necessary for technology marketing firms to identify vulnerabilities in the marketplace and fix them before competitors or disruptive innovation products attack the new technology products.[45]

Among growing market competition, many companies are introducing new products with short product life cycles and quick market penetration attributes. While new products offer tremendous value, product introductions and their transitions to market pose enormous challenges to managers. The new product development process should analyze the risks

[45] Bonabeau, E. (2007). Understanding and managing complexity risk. *MIT Sloan Management Review, 48*(4), 62–68.

impacting a transition and identify factors across departments in the business organization tracking those risks, monitor the evolution of these factors over time, and map scenarios of risks and responses. This process helps managers to understand the expectations of the firms, lessens the chance and impact of unanticipated outcomes, and synchronizes responses among different departments. It assists managers in designing and implementing appropriate policies to enhance the sales for new products and ramp down sales for existing products, balancing the supply and the demand for both so that the combined sales can grow smoothly.[46]

There are many marketing concepts including market orientation, marketing competencies and resources, and competitive marketing strategies that explain success among small agro-food companies in international markets. Some research studies indicate that the influential impact of adopting a market orientation, developing competencies in advantage-generating consumer food products, channel and relationship management areas, leveraging strategically relevant managerial, production and brand resources, and deploying appropriate competitive marketing strategies significantly affect the process of new products introductions and variability in their cyclicality.[47] Consumer-oriented innovation is an increasingly important source of new product development and competitive advantage in reference to the speed with which product innovations are introduced to the market. In many cases, aesthetic properties are as important as technical functions. When one considers the subjective part of the requirements, the feelings, impressions, sensations, or preferences of the consumers must be quantified and modeled in advance. This is a major challenge in new consumer products design.

Various factors including timing, logistics, inventory, and competitive strategies influence new consumer products in the market. Pricing is one of the major factors that affect the performance of newly introduced products at a given time and market as it stimulates the demand upwards or downwards.[48] Fluctuations in demand are attributed to diverse factors,

[46] Erhun, F., Concalves, P., & Hopman, J. (2007). Art of manufacturing new product transitions. *MIT Sloan Management Review, 48*(3), 73–80.

[47] Ibeh, K. I. N., Essam, I., & Panayides, P. M. (2006). International market success among smaller agri-food companies: Some case study evidence. *International Journal of Entrepreneurial Behavior and Research, 12*(2), 85–104.

[48] Calantone, R. J., Benedetto, C., & Anthony, D. (2007). Clustering product launches by price and launch strategy. *Journal of Business and Industrial Marketing, 22*(1), 4–19.

mainly competitive conditions, consumer preferences, and distribution systems. It has been observed that seasonality in new product introduction is reflected in one of the three main strategy manifestation—diversification of the product mix, change of the consumer mix, and aggressive pricing. There are three kinds of demand variability including structural (e.g., seasonality), managerial (e.g., promotions), and random (i.e., unpredictable) among the consumer food products that affect consumers' perceptions, product attractiveness, and buying decisions. It has been observed that while structural variability and managerial variability govern the market demand, random variability influences consumer satisfaction and buying behavior in reference to competitive advantages on existing brands.[49] Introduction of new technological products makes it important for marketers to understand how innovators or first adopters respond to persuasion cues. It has been observed in a study that innovativeness and perceived product newness, which are the constituents of new product attractiveness, are independent constructs that have independent effects on consumer's attitude towards the brand and purchase intent for the new product.

Introduction of new brands in a product category in each market is subject to seasonal variation in market demand derived by consumer preference, advertising recall, product attribute positioning, purchase intent, availability of the product, perceived use value, and overall competitive advantage of the new products. Analysis of the variables in the study would help managers develop appropriate strategies to launch new products and optimize the profit of the firm in a synchronized pattern emerging from market demand and seasonality. A company may also need to consider emphasizing integrated promotion strategy for new brands in reference to attributes, awareness, trial, availability, and repeat buying (AATAR) principle. In highly competitive markets, research methodologies need to be adapted to understand the end users' needs with greater clarity than hitherto when new products were developed. Integrating marketing and sensory analysis to measure customer preferences for the extrinsic and intrinsic attributes of new products can help consumers by augmenting perceptions on quality.[50]

[49] Caniato, F., Kalchschmidt, M., Ronchi, S., Verganti, R., & Zotteri, G. (2005). Clustering consumers to forecast demand. *Production Planning and Control, 16*(1), 32–43.

[50] Rajagopal. (2008). Consumer response and cyclicality in new product management. *Journal of Customer Behaviour, 7*(2), 165–180.

PART II

Challenge Based Research

CHAPTER 4

A Challenge-Based University: Learning, Research, Innovation, and Entrepreneurship

The challenge-based approach must be driven by the collective of academic institutions, companies, entrepreneurs, society, and government. It must consider global and local needs that can be addressed with global, open, and innovative knowledge to integrate solutions that can have local impact. The best references to understand and identify global needs are the Sustainable Development Goals defined by UN and the World Business Council for Sustainable Development imperatives (Climate, Equity, and Nature). But these development goals or imperatives must be addressed by the collaboration between stakeholders, policymakers, and implementing bodies to help local organizations conducting the challenge-based approach.

The C^3 Model

The C^3 model consists of a triadic interconnected paradigm, which converges citizens, communities, and cities. This is a model that puts people first. As explained in Chapter 1, the RISE paradigm integrates people's participation in the context of Research (challenge-based), Innovation (low-cost and incremental), Sustainability (energy, emission, environment), and Entrepreneurship (micro, small, and medium enterprises)

A. Molina and Rajagopal, *Challenge-Based Learning, Research, and Innovation*, Palgrave Studies of Entrepreneurship and Social Challenges in Developing Economies,
https://doi.org/10.1007/978-3-031-29156-2_4

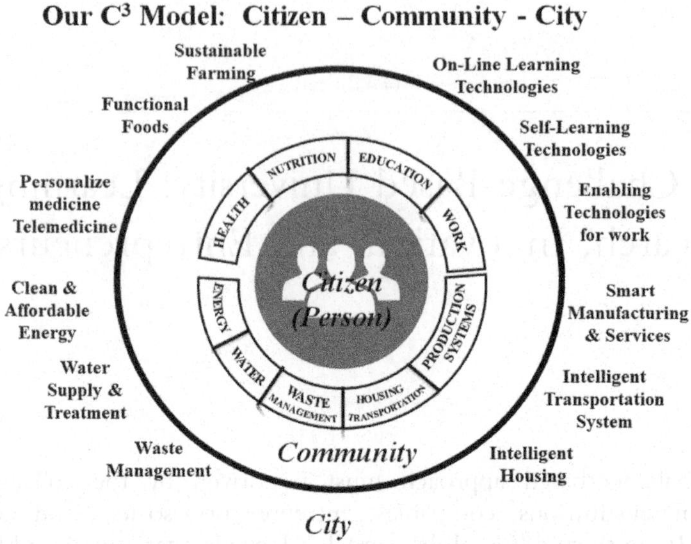

Fig. 4.1 The citizen, community, and city model of needs (C^3 model) (*Source* Author [Arturo Molina])

to create and enhance social value. Also, the concept of Advancement of People's Action and Responsive Technologies (APART) is being practiced with the extensive usage of research and innovation in the context of low-cost solution with social value and industrial challenge to address sustainability (environment, economy, social). Deriving from social and industrial research output, people and companies have learned to follow a new pace in business led by the voice of crowd and collective intelligence.

Our model to implement the APART concept is presented in Fig. 4.1. This model includes the needs (requirements) to be tackled for Citizen (Person), Community (Family, Neighbors, Blocks, Social networks, etc.), and City. The citizen (person) is the center of the model that requires to satisfy minimum services of products to have a quality of life comprising health, nutrition, education, and work. Later people create communities that also require access to clean energy, potable water, services of waste management, housing and transportation, and production system to have a job for an income. Researchers collaborating with Industry have to provide solutions to those needs of citizens and communities, some examples of such technological solutions include personalized medicine and telemedicine, functional foods, sustainable farming, on-line learning technologies, self-learning technologies, enabling technologies for work, usage of clean and affordable energy, access to water supply and treatment, waste management, intelligent housing, intelligent transportation system, smart manufacturing, and services.

Challenge-based approaches must transform existing business models to be centered in people's needs using a co-creation and co-development approach.[1] The research output stimulates firms to design and implement agile business models[2] to provide solutions to Citizens, Communities, and Cities. The challenge-based approach supports research, innovations, and entrepreneurship for social development ranging from sustainable farming to cleaner and affordable energy to the people across geo-demographic segments.[3] The challenge-based approach requires the collaboration between different stakeholders (universities, companies, government, society) to co-design, co-create, and co-develop solutions to improve food production, use of sustainable energy, reasonable management of water, cope with waste management problem but also to enhance the quality of life of people (improve health and nutrition, enhance education, and skills and competence for work).[4] The goal is to put people first to address challenges that are limiting their human flourishing.

[1] David Romero & Arturo Molina (2011) Collaborative networked organisations and customer communities: value co-creation and co-innovation in the networking era, *Production Planning & Control,* 225–6, 447–472, https://doi.org/10.1080/09537287.2010.536619

[2] Dong, W. X. (2016). Crowd intelligence: Analyzing online product reviews for preference measurement. *Information & Management, 53*, 169–182.

[3] Rajagopal (2019), *Contemporary marketing strategy: Analyzing consumer behavior to drive managerial decision making*, New York: Palgrave Macmillan.

[4] Laurett, R., Paço, A., & Mainardes, E. W. (2021). Sustainable development in agriculture and its antecedents, barriers and consequences—An exploratory study. *Sustainable Production and Consumption, 27*, 298–311.

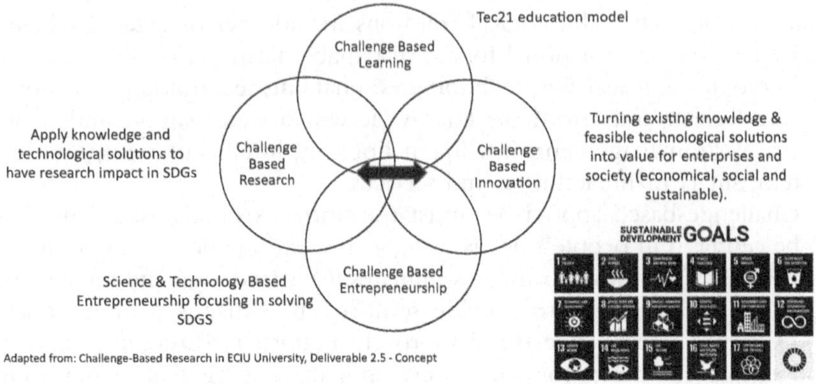

Fig. 4.2 A challenge-based University (*Source* Author [Arturo Molina])

Fundamental Definition of Challenge-Based Learning, Research, Innovation, and Entrepreneurship

The Challenge-based approach at universities has been used in the well-known paradigm of Learning (Gutierrez-Martinez et al. 2021). However, on May 24, 2022, ECIU University[5] presented its Challenge-Based Research strategy to stakeholders and policymakers at a hybrid event in Brussels with the paper Challenge-Based Research for a Stronger and more Sustainable Europe. Tecnologico de Monterrey is an associate member of this initiative and has defined a new strategy of a Challenge-Based University for 2030, see Fig. 4.2. This strategy integrates four Challenge-Based Approaches: Learning, Research, Innovation, and Entrepreneurship. The strategy includes the perspectives of PNS factors comprising embedded Problems, Needs, and Solutions within the society in the context of cost–benefit-profit and cost-time-risk factors associated with innovation and technology. The goal is to address the triple bottom line (TBL) which comprises Planet, People, and Profit, which encourages sustainable innovations, technology, manufacturing, and services.

[5] For details, see https://www.eciu.org/news/the-future-of-research-is-challenge-based.

Challenge-Based Learning: Education 4.0

A reference model for Education 4.0 has been defined at Tec de Monterrey including six categories of key enablers that are used during the design and implementation of today's teaching–learning programs (See Fig. 4.3). The following factors affect the educational process, quality, and applications in the contemporary context:

i. Key competencies. Identifying crucial transversal and disciplinary competencies necessary to be developed by today's students.
ii. Innovative teaching–learning methods. Incorporating active learning methods in educational programs with different delivery modalities (face-to-face, remote, and hybrid).
iii. 4.0 Technologies and current Information and Communication Technologies (ICTs). Implementing current and emerging ICTs

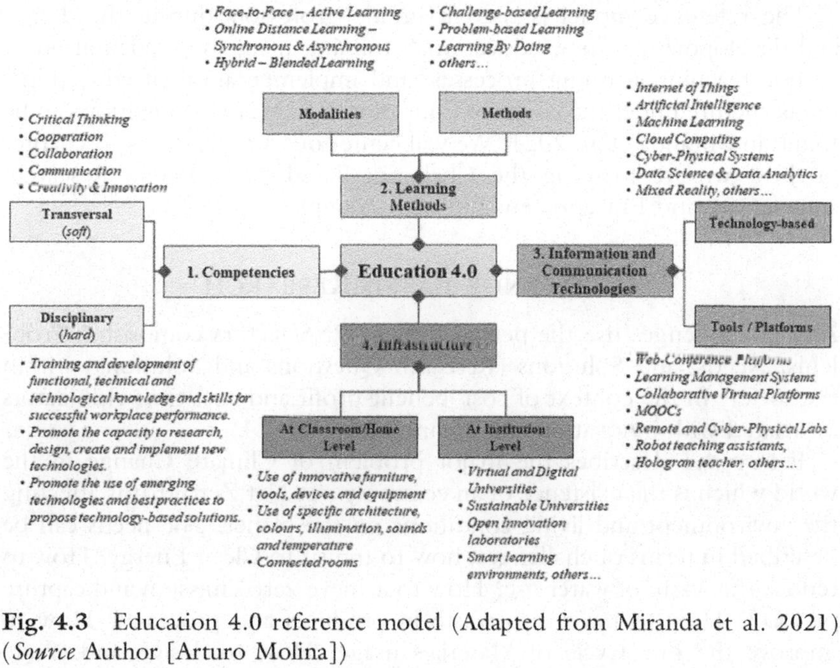

Fig. 4.3 Education 4.0 reference model (Adapted from Miranda et al. 2021) (*Source* Author [Arturo Molina])

considering 4.0 Technologies for remote collaboration and interaction, digital presentations and easy exchange of information and data, rapid prototype development and common use of digital technology as platforms for rapid product development.

iv. Modern Infrastructure. Employing innovative infrastructure such as facilities, flexible furniture, online services, and platforms to improve teaching–learning processes at two levels: at classroom/home level and at institutional level.
v. Key stakeholders. Include the participation in teaching–learning processes of key stakeholders inside and outside of the institution; therefore, leading actors from government, companies, academia, and society can be considered during teaching–learning processes.
vi. Sustainability. Enabling sustainable education and training systems by providing high-quality, affordable education with high social impact.

The reference model is used to guide professors during the design and development of new educational/training programs, redefinition of ad-hoc teaching–learning processes, and implementation of educational infrastructure under the vision of Education 4.0. More information can be found in Miranda et al. 2021. We will center our attention in this chapter on how we are focusing the Challenge-Based Approach in Research, Innovation, and Entrepreneurship with examples.

Challenge-Based Research

All our challenges use the perspectives of PNS factors comprising Problems, Needs, and Solutions (Research Questions and Solutions) within the society in the context of cost–benefit-profit and cost-time-risk factors associated with innovation and technology (Fig. 4.4).

Figure 4.4 describes the major problem of Climate Change in the world which is the existence of an economy not Net Zero that is affecting the environment and living conditions on the planet. The needs can be described in terms of challenges: how to transit to Clean Energy? How to reduce the waste of water use? How to achieve zero emission and capture of CO_2? How to have zero waste in products and processes? How to improve the Life Cycle of Materials usage? How to design and create sustainable economic business models? How to promote a Sustainable consumption culture?

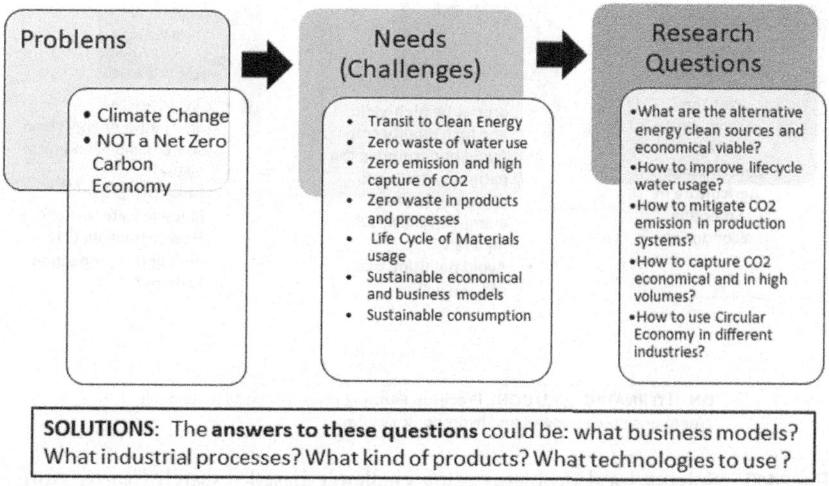

Fig. 4.4 The PNS factors—problems, needs, and solutions (*Source* Author [Arturo Molina])

All these challenges that need to be addressed by research questions and solutions are described in the above figure in the context of Planet, People, and Profit: what are the alternative energy sources that are economically viable? How to improve life cycle of water usage? How to mitigate CO_2 emission in production systems with alternative cost-effective technologies? How to capture CO_2 in an economical manner and in high volumes? How to use Circular Economy in different industries non-zero waste? Alternative solutions can be found while using different research models: applied research, experimental research, and action-research. All these models could seek solutions on new sustainable business models, greener industrial processes, new net-zero products, or usage and development of disruptive technologies (nano-bio-info-cogno). This approach can be focused more if the problem is a regional problem, for example in Agriculture in emerging economies. The regional problem of sustainable agriculture in emerging economies can be solved with techniques of sustainability in agriculture using low cost intelligent green houses (Fig. 4.5).

In this example, the final solutions to this challenge were the design and development of a low-cost greenhouse using hydroponic systems

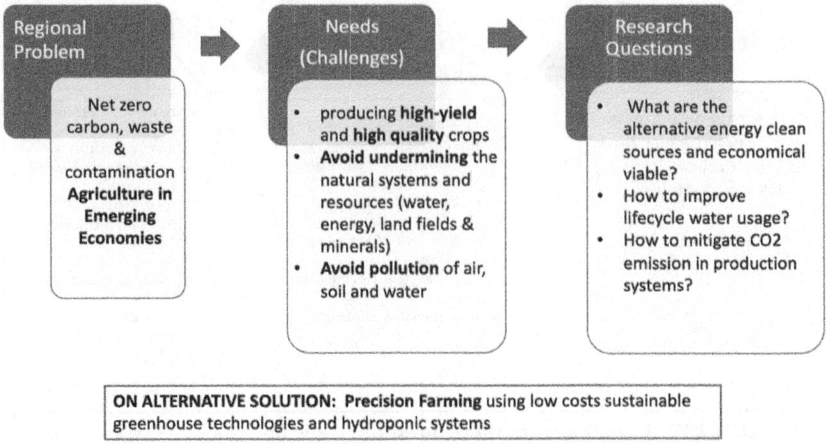

Fig. 4.5 Solving local problems using challenge-based research (*Source* Author [Arturo Molina])

(Ponce et al., 2014). Figure 4.6 describes the solution proposed in a prototype system of a greenhouse system using low-cost technologies that demonstrated the impact of reducing emission, water consumption, and improving crop production.

Challenge-Based Innovation: Social-Ecological, Industry and Government

The major challenge in innovation is to identify the problem, articulate the stakeholder's needs, explore alternative solutions, develop multiple prototypes, and define Minimum Viable Products (MVPs) using alternative core technologies, and test the products and services at the right target segment. Economic viability and technological feasibility drive innovations to discover, design, development, and efficiency in delivering the innovation. In the following sections, different types of Challenge-Based Innovations are described and explained using different case studies.

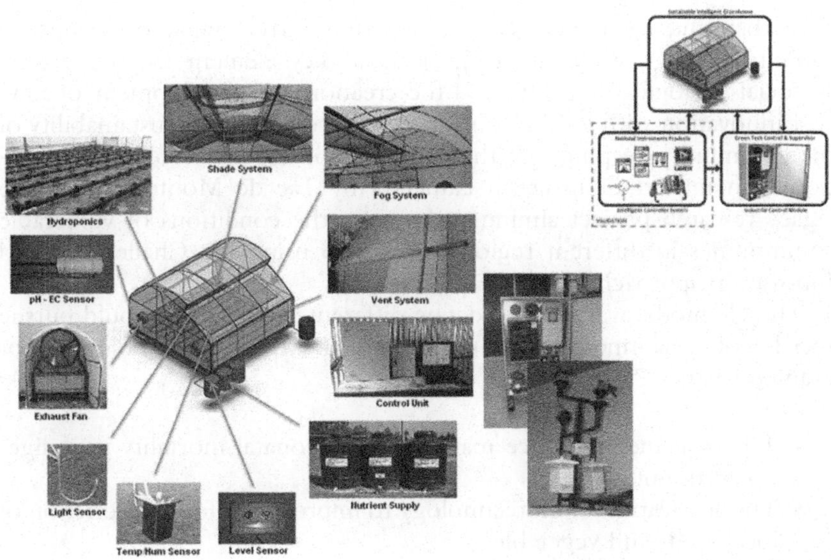

Fig. 4.6 Sustainable agriculture in emerging economies (*Source* Author [Arturo Molina])

Challenge-Based Social-Ecological Innovation

In Chapter 2, we discussed the emergence of social-ecological innovation as a relevant approach to build resilience in communities in local sub-urban and rural areas. Social-ecological innovation is largely based on the review of opportunities with a focus on desirability, feasibility, and viability of the innovation to commercialize and make it adaptable to the social and economic development.[6] An important goal is to contribute to the sustainable development of ecosystems but the improvement of quality of life of the people living in these areas. Eco-innovations encouraged in local markets contribute to the resilience of ecosystem services in sub-urban and rural socio-economic and ecological landscapes. Crowdsourcing of innovative ideas, collective intelligence to improve the resources utilization, and management of green space in

[6] Chen, H. C., Knierim, A., & Bock, B. B. (2022). The emergence of social innovation in rural revitalization practices: A comparative case study from Taiwan. *Journal of Rural Studies*, *90*, 134–146.

sub-urban and rural social-ecological systems have emerged as effective tools to manage sustainability projects. A key element for the success of social-ecological innovation is the creation and development of low-cost innovation with local resources to achieve long-term sustainability of the community keeping safe the natural resources and ecological conditions. An important program launched by Tec de Monterrey was the legacy research project aiming to improve the conditions of vulnerable communities in different regions in Mexico using the Challenge-Based Innovation approach.

The C^3 model was used to define different projects that could pursue social-ecological innovation by using low-cost advanced technologies. For example (Fig. 4.7):

- Telemedicine to reduce maternal and neonatal mortality in indigenous communities.
- The application of biotechnology to improve the food production of local seeds and vegetables.
- Introduction of mobile technology to improve the mathematical and reading skill of K-12 children.

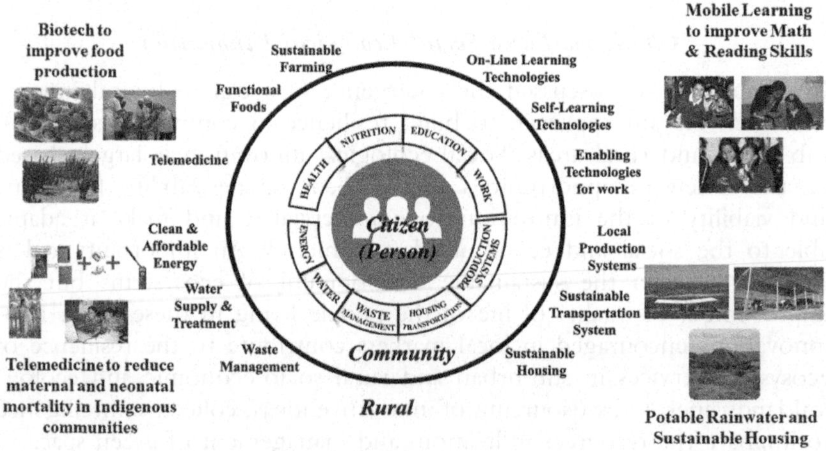

Fig. 4.7 Vulnerable communities action research and innovation with impact of improving the quality of life: Some examples (*Source* Author [Arturo Molina])

- The use of natural local materials for the construction of sustainable housing and incorporation rain capture systems to have access to potable water.

Innovation is the critical dimension of economic change in these rural communities to have alternatives for improving the living standards without risking the local ecosystems and natural resources.

Challenge-Based Innovation in Industry

Industry innovation is described in detail by the Oslo Manual OECD,[7] where a company can achieve different types of innovation: marketing, process, product, and organization. Sustainable manufacturing in México and other manufacturing countries is a priority for the survival of companies. Successful innovation in sustainable manufacturing is related to the reduction of CO2 emission, scrap, energy, water, and improvement of production operations by increasing quality, volumes, reduction of time and cost. Industry is moving towards the use of technologies of Industry 4.0 to achieve their productivity and sustainability key performance indicators (KPIs). Challenge-Based Innovation for industry can be accomplished by co-designing and co-developing solutions to achieve such KPIs.

Successful innovation leads to stakeholders' involvement and profits, which can be achieved through the co-creation and co-development of solutions that can achieve the customers and consumers expectations. The aligning of all important actors in the supply chain is a must for a successful innovation process. In the example presented in Fig. 4.8 (Molina et al., 2021), a set of Industrial stakeholders in a company identifies an opportunity in process innovation to improve the productivity of a production line to increase its volume per year. The research and innovation take place by the identification of existing digital technologies that can evaluate alternative solutions in the production line to meet the productivity criteria. Also, the evaluation of key performance indicators related to reduction of emission, water usage, energy efficiency, and reuse of materials has been incorporated into the mathematical and digital/simulation models. The technological transfer of such solutions

[7] https://www.oecd.org/sti/inno/oslo-manual-2018-info.pdf.

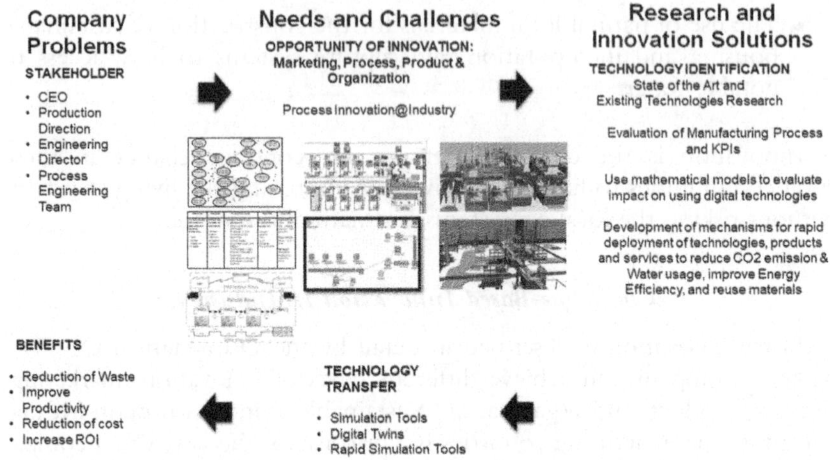

Fig. 4.8 Example of industry innovation in a cycle that impacts on Profit (*Source* Author [Arturo Molina])

takes place in the factory and the benefits attained are reduction of waste, improvement of productivity (volume per year), reduction of costs, and crease of ROI (Return of Investment and associated profit).

Challenge-Based Innovation in Government

In Chapter 2 it was noted that energy market transition, which is enabled by new affordable energy technologies and digitalization, opens novel opportunities for developing innovative energy solutions through collective intelligence and public–private co-creations. The new technologies emerging through co-creation facilitate stakeholders to buy low-cost renewable energy and create smart technologies. In Mexico, the law of transition to clean energy from the government launched a special program to help in this transition to the Mexican government and state-owned companies including the state electricity company (Fig. 4.9).

The problems identified in this transition was lack of enough human talent specialized in sustainable energy and management, insufficient infrastructure for education, research, and technology development, and absent of national innovative and smart technologies for the supply chain

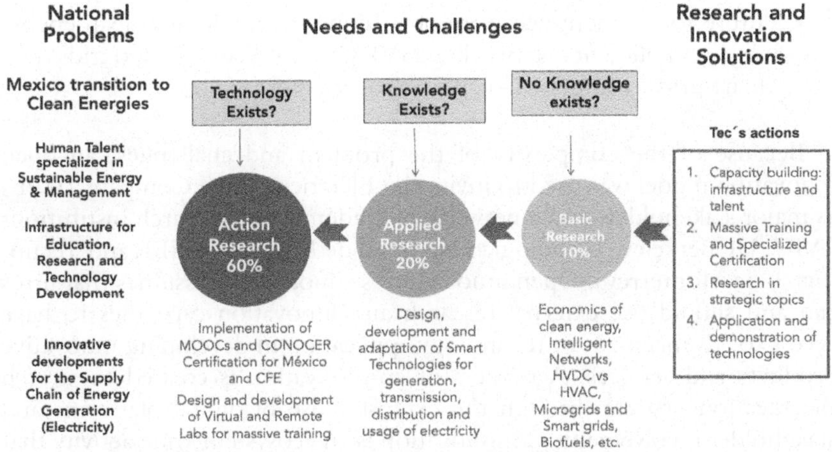

Fig. 4.9 Binational laboratory on smart sustainable energy management and technology training (Sponsored by National Council of Science and Technology, Mexico) (*Source* Author [Arturo Molina])

of energy generation, transmission, distribution, and usage. The challenges identified in this project were as stated below (Lozano et al. 2022):

- How to use existing technology to maximize the outreach of people to train in specialized themes related to energy and sustainability.
- How to use state-of-the-art knowledge in applied research to find solution to nowadays energy's needs in Mexico.
- How to identify long-term research areas to have an impact in future needs of Mexico's energy needs.

Solutions that were proposed have been included as:

- Implementation of MOOCs (Mass Online Open Courses) and CONOCER Certification for México and CFE. Design and development of Virtual and Remote Labs for massive training.
- Design, development, and adaptation of Smart Technologies for generation, transmission, distribution, and usage of electricity.

- Future topics identified were new economic model for clean energy usage, Intelligent Networks, HVDC vs HVAC, Microgrids and Smart grids, Biofuels, Green Hydrogen, etc.

Because of the complexity of the problem and challenges, an open innovation model was used to invite the Electricity State Company (CFE) as major stakeholder, and a network of academic and research institutions (ASU, UCBerkeley, Tecnologico Nacional de México, INEEL and Tecnologico de Monterrey). Open innovation is a model that assumes that firms can and should use external research and innovation capacities to have access to advancement of technology application in developing innovative products and services. A process of co-innovation is created to stretch the ideation process through the extensive use of digital platforms and stakeholder involvement. Co-innovation is an ecosystem-wide activity that involves multiple stakeholders, who collaborate towards a shared social goal and explore niche strategies to commercialize eco-innovations.

References

Cai, P. (2021). Thinking skills development in mobile learning: The case of elementary school students studying environmental studies. *Thinking Skills and Creativity*, 42, Art. 100922 (*in press*). https://doi.org/10.1016/j.tsc.2021.100922

Stephan, U., Patterson, M., Kelly, C., & Mair, J. (2016). Organizations driving positive social change: A review and an integrative framework of change processes. *Journal of Management, 42*(5), 1250–1281.

Gutiérrez-Martínez, Y., Bustamante-Bello, R., Navarro-Tuch, S. A., López-Aguilar, A. A., Molina, A., & Álvarez-Icaza Longoria, I. (2021). A challenge-based learning experience in industrial engineering in the framework of education 4.0. *Sustainability*, *13*, 9867. https://doi.org/10.3390/su13179867

Miranda, J., Navarrete, C., Noguez, J., Molina-Espinosa, J.-M., Ramírez-Montoya, M.-S., Navarro-Tuch, S. A., Bustamante-Bello, M.-R., Rosas-Fernández, J.-B., & Molina, A. (2021). The core components of education 4.0 in higher education: Three case studies in engineering education. *Computers & Electrical Engineering*, *93*, ISSN 0045–790 https://doi.org/10.1016/j.compeleceng.2021.107278.

Ponce P., Molina A., Cepeda P., Lugo E., & MacCleery B., (2014). *Green house design and control*. CRC Press, ISBN-10 978–1–138–02629–2 (Hardback).

Molina A., Ponce P., Miranda J., & Cortes D., (2021). *Enabling systems for intelligent manufacturing in industry 4.0—Sensing, smart and sustainable systems for the design of S3 products, processes, manufacturing systems, and enterprises*. Springer, ISBN-978-3-030-65549-5.

Lozano F.J., Mendoza A., & Molina A., (2022). *Energy issues and transition to a low carbon economy: Insights from Mexico*, Springer; Edición 2022 ed. (11 agosto 2021), ISBN-10 978-3-030-75660-4.

CHAPTER 5

Linking Research and Business: Raising Social Well-Being

The Use of C³ Model

In Latin America, like other developing regions Asia and Africa there is a need to focus the attention to solve major basic problems like poverty, community health, housing, energy, food production and quality, and education. An excellent proposal is given by Manfred Max-Neef's model of human needs (2010) to tackle these problems using a model that contains a list of needs: subsistence, protection, affection, understanding, participation, creation, leisure, identity, and freedom. We have used the Max-Neef's needs to guide the instantiation of our C³ Model regarding the needs of citizens (people), communities, and cities (Fig. 5.1). It is important to understand the needs of the citizen in terms of axiological needs to help in the identification of possible solutions. For example, the need of subsistence could be related to the individual´s needs for health and nutrition, and community´s needs of energy, water, waste management, housing, transportation, and work (production systems). On the other hand, the need of protection is related to individual´s needs of health care and access to health systems, and community´s needs of access to clean energy, potable water, sustainable housing, and transportation.

The full matrix is described in Fig. 5.2 which demonstrates the interaction and axiological needs of subsistence, protection, affection,

A. Molina and Rajagopal, *Challenge-Based Learning, Research, and Innovation*, Palgrave Studies of Entrepreneurship and Social Challenges in Developing Economies,
https://doi.org/10.1007/978-3-031-29156-2_5

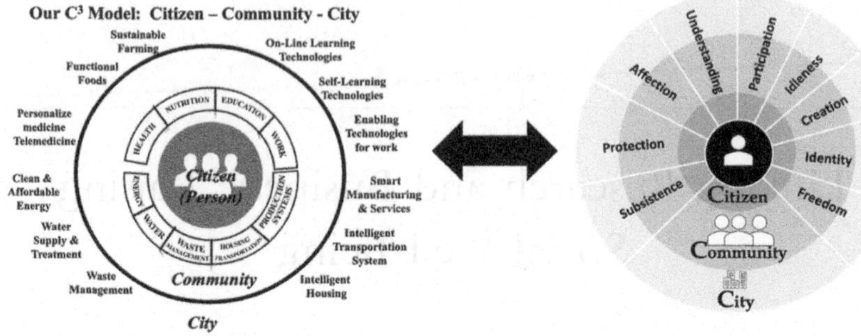

Fig. 5.1 C^3 model instantiated using the matrix of needs of Max-Neef (*Source* Author [Arturo Molina])

understanding, participation, creation, leisure, identity, and freedom and the existential needs of being, having, doing, and interacting; each box allows to describe in more detail feasible satisfiers to solve the relationship of an axiological need (e.g., subsistence) with the existential need of being (physical health), having (food), doing (feed), and interacting (living environment).

For example, a person that needs quality of life (Subsistence) must be with physical health, have access to food, require to be able to feed themselves, and interact with a sustainable and living environment that will be able to grow such nutritional foods at low cost, with local resources and keeping natural resources safe. This ideal solution requires initiatives of research and innovation to find alternative technologies, products of services that will satisfy such need, for example: biotechnological functional foods. It is important to mention that each box describes satisfiers and no needs. Food, shelter, or work are satisfiers (solutions) for subsistence. Protection can be satisfied by being careful about the activities that a person realizes, having access to social security, preventing acts of danger to nature, and dwelling in a safe environment where the rule of law applies. Investigate, study, experiment, or educate are activities (doing) that satisfies the need for understanding. The relation between needs and satisfying elements is multiple. Different needs can be addressed by a satisfier, or a need can be resolved by multiple satisfiers. The fact that elements driving satisfaction can give a solution to a different needs might direct the effort to focus on such satisfier to develop a product or technology.

Needs according to existential categorice Needs. according to axiological categories	BEING (registers attributes personal or collective, that are expresed as nouns)	HAVING (registers attributes personal or collective, that are expresed as nouns)	DOING (registers actions, personal or collective, that can be expressed as verbs)	INTERACTING (registers locations and milieus (as times and spaces). It stands for the Spanish ESTAR or the German BEFINDEN, in the sense of time and space. Since there is no corresponding word in English, INTERACTING was chosen à faut de mieux)
SUBSISTENCE	(1) Physical health, mental health, equilibrium , sense of humor, adaptability	(2) Food , shelter, work	(3) Feed, procreate , rest, work	(4) Living environment, social se tting
PROTECTION	(5) Care, adatability, autonomia, equilibrium, solidarity	(6) Insurance system, savings, social security, health systems, rights , family, work	(7) Cooperate, prevent, plan, take care of, cure, help	(8) Living space, social environment, dwelling
AFFECTION	(9) Self-esteem, solidarity, respect, tolerance, generosity, receptiveness, passion, determination, sensuality, sense of humor	(10) Friendships, parterships, relationships with nature	(11) Make love, caress, express emotions, share , Take care of, cultivate, appreciate	(12) Privacy, intimacy, home, space of togethermess
UNDERSTANDING	(13) Critical conscience, receptiveness, curiosity, astonishment, discipline, intuition, rationality	(14) Literature , teachers, method, educational policies, communication policies	(15) Investigate , study, experiment, educate , analize meditate	(16) Settings of formative interaction, schools, universities, academies, groups, communities, fa mily
PARTICIPATION	(17) Adaptability, receptiveness, solidarity , willingness, determination, dedication, respect, passion, sense of humor	(18) Rights, responsibilities, duties, privileges, work	(19) Become affiliated, cooperate , propose, share, dissent, to obey, interact, agree on, express opinions	(20) Settings of participative interaction, parties, associations, churches, communities, neighborhoods, family
IDLENESS	(21) Curiosity, receptiveness, imagination, recktessness, sense of humor, tranquility, sensuality	(22) Games , spectacles, clubs, parties, peace of mind	(23) Daydream , brood , dream, recall old times, give away to f antasies, remember, relax, have fun, play	(24) Privacy, intimacy, spaces of closeness, free time , su rroundings , landscapes
CREATION	(25) Passion, determination, intuition, imagination , boldness, rationality, autonomy, inventiveness,	(26) Abilities, skills, method, work	(27) Work, invent , build , des ign, compose, interpret	(28) Productive and feedback settings, workshops, cultural groups, audiences, spaces for expression, temporal freedom
IDENTITY	(29) Sense of belonging, consistency, differentiation, self-esteem, assertiveness	(30) Symbiosis, language, religion, habits, customs, reference groups, sexuality, values, norms, historical memory, work	(31) Commit oneself, integrate oneself, confront, decide on, get to know oneself, recognize oneself , actualize oneself, grow	(32) Social rhythms, everyday settings, settings which one belongs to , maturation stages
FREEDOM	(32) Autonomy, self-esteem, determination, passion, assertiveness, openmindedness, boldness, rebelliousness, tolerance	(34) Equal rights	(35) Dissent, choose , be different from, run risks, develop awareness, commit oneself, disobey	(36) Temporal/spatial plasticity

Fig. 5.2 Adaptation of the matrix of Manfred Max-Neef's needs and satisfiers (*Source* Author [Arturo Molina])

Building Solutions for People's Needs Using Program Logic Models

Research and innovation traditionally at universities had followed a "push" approach where researchers look for interesting scientific questions to be answered, and they undertake research projects trying to answer those questions. In some cases, the answer to these questions can be transformed into technological developments that can be pushed to the market as innovative products or services. IPR (Intellectual Property Rights) can be filled to protect these discoveries, and then technology packages can be prepared to be commercialized. Sometimes researchers develop further their technological innovations to pursue prototypes that can achieve TRL 4 (Technology Readiness Level) according to NASA.[1]

For example, a "push" approach to have an impact on subsistence of people using a logic model is described in Fig. 5.3. With the research on functional foods to increase the quality of the food produced, this research will aim to develop new functional foods that will have 3 major characteristics: high-quality nutrients, flavor, and functional activity (*e.g.*,

[1] For details see https://esto.nasa.gov/trl/

improve the immunology system of a person). If we change the nutritional diet in children between 0–5 years, by using this new functional food, we could have an impact on their lives by improving their nutrition and health. The benefit will be to increase their life expectancy, improve their physical health, and allow them to have a brain developed to have learning abilities and skills. Figure 5.3 exhibits a program logic model to represent a "Push" approach for research and innovation and have an impact of health and nutrition of children aged 0–5 years.

If we change the model to a challenge-based approach which was based on the Neef's matrix, then we could identify the needs and then build up the project using a logic model as described in Fig. 5.4. Subsistence is vital for the development of regions such as Latin America, but it requires to improve the life expectancy and health of the people living in vulnerable communities. Therefore, it is important that challenge-based research tackled the problem of subsistence by improving the nutrition and health of children under 5 years of age. Changing the nutritional habits of children in such communities is critical to the success of the project; therefore, an important part of the project will be to ensure that changes are made to feed children with new types of food or formulas. Once the context for the research is established (problem and needs), alternative solutions can be proposed by researcher to undertake action research actions to provide products and services that are sustainable in terms of economic (produced locally at low cost), environmental (without harming the ecosystem), and social (changing cultural and eating habits).

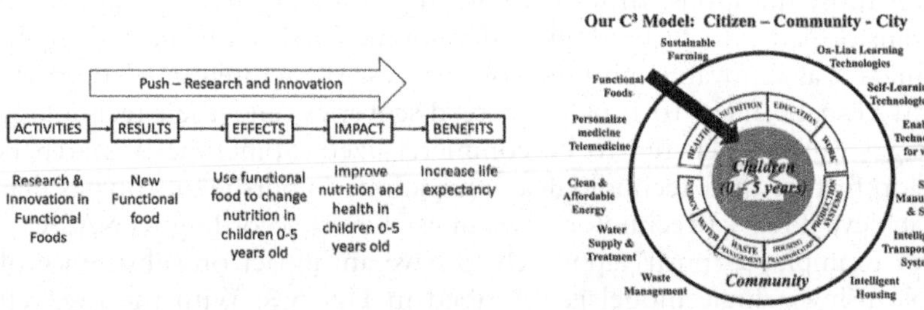

Fig. 5.3 A program logic model with a PUSH approach (*Source* Author [Arturo Molina])

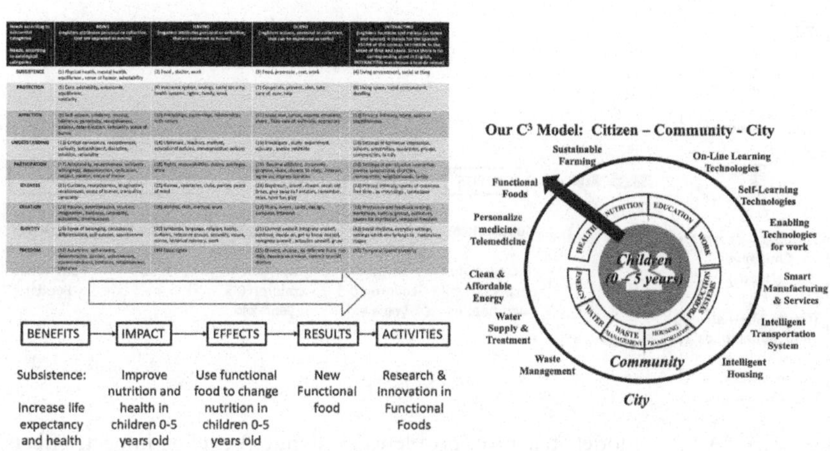

Fig. 5.4 A program logic model with a PULL Approach (*Source* Author [Arturo Molina])

Figure 5.4 illustrates a program logic model to represent a "Pull" approach for research and innovation and have an impact of health and nutrition of children aged 0–5 years.

Program Logic Models

The program logic models exhibit a customer centricity for challenge-based research and innovation. The starting point to develop a program logic model is a problem. We have included then the definition of a challenge (need). A program logic model has the following structure (Vallejo et al. 2017), see Fig. 5.5:

1. *Benefits:* the achievements of the project according to its main objectives,
2. *Impacts:* the consequences of changes in the community/person or activities,
3. *Effects*: changes the project is going to cause in the community/person,
4. *Results*: the outputs produced by the activities of the project, and

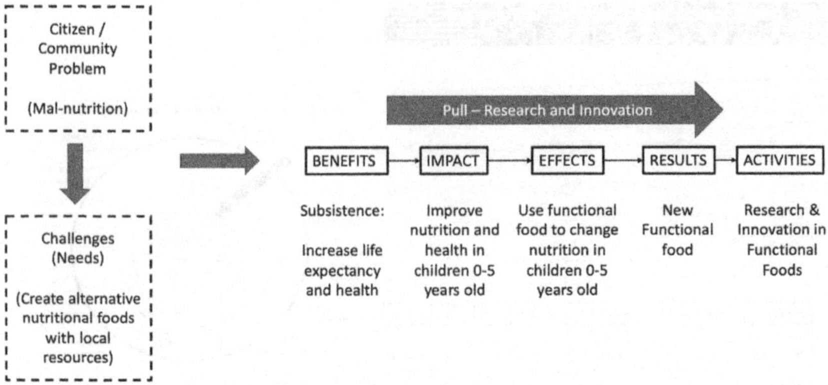

Fig. 5.5 A logic model structure: problem/challenge, benefits, impact, effects, results, and activities

5. *Activities*: the actions or tasks carried out in any project applying different methodologies or resources—human capital and technological capital.

A Reference Model for Challenge-Based Research and Innovation: Social and Ecological Initiatives

Figure 5.6 describes a reference model to define challenge-based research and innovation projects for social–ecological initiatives. This type of project can be defined by national governments, international funding agencies, Non-governmental organizations or civil associations, and universities. At a first stage, it is critical to clearly define the citizen/community problem and then the writing of the challenge (need) which can be done using the Max-Neef matrix. Once we have defined the context, then the program logic model can be developed by defining the expect outcomes (benefits, impacts, and effects) of the challenge-based research and innovation project. Outcomes are the expected changes in the population served that result from a program's activities and fall along a continuum, ranging from short- to long-term results:

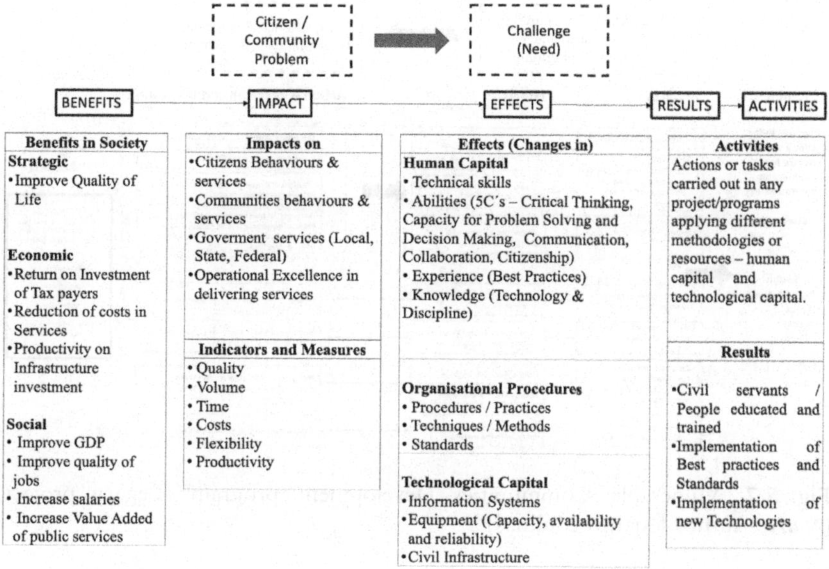

Fig. 5.6 Program logic models reference model for social ecological projects (*Source* Author [Arturo Molina])

- Long-term (benefits): changes in condition or status in life (e.g., improve quality of life—nutrition and health)
- Medium-term (impact): changes in behavior or action (e.g., changes in citizens behavior by adopting healthy food practice and/or improving government services to provide access to healthy food)
- Short-term (effects): changes in human capital knowledge, skills, and/or attitudes; changes in practices or standards or public policies; and use of information systems to improve information about nutrition facts in vulnerable communities (e.g., increase knowledge in rural communities about local healthy choices).

The example given in Fig. 5.7 is related to the case presented in Chapter 4 vulnerable communities:

- Problem: lack of sustainable development options for rural vulnerable communities,

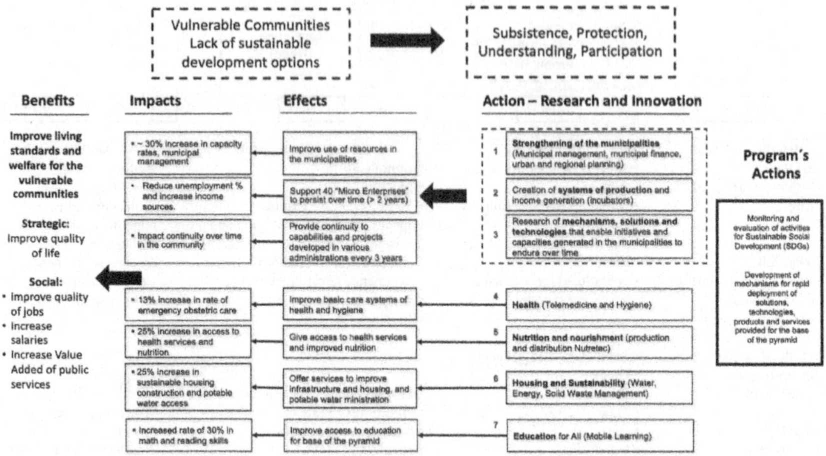

Fig. 5.7 Vulnerable Communities Development program (Legacy project) (*Source* Author [Arturo Molina])

- Challenge: subsistence (food), protection (health system), understanding (education), and participation (settings of participative interaction citizens/community, government, and academy),
- Benefits: improve living standards and welfare for vulnerable communities, improve quality of life, improve quality of jobs, increase salaries, and increase value-added public services, and
- Impacts:
  - o Government services—increase in 30% in capacity rates' municipal management,
  - o Community services include the following impact:
    - Reduce unemployment % and increase income sources
    - Health—13% increase in rate of emergency obstetric care, and
    - Health and nutrition—25% increase in access to health services and nutrition.
  - o Community behavior impact can be seen as discussed below:
    - Impact continuity over time in the community;
    - 25% increase in sustainable housing construction and potable water access.

o Citizen behavior: education—increased rate of 30% in math and reading skills.

The effects and actions-research and innovation initiatives are described in Fig. 5.7. The changes required to have the desirable benefits and impacts are related to the capacity of the municipality leaders and staff (improve knowledge and technical skills), creation of supporting services for micro-enterprises (new practices), improving basic care systems for health and hygiene, and giving access to health services and improve nutrition. To have a better healthy environment, there is a need for improving the infrastructure and housing, and to have potable water reliable systems. Finally, education is important to improve the quality of jobs and opportunities for all people. The seven initiatives that were deployed were:

- Strengthening of the municipalities (municipal management, municipal finance, urban, and regional planning),
- Creation of systems of production and income generation (incubators),
- Research of mechanisms, solutions, and technologies that enable initiatives and capacities generated in the municipalities to endure over time,
- Telemedicine to reduce maternal and neonatal mortality in indigenous communities,
- The application of biotechnology to improve the food production of local seeds and vegetables,
- The use of natural local materials for the construction of sustainable housing and incorporation rain capture systems to have access to potable water, and
- Introduction of mobile technology to improve the mathematical and reading skill of K-12 children.

There is a need for a collaborative process to create initiatives that could be successful. They must follow a co-creation and co-development with the local government and community using design thinking approaches, and several on-site meetings with all stakeholders.[2]

[2] More about this project can be found in https://www.youtube.com/watch?v=kqFStgcW3UE.

Program Logic Models for Industry Innovation: Marketing, Process, Product, and Organization

The reference model used for challenge-based research and innovation for industry is in Fig. 5.8. The company must identify a problem of the citizens/communities/industry. In this case the citizens are customers of the company products/services; therefore, it is very important to define the profile of the persona: geography, demographics, socio-economical, physiographic, and behavioral (Revella, 2015). Then it is possible to define the challenge (need) using the Max-Neef matrix to pursue a type of innovation that is required to satisfy the need and solve the problem i.e., marketing, process, product, or organization.

Because any action taken by the company must have a benefit, it is important that once the problem/challenge/type of innovation has been defined the program logic model can be built around three types of benefits for the company (Molina, 2003):

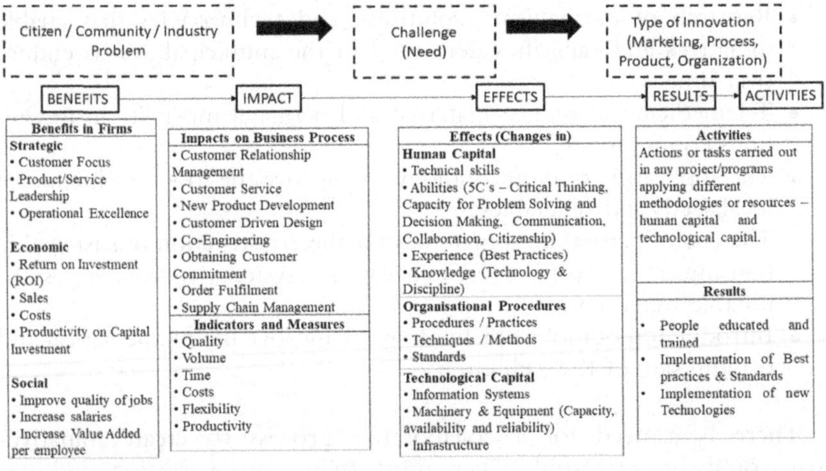

Fig. 5.8 Reference model for challenge-based research and innovation for industry (*Source* Author [Arturo Molina])

- Strategic: customer focus (marketing innovation), product/service leadership (product innovation), and operational excellence (process and organization innovation).
- Economic: increase ROI and sales, reduce cost, and improve productivity on capital investment
- Social: improve quality of jobs, increase salaries, and increase value added per employee.

Once the benefits are defined, the focus should be in what process or processes must be undertaken to achieve such benefits and address the challenge and customer needs. The eight core business in a company are executed by the company to deliver a product (Molina et al., 2021). For innovation on:

- Marketing: customer relationship management and customer service
- Product: new product development, customer driven design, and co-engineering
- Process: obtaining customer commitment, order fulfillment and supplier, and relationship management.
- Organization: any process in the company that is a core process sustained by core competencies.

Then the company must change its human capital, organization procedures, and technological capacities to align its strategy to execute such process in a way that the impact and benefits are achieved to give a solution to the challenge and problem of the customer. Developing of new products for many companies does not occur as a chance or coincidence; innovative products emerge through careful attention to the user/customer needs, innovation capabilities of the business, and growing market criteria. Co-creation and co-development with end users create products that gain market more rapidly. Also, co-engineering working in collaboration with suppliers is a must. The companies must follow a set of activities collecting user feedback, lead user engagement, modified prototype development, product testing, pricing, distribution strategy, and integrating manufacturing and services. Therefore, the approach usually taken by industry encompasses the development of a product-service portfolio based on user´s requirements that delivers benefits from the functionality of products or services offered by the firm. Any product/service generally solves a problem for the user/customer.

Let´s take the example of the apps for the mobile phone. The apps usually are created to tackle certain needs. Figure 5.9 depicts an industrial case of a mobile application to control the energy equipment for a digital twin and also the book related to that application. We can identify using the Max-Neef matrix different needs and the apps that are the satisfiers of such requirements. For a company to seize these opportunities, we must determine the problem, challenge, and what type of innovation wants to pursue to respond to the market´s niche: marketing, process, product, or organization. Let´s describe in more detail the example presented in Chapter 4 related to the educational product related to education on Smart Grids. Figure 5.9 depicts the case study. The problem was defined as obsolete educational equipment (Fig. 5.10). The challenge is the need to update equipment with digital technologies to improve understanding and participation of the students and professors at universities / educational institutions about smart grids and sustainable energy.

The activities carried out by the collaborative team of industry and university was:

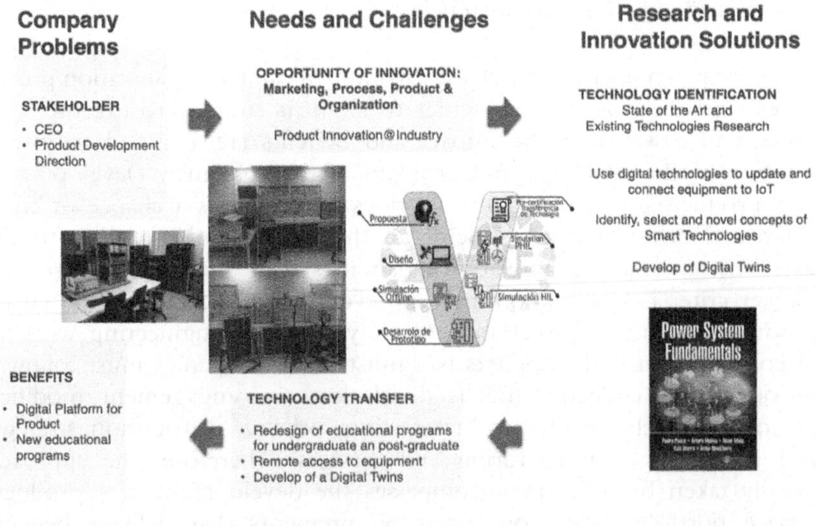

Fig. 5.9 Industry Innovation in products to meet customer and user's requirements (*Source* Author [Arturo Molina])

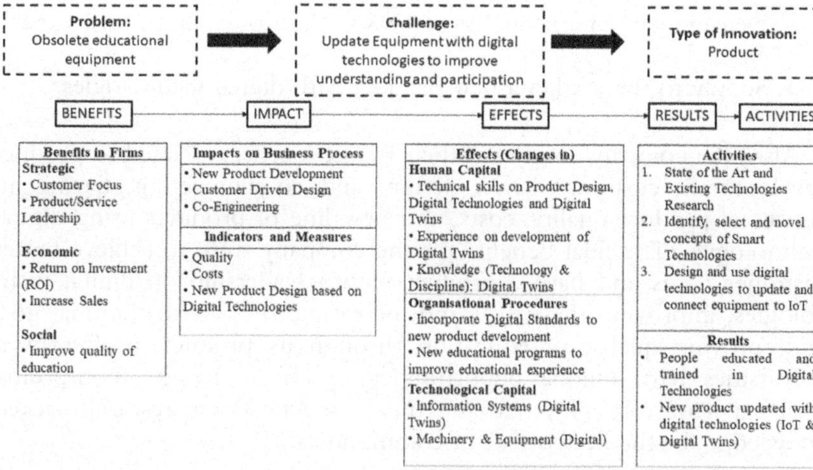

Fig. 5.10 Case study of updating equipment with digital technologies to meet customer and users requirements (*Source* Author [Arturo Molina])

1. Research on state-of-the-art and existing technologies,
2. Identification and selection of novel concepts of smart technologies, and
3. Design and use digital technologies to update and connect equipment to IoT (Internet of Things).

The results of these activities were:

1. People from industry educated and trained in digital technologies,
2. Creation of new product updated with digital technologies (IoT and digital twins), and
3. Development of educational program including book to execute the educational programs.

This innovation project allowed the company to:

1. Improve their human capital capabilities and skills in digital technologies,
2. Incorporate digital standards to their new product development,

3. Deliver new educational programs to improve educational experiences, and
4. Supply to the market a new product with digital technologies.

Also, the company improved their business process related to product development, customer-driven design, and co-engineering, having an impact of product quality, costs, and new line of products using digital technologies. The final benefits for the company were to achieve better customer focus and have a product with a leadership on digital technologies, improving their ROI and increasing sales. With the final goal of improving quality of education through its product, professors at universities have unique opportunities to effect change, repurposing their expertise to deploy relevant, timely, practical, and research-backed knowledge for the betterment of communities.

References

Max-Neef, M. (2010). *Development and human needs*, 1st Edition. Routledge, ISBN 9781315258003.

Vallejo, C., Romero, D., & Molina, A. (2017). Implementation of best manufacturing practices using logic models and system dynamics: Project design and project assessment views. *Information Systems and e-Business Management, 15*, 535–575. https://doi.org/10.1007/s10257-016-0327-6

Molina, A. (2003). Developing the enterprise concept—The business plan. In Bernus, P., Nemes, L., Schmidt, G. (Eds.), Handbook on enterprise architecture. *International Handbooks on Information Systems*. Springer. https://doi.org/10.1007/978-3-540-24744-9_9

Adelle, R. (2015). *Buyer personas: How to gain insight into your customer's expectations, align your marketing strategies, and win more business*, Wiley. ISBN-10: 1118961501.

Molina et al. (2021, February 8). *Enabling systems for intelligent manufacturing in industry 4.0: Sensing, smart and sustainable systems for the design of S3 products, processes, manufacturing systems, and enterprises*, Springer; Edición 1st ed. ISBN-13: 978–3030655464.

CHAPTER 6

Research, Technology, and Institutions: Fostering Role, Relationship, and Responsiveness

A New Model from Ideas to Business and Society Development

Traditionally, there are three missions of universities, namely education, research, and outreach for the benefit of society development in economic, social, and cultural aspects (Compagnucci & Spigarelli, 2020). A reference framework has been developed by the authors to carry out these three missions of a university in collaboration with Industry which is depicted in Fig. 6.1. The concepts included are investigation (research), innovation, technology transfer, business, and society development. In the next sections, this reference model is explained in detail including examples of how to undertake the third mission of a university.

Knowledge Creation

Research is carried out in a university for knowledge creation and is undertaken by professors, researchers, and students. In this process education and training of scientific talent is accomplished by building core knowledge and skills in the students (undergraduate, post-graduate) and post-doctoral researchers. Also core technologies can be taught and used during research to educate and train highly specialized talent. The

A. Molina and Rajagopal, *Challenge-Based Learning, Research, and Innovation*, Palgrave Studies of Entrepreneurship and Social Challenges in Developing Economies,
https://doi.org/10.1007/978-3-031-29156-2_6

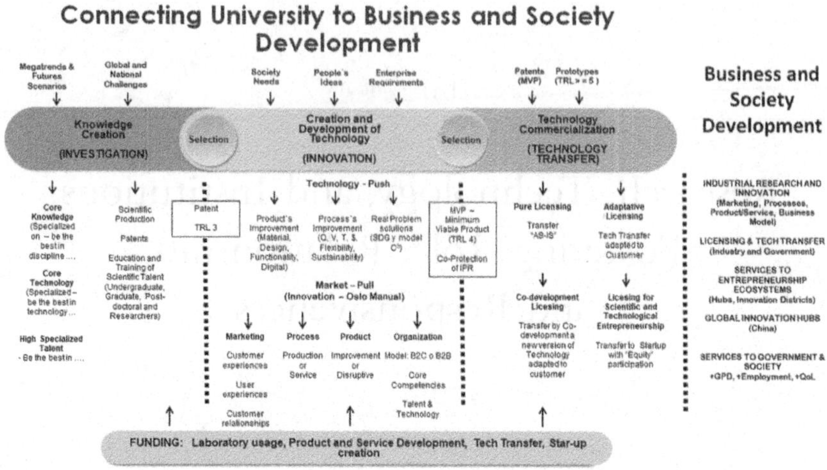

Fig. 6.1 Connecting universities to business development (*Source* Author [Arturo Molina])

outcomes of research are scientific publication, patents, and prototypes. The research topics can be defined using megatrends, state-of-the-art studies, and future scenarios of needs in society. On the other hand, it is becoming very common to take into consideration global and national challenges such as sustainable development goals. Research is driven by the creation of new knowledge and ground-breaking discoveries. From all these activities, usually patents and prototypes can achieve TRL.[1] These prototypes can be used for the pipeline for the creation and development of technologies that can deliver new innovations. These types of inventions are used by the companies to identify which one could be used to achieve a marketing, product, process, or organization innovations.

Innovation, Creation, and Development of Technology

The sources of innovation can be society needs, people´s ideas, and enterprise requirements. All these sources can lead to the creation of new

[1] According to NASA. For details see https://esto.nasa.gov/trl/.

products or services in companies. As we discussed in previous chapter, innovation can be undertaken using a technology-push or market-pull approach. Firms can use the technology-push approach in collaboration with universities to improve (Fig. 6.1).

- Product´s attributes and functions (material, design, functionality, digital),
- Process´s performances measures (quality, volume, time, costs, flexibility, productivity, sustainability), or
- Solve peoples' or communities' problems (sustainable development goals, Max-Neef's needs and satisfiers or citizen-communities-cities challenges).

On the other hand, companies can use the market-pull approach to innovate in:

- Marketing to be disruptive in customer experiences, user experiences, or customer relationships.
- Process either core process in the company or services, by having an impact on their key performance indicators.
- Product to improve or disrupt in product´s attributes and functions.
- Organization to make strategy on the business model (for example B2C or B2B), building, and delivering of core competencies (talent and technology).

Different alternatives to achieve the innovation process using both approaches are described in Fig. 6.2. The technology-push approach uses as a driver the existence of a technology or product, and the market-pull is based on the definition of the problem or segment to be solved. The alternatives can be described as (Cooper & Vlaskovits, 2013; Ponce et al., 2016):

1. Type 1—Technology: The research has already developed a technology that can be used to solve a problem. There is a need to identify a segment (citizens or communities) where this problem is important, and a product must be created and delivered.
2. Type 2—Technology for Product: The research has developed a technology that can improve a product to have a positive impact

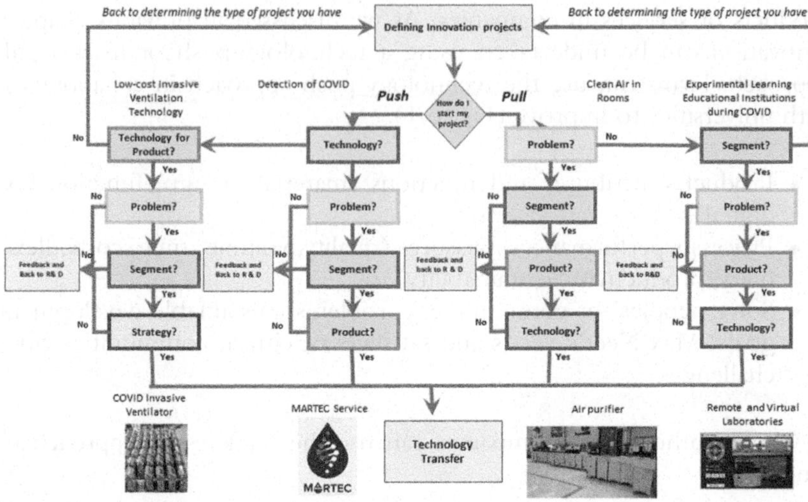

Fig. 6.2 Alternatives for innovation project in a collaboration model university-industry (*Source* Author [Arturo Molina])

on key attributes. The product is already solving a problem but with enabling technology a new satisfier is incorporated to the solution. The segment is already defined, but there is a need to define a strategy to communicate the benefits of the product enhanced by the technology.

3. Type 3—Problem centered: A problem has been identified within a specific segment of the population. There is a need to design and create a product that could satisfy such market using alternative technologies.
4. Type 4—Segment centered: A segment of the population wants to be addressed to improve their economic, social, or sustainable situation. A specific problem must be identified to be solved by a product and related technology.

As mentioned in Chapter 3, evidenced during the COVID-19, social (educational) institutions took the lead in creating awareness about the capacity to innovate offering solutions to multiple challenge faced by society. The cases to exemplify the alternative innovation projects are related to COVID-19:

1. Type 1—Technology
    a. What technology do you have that has proven to be functional? Extraction process of SARS-CoV-2 RNA in waste waters.
    b. To which existing problem do you want to apply your technology? COVID-19 detection at low cost and with certainty in waste waters.
    c. Who is the user of my technology? Who is my customer (who is willing to pay for my technology)? What characteristics do they have that can determine a market segment? Universities, companies, and government that require a fast-low-cost method to detect COVID-19 in facilities.
    d. What is the Product? Urban metabolism system for detection of SARS-CoV-2 in wastewater.
    e. Result: A system named MARTEC was implemented at Tecnologico de Monterrey to detect COVID-19 in waste waters allowing the risk managers of the institute to monitor buildings to detect focus of infection in the opening of university facilities. The system was also implemented in different factories allowing them to early detect risks of outbreaks (Sosa-Hernández et al., 2022) (Fig. 6.3).
2. Type 2—Technology for product
    a. What technology do you have that has proven to be functional? Alternative low-cost technology to be used in intrusive ventilators: ambush, piston, and micro-turbine.
    b. To which existing problem do you want to apply your technology? Lack of invasive ventilators to care for patients with COVID-19.
    c. Who is the user of my technology? Who is my customer (who is willing to pay for my technology)? What characteristics do they have that can determine a market segment? COVID-19 patients, Mexican Government, and public health institutions with limited access to invasive ventilators.
    d. What is the product? A low-cost piston-invasive ventilator.
    e. Result: A university-industry collaboration project for rapid development of an invasive ventilator was executed during 6 months to design, develop, and manufacture 202 ventilators that were

donated to public health institutions in Mexico, LATAM, and the Caribbean (Revista TecReview, 2020, August 7) (Fig. 6.4).

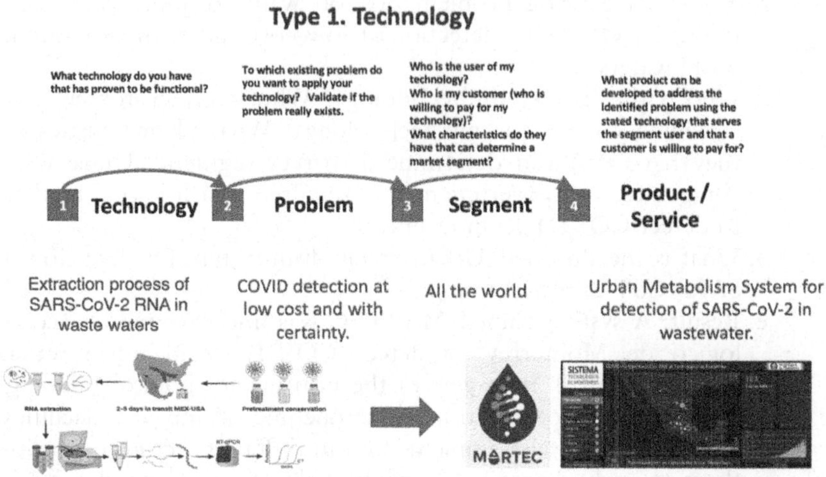

Fig. 6.3 Type 1—Technology: Urban metabolism for detection of SARS-CoV-2 in waste waters

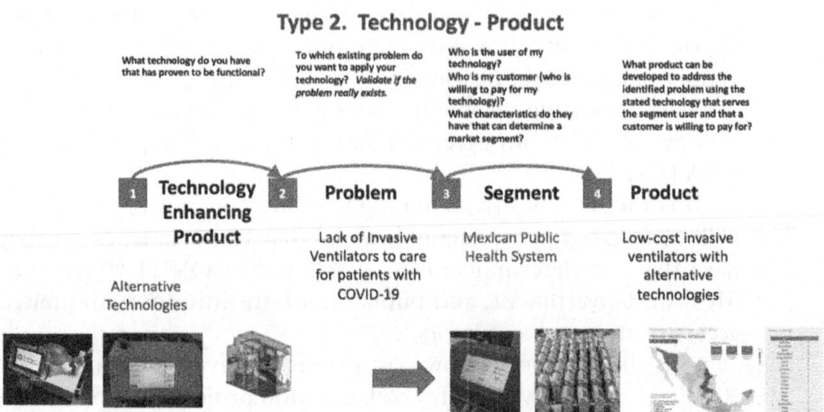

Fig. 6.4 Type 2—Technology enhancing product: invasive ventilator (*Source* Author [Arturo Molina])

3. Type 3—Problem centered

   a. What is the problem to be addressed according to the segment (user/customers) identified? Air purification in rooms to reduce risk of COVID-19.
   b. Who has this problem? How do I describe the profile of the person who has the problem? Can I group people who share similar problems? All persons in rooms during COVID-19 in reactivation of person-to-person activities.
   c. What solutions are currently available? Can I improve the current solutions? What features should my product have to solve the problem with more benefits? Filters for air conditioning and other air purifications devices. The solution was improved with a new device (low cost, low noise, easy to use, right size).
   d. What technology exists, and do I know that can be used to deliver the proposed solution? Nano-filters (patent) that could be used in new air filter device.
   e. Result: A university-industry collaboration project for rapid development of air purifier was executed during 8 months to design, develop, and manufacture. A new product was delivery to the market SAFE-AIR (Fig. 6.5).

4. Type 4—Segment centered

   a. Who is my user? What is their profile? What are their needs? People with hands-on training needs. University students that require learning by experimentation in the laboratories, and professors that require in their classes to teach using laboratories. The customers are Educational Institutions.
   b. What is the problem to be addressed according to the target population? No access to labs during COVID-19. Lack of hands-on training for university students during COVID-19 and high cost of remote laboratories.
   c. What products/services can be developed to address the identified problem? Remote laboratories and virtual laboratories.
   d. What technology can be used to develop the identified product/service? Internet of Things, tele-operation, augmented reality, and virtual reality.

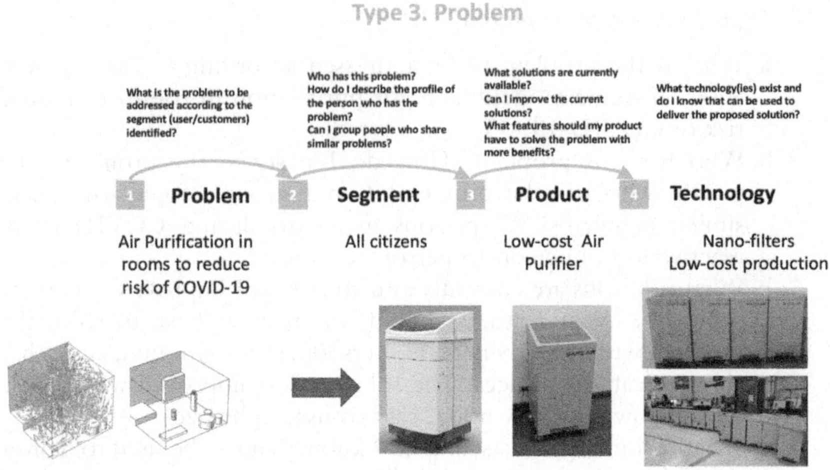

Fig. 6.5 Type 3—Problem centered: air purifier (*Source* Author [Arturo Molina])

e. Result: A pilot project of virtual and remote labs was scaled to give service to Tec de Monterrey students and other international universities. The labs offered hands-on experience to students remotely. A spin-out was created from this project namely LAIBOYAN[2] (Fig. 6.6).

All these cases required university-industry collaboration to deliver products to market, in systematic manner following the reference model.

Technology Transfer—Technology Commercialization

An excellent reference for Intellectual Property Rights (Patents) and technology transfer alternatives can be found in DeMatteis (2005) and Ponce et al. (2016). Using these books as references a definition of 4 types of licensing has been defined. The following section will describe each type of licensing with an example:

[2] For details see http://www.laiboyan.mx/.

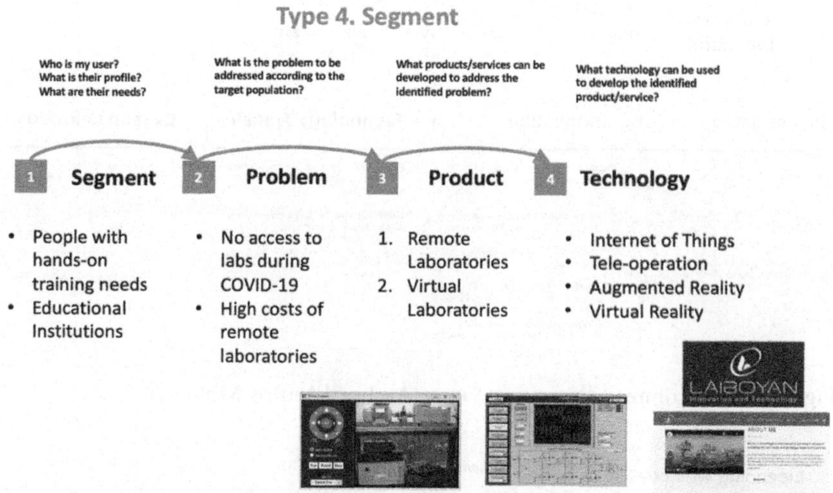

Fig. 6.6 Type 4—Segment centered: remote and virtual laboratories (*Source* Author [Arturo Molina])

1. **Pure Licensing:** Transfer "AS-IS". The patent is licensed to a partner as it is, without any further involvement from inventors. The license can be exclusive or non-inclusive. The licensee can be a manufacturing or marketing partner.
2. **Customized Licensing:** The license is offered to partner with the involvement of inventors to customize technology/product to fulfill requirements of the partner in their business model. The patent is organized in a technology transfer package. The example presented in Fig. 6.7 is of a manufacturing process to produce liquid fructose directly from sugar cane (Serna-Saldivar & Rito-Palomares, 2008).
3. **Licensing with Co-development:** A collaboration agreement is signed by university and industry partner to co-develop an improved version of the technology/product to satisfy market´s requirement and achieve faster commercialization of the product based on the marketing plan of the partner. The case described in Fig. 6.8 is a natural inhibitor extracted from the avocado seed for antimicrobial activity (Villarreal-Lara et al. 2019).
4. **Licensing for Scientific and Technological Entrepreneurship:** The license is giving to the inventors that want to pursue the

Fig. 6.7 Customized licensing (*Source* Author [Arturo Molina])

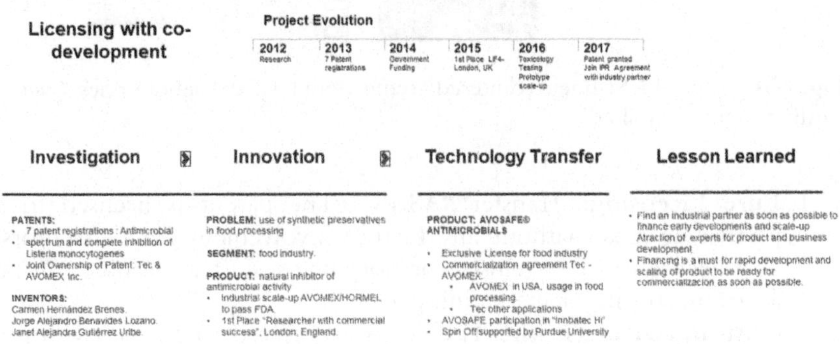

Fig. 6.8 Licensing with co-development (*Source* Author [Arturo Molina])

creation of a start-up. The most common commercial agreement is to ask for an up-front payment and equity from the spin-off to the university[3] (Fig. 6.9).

Business and Society Development

The third mission of the university is the active role of a university in supporting regional business and social development using its

[3] For details see https://patents.justia.com/assignee/onko-solutions-llc.

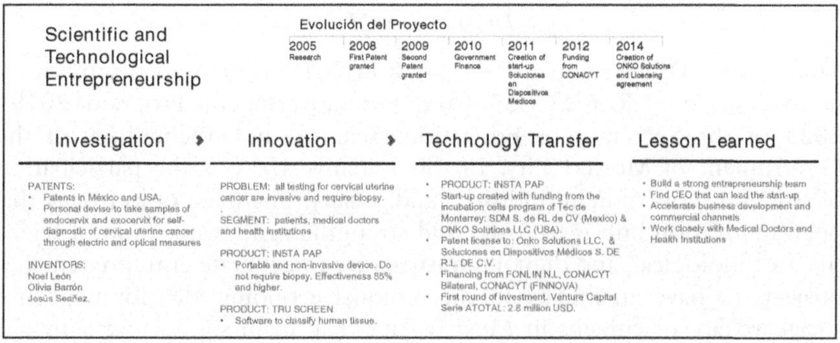

Fig. 6.9 Licensing for scientific and technological entrepreneurship (*Source* Author [Arturo Molina])

capacity for research, development, and innovation to have economic and social impact (Etzkowitz et al, 2000; Klofsten et al, 2019; Sánchez-Barrioluengo, 2014). The strategy defined by Tecnologico de Monterrey to accomplish the third mission of the university has been defined in the following strategic projects OECD/IDB (2022):

1. Creation of Interdisciplinary Institutes of Investigation to tackle global challenges such as education—innovative technologies, health—obesity, and sustainability—advanced materials for sustainable manufacturing.
2. Support industrial research and innovation using challenge-based innovation in industry projects to develop new products, services, and technologies.
3. Licensing technologies and undertaken technology transfer projects to industry and government partners.
4. Creation of entrepreneurship ecosystems at regional, national, and global level to promote challenge-based entrepreneurship by developing innovation hubs and innovation districts.

Examples of projects related to fostering entrepreneurship ecosystems are described to explain in more detail the impact on business and social developments.

Innovation Hub

This hub—CDIT Vallejo-i was created in 2019 as part open innovation network called "*Red ECOS*" from the Government Program 2019–2024 of the Secretary of Education, Science, and Technology of the Government of Mexico City. In this initiative there is the participation of academy, government, industry, and society. The main objective of this open innovation hub is to foster and strengthen the connection of scientific, technological, and digital infrastructure to generate entrepreneurship projects to have an impact in the regional economic development and social welfare of citizens in Mexico City. The main supporting activities of the HUB to the stakeholders are:

1. Access to economic and strategic information for research and business development (technological roadmaps, megatrends),
2. Identification of priorities/problems in Mexico City to be addressed,
3. Provide educational and training programs to guide entrepreneurship initiatives,
4. Support technological solutions by academic institutions and industry experts,
5. Service to define intellectual property (IP) strategies, IP registration, and management, and
6. Support for technology transfer activities and entrepreneurship endeavors which includes knowledge transfer, funding, licensing, project management, and incubation.

Tecnologico de Monterrey is participating in this innovation hub by coordinating and operating the activities related to Technology Transfer and Entrepreneurship using the reference framework described in Fig. 6.1. The name of the center is CAETS (Centro para el Aprendizaje en Emprendimiento Tecnologico y Social—Technological and Social Entrepreneurship Learning Center). The objective of the center is to educate and train researchers, entrepreneurs, and citizens in different model of entrepreneurship and guide them throw their start-up process. More details of this center can be found in Miranda et al. (2020a, 2020b).

The impact indicators defined for this Hub are: participants in different educational programs, number of scientific technology-based projects, number of start-ups, impact on companies indicators (employment, value added per employee), and economical grow in Vallejo and Mexico City.

Innovation District @Monterrey

The Innovation District is a strategy of Tec de Monterrey to create districts in different regions of Mexico, where campus of the university exists, to foster an innovation and entrepreneurship environment to attract high specialized human talent, researchers, entrepreneurs, investors, and high-tech companies to solve most challenging human problems and create economic and social development in these areas. The first districts are at Monterrey,[4] and Distrito Innovación Tlalpan at Mexico City. The impact indicators defined for this district are high-tech employment, number of start-ups, number of high-tech companies installed in the districts, and economic growth in districts.

Innovation Hub Tec-China

Located in the city of Hangzhou, in the province of Zhejiang, the Innovation HUB Tec-China is a global space promoted and supported by Tecnológico de Monterrey since 2018 to create opportunities of collaboration in research, innovation, and entrepreneurship between Mexico and China. Services provided by the Innovation Hub Tec-China are:

1. Identification of technological opportunities to be developed and transfer between the countries,
2. Talent development via formal education, technical boot camps, and research exchange programs,
3. Investor and funding attraction for technological developments and start-ups,
4. Fostering and supporting the creation of start-ups, joint venture, and landing in both countries, and
5. Identification of industry, government, and academia partners in China and Mexico.

The final goal is to develop innovations and accelerate scientific start-ups, detonating entrepreneurship, and talent attraction fundamental for the knowledge economy in both countries.[5] The impact indicators

[4] For details see https://distritotec.itesm.mx/.

[5] For details see https://www.facebook.com/InnovationHUBTecChina/.

defined for this global innovation hub are: talent development (participants in educational and training programs), collaboration projects, funding, number of start-ups, and joint industry agreements.

Key Performance Indicators

The different Key Performance Indicators (KPIs) are used in the reference model to evaluate the success of the process of investigation, innovation, technology transfer, and business and social development. Using this KPIs a better management process can be implemented to evaluate the impact of the funding or investment carried out in this reference model.

References

Compagnucci, L., & Spigarelli, F. (2020) The third mission of the university: A systematic literature review on potentials and constraints. *Technological Forecasting and Social Change, 161*, 120284. ISSN 0040-1625. https://doi.org/10.1016/j.techfore.2020.120284

Cooper, B., & Vlaskovits, P. (2013). *The lean entrepreneur*. Wiley. ISBN 978-1-118-29534-2.

DeMatteis, B. (2005). *From patent to profit*. Square One Publishers. ISBN 0-7570-0140-8.

Etzkowitz, H., Webster, A., Gebhardt, C., & Terra, B. R. C. (2000). The future of the university and the university of the future: Evolution of ivory tower to entrepreneurial paradigm. *Research Policy, 29*(2), 313–330. ISSN 0048-7333. https://doi.org/10.1016/S0048-7333(99)00069-4.

Klofsten, M., Fayolle, A., Guerrero, M., Mian, S., Urbano, D., & Wright, M. (2019). The entrepreneurial university as driver for economic growth and social change—Key strategic challenges. *Technological Forecasting and Social Change, 141*, 149–158. ISSN 0040-1625. https://doi.org/10.1016/j.techfore.2018.12.004.

Miranda, J., Rosas-Fernández, J. B., & Molina, A. (2020a). Collaborative networking to enable innovation and entrepreneurship through open innovation hubs: The entrepreneurship learning centre of Mexico City. In L. M. Camarinha-Matos, H. Afsarmanesh, & A. Ortiz (Eds.), *Boosting collaborative networks 4.0. PRO-VE 2020*. IFIP Advances in Information and Communication Technology (Vol. 598). Springer. https://doi.org/10.1007/978-3-030-62412-5_26

Miranda, J., Rosas-Fernández, J. B., & Molina, A. (2020b). *Achieving innovation and entrepreneurship by applying education 4.0 and open innovation*. 2020 IEEE International Conference on Engineering, Technology and Innovation

(ICE/ITMC), pp. 1–6. https://doi.org/10.1109/ICE/ITMC49519.2020.9198638.

OECD/IDB. (2022). *Innovative and entrepreneurial universities in Latin America*. (Chapter 4 Case studies in Mexico, OECD Skills Studies). OECD Publishing. https://doi.org/10.1787/ca45d22a-en.

Ponce, P., Polasko, K., Molina, A., Ramírez, M., & Mora P. (2016, December 7). *Intellectual property basic manual for researchers in universities*. Bentham Science Publishers. Technology & Engineering. eISBN: 978-1-68108-403-9, 2016, ISBN: 978-1-68108-404-6. https://doi.org/10.2174/97816810840391160101

Revista TecReview. (2020). https://tecreview.tec.mx/2020/08/07/tecnologia/ventilador-automatico-mexicano-vsz-20-2-contra-la-covid-19/

Sánchez-Barrioluengo, M. (2014). Articulating the 'three-missions' in Spanish universities. *Research Policy 43*(10), 1760–1773. ISSN 0048-7333. https://doi.org/10.1016/j.respol.2014.06.001.

Serna-Saldivar, S. R., & Rito-Palomares, M. A. (2008, October 14). *Production of invert syrup from sugarcane juice using immobilized invertase*. Publication of US7435564B2.

Sosa-Hernández, J. E., Oyervides-Muñoz, M. A., Melchor-Martínez, E. M., Driver, E. M., Bowes, D. A., Kraberger, S., Lucero-Saucedo, S. L., Fontenele, R. S., Parra-Arroyo, L., Holland, L. A., Peña-Benavides, S. A., Newell, M. E., Martínez-Ruiz, M., Adhikari, S., Rodas-Zuluaga, L. I., Kumar, R., López-Pacheco, I. Y., Castillo-Zacarias, C., Iqbal, H. M. N., ... Parra-Saldívar, R. (2022). Extensive wastewater-based epidemiology as a resourceful tool for SARS-CoV-2 surveillance in a low-to-middle-income country through a successful collaborative quest: WBE, mobility, and clinical tests. *Water, 14*(12), 1842. https://doi.org/10.3390/w14121842

Villarreal-Lara, R., Rodríguez-Sánchez, D. G., De La Garza, R. I. D., García-Cruz, M. I., Castillo, A., Pacheco, A., & Hernández-Brenes C. H. (2019). Purified avocado seed acetogenins: Antimicrobial spectrum and complete inhibition of Listeria monocytogenes in a refrigerated food matrix, CyTA. *Journal of Food, 17*(1), 228–239. https://doi.org/10.1080/19476337.2019.1575908

CHAPTER 7

Research-Based Innovation: Economics, Transferability, and Consumerism

The economics of innovation is founded on the end user preferences and propensity to support innovative products and services, which contributes to the returns on investment besides the cost, time, and risk (CTR) factors associated in the innovation process. The prolific investment in innovation among the micro, small, and medium firms is largely governed by the AATAR factors comprising awareness (customer centricity and collective intelligence), attributes (complementarity with existing innovative products), trial (effective demonstration of prototypes), availability (commercialization of innovations), and repeat buying (gaining customer confidence, perceived use value, and social consciousness). However, most firms operating in the niche and within a conventional business ecosystem have never known their customers holistically but continued with their innovation processes by investing increasing capital and human resources. Such firms face hit-or-miss actions in business with no guarantee on returns on investment and cost recovery in the failed innovations. To overcome such blind business drives, innovative entrepreneurs must focus on building customer profiles and look for convergent manufacturing and marketing models by analyzing correlations across the CTR and cost, benefit, and profit (CBP) factors. To develop innovative products that people want to buy, firms instead need to launch innovative products

A. Molina and Rajagopal, *Challenge-Based Learning, Research, and Innovation*, Palgrave Studies of Entrepreneurship and Social Challenges in Developing Economies,
https://doi.org/10.1007/978-3-031-29156-2_7

and services on pilot destinations, explore market opportunities within the niche, and develop alliances with large firms and collaborators to grow both vertically and horizontally. Consumers just do not buy products today, and they buy solutions and if a product lives to the expected perceived value of customers, it contributes in building both product and brand loyalty among consumers. However, driving innovative products to contribute consistent value for money is never a simple about function as they have powerful social and emotional dimensions. The crowd behavior in which customers try social and sustainable innovative products are more critical than common buying characteristics. As sales for such products are stimulated by social behavior and collective intelligence, such products have a weak start in the market and transform the consumption process over time. The key to successful innovation is exploring PNS factors that are congruent to the consumer preferences for innovative products, experiences, and processes within the market ecosystem.[1]

Technology, Entrepreneurship, and Economics

Technology-led innovations and business models can be successful provided it is user oriented. The agile use of technology, however, can erode customer care. Firms must listen empathetically to the requirements of consumers to cater technology to them, managers, and frontline employees. However, impulsive innovations targeted primarily at lowering the costs and increasing use values have made many companies impervious to their customers. Such a situation drives estrangement of employees from customers and firms face difficulty in diffusing, launching, and serving the technology to the consumer segments. Several innovation-driven firms have shown intricate relations between businesses and consumers they serve. These firms enrich consumers by upholding their commitment, involvement with consumers empathetically, understanding the ways in which current technology is valued by consumers, and co-promoting the technology-led products through social networks and informal ways to help consumers in developing sustainable storyboards and inculcate trust on the firm and technology service providers.[2]

[1] Christensen, C. M., Hall, T., Dillon, K., & Duncan, D. (2016). Know your customers' "jobs to be done". *Harvard Business Review*, *94*(9), 54–62.

[2] Gorry, G. A., & Westbrook, R. A. (2011), Once more, with feeling: Empathy and technology in customer care, *Business Horizons*, *54*(2), 125–134.

A young women entrepreneur[3] of India has developed the low-cost housing prototype using O-pod type sewage pipes and commercialized this entrepreneurial venture through the social institutions in the Telangana State of India. This low-cost housing option was improved through challenge-based research conducted with the social institutions to build pod-style homes from sewage pipes. Such low-cost social innovation to provide housing to the people lying below the poverty line in India comes with a bedroom, kitchen, hall, washroom, and shelves. The pod house is equipped with electricity, water, and drainage. This social innovation has significantly contributed to solving housing problems among the poor. One of the appropriate ways to examine the effect of technology in society is to draw up a demographic profile of the industry. Markets dominated by small, single-industry businesses or small regional competitors differ significantly from those dominated by national or multi-industry companies.

Public policies and social institutions have encouraged partnership of micro, small, and medium firms with large firms to work on local development projects exploring the PNS factors jointly. Such synergy across the firms has been the driving force behind challenge-based research to promote innovation and attract markets in the developing economies. The transformational entrepreneurship theories suggest frugal and reverse innovations are consistent with the existing demand and contribute to social and economic growth. Unlike classical theories that emphasize markets attract innovation, the transformational entrepreneurship concept advocate customer-centric innovation congruent with the PNS factors. Challenge-based research motivates social applied innovations to support holistic development and growth in the economy, social values, and lifestyle in the developing countries. However, the global competition and changing consumer behavior on experimenting frugal, reverse, and disruptive innovations have raised new theoretical concepts on the relationship of launching new products with the market demand based on the PNS factors. The partnership among the local and global firms encouraged by the government and market forces helps in converging the local innovations with changing international market dynamics and customer

[3] Perala Manasa Reddy, a civil engineer graduate from Telangana State of India has launched the firm Samnavi Constructions and innovated the OPods— a low-cost housing solution, which is built using large sewage pipes. For details see https://www.youtube.com/watch?v=0LJh-FbsVEs.

values. Such collaborative challenge-based innovations continuously drive both social and commercial products to render desired benefit to small firms, from economies of scale and scope. Many economists believed that more large firms would lead to more economic growth and that the share of small firms eventually would disappear or reduce to only a small fraction. Globalization has induced extensive cross-culture working ambience and driven most firms to multi-dimensional manufacturing and marketing operations to sustain in the competitive marketplace. Hence, most firms have become increasingly complex and ungovernable causing decline in performance, unclear accountability, and opaque decision process that raise questions on the sustainability of the firm. To avoid frustration and inefficiency, executives need to systematically address the causes of complexity using a simplicity-minded strategy in their companies by streamlining the structure, pruning non-responding products before introducing new products to create space, build disciplined processes, and improving managerial behavior.[4]

Innovation and its commercialization are the top priorities for every emerging enterprise and to achieve success through frugal and radical innovations, firms must put as high energy and investment into marketing new offerings as they do in generating them. Commercializing innovation and marketing innovative products and services are central to strategic decisions and sustainable approaches rather than merely tactical functions of acquiring and retaining customers, as many firms tend to practice today. The full, business-growing power of the marketing strategies for both frugal and radical (disruptive) innovations are penetrated ambidextrously in the upstream and downstream markets through social media and collective intelligence. Nonetheless, the major focus in commercializing innovation is to co-create and coevolve markets by engaging customers and stakeholders. Such a marketing strategy would help firms in developing value-based stakeholder-led decisions to gain benefits over the competitors. Understanding the PNS factors and consumption drivers, identifying customers, and working with the go-to-market approach offer several competitive benefits to the firms to market innovative products irrespective of their scale of business. It is also important to explore and analyze the consumption ecosystem congruent to the innovations, especially those that support the breakthroughs. Marketers, therefore, need to

[4] Ashkenas, R. (2007). Simplicity minded management. *Harvard Business Review*, *85*(12), 101–109.

be included in development discussions earlier in the innovation process and must be engaged in implementing the tasks of project charter.[5]

The technology-marketing grid has several factors that pose conflicts and challenges to the innovation and technology development firms during different levels of process. The complexity grid comprises twelve commonly observed points of conflicts, which has independent effects of each point as well as in a matrix form. The conflict points in the grid include ideation, resources management, process management, capabilities and competencies, technology marketing, growth and next-generation innovation and technology issues, involvement, organizational policies, operational efficiency, competitive decision, business environment, and organizational culture, all of which nurture the innovation and technology development projects in the firm. In the complexity grid ideation process and the extent of involvement of employees, consumers and market players stage cognitive and organizational conflicts and challenges while management of resources and organizational policies raise various challenging issues during different phases of innovation and technology development. Similarly, the process and operational efficiency commonly drive various issues of concern in reference to capabilities and competencies and work culture of the organization. Firms face many conflicts during the innovation process on marketing of the technology-led products and the existing business environment. Moving innovation and technology to next generation is also not an easy step-up as firms often get snared in the unwise competitive decisions to push the innovation and technology-led products in the marketplace.

The frugal innovation with focus on PNS factors and achieving economies of scale has significantly contributed to the social and economic development within the niche. Consequently, disruptive innovation has increasingly become a core attraction to the large firms to collaborate, converge, and commercialize (3Cs) not only to motivate business alliances but also to build the business strategy cube. The business strategy cube has triadic business strategies comprising design-to-market, design-to-society, and design-to-value perspectives. Such micro–macro business alliances within various social development sectors including health, housing, energy, transportation, and machinery and robotics across sectors have bridged economics to engineering

[5] Yohn, D. L. (2019). *Why great innovations need great marketing*. Harvard Business Review Digital Article, Cambridge: Harvard Business School Press.

and technology. This change is occurring as most firms in the world are facing contemporary challenges such as intense global competition, rising market volatility, constantly changing consumer demand, and shortened product life cycles. Such socioeconomic and business conditions have driven disruptive innovation and disruptive innovation-based entrepreneurship to resolve social challenges, which are increasingly becoming a strategic means for achieving sustainable company growth and competitiveness.[6] The concept of disruptive technology can be either necessarily radical, frugal, or superior to the existing technology. A challenge-based research design is generated through a process of social, economic, and political negotiation and value-based stakeholder focus. Accordingly, low-cost technologies with high perceived use value and ease-of-use perception become to serve the social and economic needs, survive, and prosper. However, penetration of social innovation and technology is slow, which causes delay in adoption and jeopardizes their success.[7]

Frugal innovation is the process of reducing the complexity and cost of products by taking cost-effective measures in manufacturing and following economies of scale. Usually this refers to removing conspicuous features from products, such as an automobile, to market it in bottom-of-the-pyramid markets and emerging markets. Designing products for such markets may also call for an increase in sustainability of innovative products and selling through modern routes to market. However, profits earned on frugal innovations are much lower than high-value, high-technology innovative products targeted to the up-front or premier markets. The user-driven innovation conforms to the consumers' needs

[6] Si, S., Zahra, S. A., Wu, X., Jeng, D. J. F. (2020). Disruptive innovation and entrepreneurship in emerging economics,
Journal of Engineering and Technology Management. 58 (in Press). https://doi.org/10.1016/j.jengtecman.2020.101601.

[7] Si, S., & Chen, H. (2020). A literature review of disruptive innovation: what it is, how it works and where it goes.
Journal of Engineering and Technology Management, 56 (In Press) https://doi.org/10.1016/j.jengtecman.2020.101568.

and would help them realize its value at relatively lower costs. Accordingly, firms can "refresh" innovation policy to embrace user-driven innovation and encourage user-driven innovation against high cost-complex market innovations.[8]

Collaborative Designing of New Products

Designing and developing new products is commonly based on the PNS factors and market trend. However, foresights on competition and consumption also have significant influence on architecting new products. Innovation foresight has become a relevant stimulus in strategy in the design thinking process, which synchronizes the discover, define, develop, and deliver stages. Most firms are engaged in commercialization of generic innovations by developing new products to meet the changes and uncertainty in the business environment. Foresight encompasses a wide range of practices and the activities that enhance the abilities of managers to explore new events and trends in the market to creative value among stakeholders and customers.[9] The globalization effect on the firms in the recent past has driven the product development process with focus on the scope of innovation contextual to future business. The innovation in new products is subjected to continuous monitoring of potential needs of consumers and changes in the market trends. The increase in the switch from a shared house phone to a personal phone has had a significant impact on product appearance as well as product use. People do not use their personal phone only for calling, but also for taking pictures, making movies, playing games, and listening to music as an agenda. This has changed consumer attitudes towards the phone. What once was a rather functional product has become a product that expresses one's personality. Therefore, consumers require their phone to be modern, easy to use, and of good quality. In the meantime, they do not want the phone to be expensive, as they would like to frequently change their handsets. Such consumer needs drive recurring shifts in demand and increase product complexity.

[8] Martin, R., & Milway, J. (2012). *User-driven innovation: Putting an end to inventing in the dark*, Working paper, Rotman School of Management, September.

[9] Fergnani, A. (2022). Corporate foresight: Real or ideal? *Academy of Management Perspectives*, *36*(2), 851–856.

Firms require developing integration of the knowledge domains from different disciplines to develop new products to meet the changing consumers demand and drive collaborative new product development (Co-NPD) process[10]. During the process of Co-NPD, knowledge management should focus on knowledge integration instead of focusing on knowledge transfer. They also stated that the effectiveness of knowledge integration required a mutual understanding of the actor's contributions. This is in line with the research on design communication, which finds that the quality of the Co-NPD project is dependent on the process of creating a shared understanding.[11] In developing collaborative product designs, managers should involve stakeholders and stakeholders in the design process by transferring knowledge, skills, and technology. During the process of co-creation of products, firms need to document experiences of customers and stakeholders and analyze the collective intelligence influencing the ideation and design process. To understand the PNS factors and social implications of innovative products, firms can obtain vital information on consumer preferences during the co-creation process through critical observations and ethnographic studies. Firms supporting co-creation need to invest resources in developing relationship marketing, customer engagement, and precision in decision-making. To critically examine and validate the PNS factors, firms should observe in proximity the consumer behavior through ethnographic approaches. The PNS factors associated with stakeholders should be analyzed through both the longitudinal and latitudinal approach. The PNS factors can be well explored by liberally talking to the stakeholders to acquire comprehensive information. The structured, in-depth, one-on-one, and situational interviews help in engineering the desired solutions for the stakeholders.

Co-NPD process was considered as a socio-organizational process. In developing collaborative new product development, there are many actors who are involved in the process. A collaborative player in the new product development executes three main activities within social process:

[10] Garcia, R., & Calantone. R. (2002). A critical look at technological innovation typology and innovativeness terminology: A literature review. *Journal of Product Innovation Management*, *19*(2), 110–132.

[11] Dong, A. (2005). The latent semantic approach to studying development team communication. *Design Studies, 26*(5), 445–461.

- Construction of the task to perform.
- Understand that the task is a part of the production system, and
- Attend complementary tasks within the system.

Thus, co-creation of new products may work on interrelated actions. This shows that the relations among the players are not predefined but constructed during the process. A result derived by an actor performing a development task may result in the necessity that another actor needs to make an interactive loop.[12] A product development manager should actively observe the activities of various teams during their regular meetings by taking notes about the most important issues concerning communication about the design content. During the regular face-to-face meeting with the separate actors, which are now mostly about planning and monitoring issues and design problems or changes, the project leader could use the notes as input for discussing the collaborative aspects with the actors. This form of storytelling will provide the project leader with knowledge about the collaborative aspects of the design process. A project leader should also learn to distill the barriers and enablers from these conversations.[13]

Analytical Attributes Technique

Review of research on product development indicates that analytical attributes technique plays vital role in product designing for both the business to stakeholders and business to business companies. The analytical attributes approach is defined as the transformation of a market opportunity into a product available for sale. This technique of new product designing also encompasses the functional fields of marketing, operations management, and engineering design. The value of this breadth is in conveying the shape of the entire research landscape. The analytical attributes techniques look inside the "black box" of product development at the fundamental decisions that are made by intention

[12] Weick, K.E., & Roberts, K.H. (1993). Collective mind in organizations: heedful interrelating on flight decks. *Administrative Science Quarterly*, *38*(4), 357–381.

[13] Maaike, K., Buijs, J., & Valkenburg, R. (2010). Understanding the complexity of knowledge integration in collaborative new product development teams: A case study. *Journal of Engineering and Technology Management*, *27* (1–2), 20–32.

Table 7.1 Attributes of Product Design

Attributes	*Functions*	*Benefits*
Dimensions	Applications	Performance
Constituents	Sensory appeal	Referrals
Services	Economics gains	Self-esteem
Process	Delighted feeling	
Trademarks	Direct benefits	
Price		

or default. In doing so, managers can adopt the perspective of product development as a deliberate business process involving hundreds of decisions, many of which can be usefully supported by knowledge and tools.[14] Analytical Attributes Approach capitalizes on the concept that any feature change in a product must involve one or more current attributes. The attributes of products that need to be considered during the process of developing new products are exhibited in Table 7.1.

Although the role of attributes in new products development is not well understood, research suggests that personality plays a critical role in the effective performance of attributes. Product attributes should be especially important for new product development which typically includes highly coordinated activities among multidisciplinary members. There are two specific types of new product development processes - incremental innovation and radical innovation (Reilly et al., 2002). Analytical Attributes Approach can be used in designing new products in the following ways:

- o Dimensional analysis uses features,
- o Checklists use all attributes, and
- o Trade-off analysis also uses determinant attributes.

Materials selection has emerged as a major issue for product design engineers. The available set of materials, rapidly growing both in type and number, has vastly expanded the number of possibilities meriting serious consideration for many engineering applications. Today, engineers are forced to look for systematic techniques for managing and analyzing

[14] Kishnan, V., & Ulrich, K.T. (2001). Product development decisions: A review of literature. *Management Science*, *47*(1), 1–21.

engineering data on the growing array of materials. While advances in materials science continue to expand the horizons of material performance, the material developer finds it increasingly difficult to establish what constitutes a desirable material. By its nature, the designer's process of material selection happens outside the ken of the suppliers of the material alternatives. Because the suppliers are frequently isolated from this process, they receive little insight into the rationale for the success or failure of their offerings. The lack of this information not only limits their ability to identify and rectify the limitations of their current offerings, but it also makes it very difficult to ascertain what success new offerings will have. Product design engineers should make the following analysis attributes in designing new products:

- Benefit analysis
- Unique sales proposition (USP)
- Use analysis
- Hierarchical design
- Functions analysis
- Weaknesses
- Attribute extension
- Relative brand profile
- Systems analysis

Inventory constraints, costs of lost production, safety and environmental objectives, strategies of maintenance adopted, and logistics aspects of spare parts are some of the criteria considered, and spare parts classification is thus defined with respect to multiple attributes. In virtue of the large number of the potential operational characteristics to be considered, the decision diagram is integrated with a set of analytic hierarchy process models used to solve the various multi-attribute decision sub-problems at the different levels or nodes of the decision tree. An inventory policy matrix can be defined to link the different classes of spare parts with the possible inventory management policies to identify the "best" control strategy for the spare stocks[15]. Most firms build their marketing strategies around the concept of the product life cycle. However, by positioning

[15] Braglia M., Grassi, A., & Montanari, R. (2004). Multi-attribute classification method for spare parts inventory management. *Journal of Quality in Maintenance Engineering*, *10*(1), 55–65.

their products in non-conventional ways, companies can extend the span of product life cycle in reference to how customers perceive them. In doing so, managers can shift products lodged in the maturity phase back and propel new products forward into the growth phase. Some non-conventional positioning strategies firms can use to shift stakeholders' thinking include reverse positioning, breakaway position, and furtive position. The reverse positioning strategy holds products in a particular stage of life cycle for a longer period while adding new ones. Breakaway positioning associates the product with a radically different category, like trendy, a brand of Swatch Company associated its watches in the category of fashion accessory. The furtive positioning strategy offers stakeholders, who are not confident on the products of the company, a new offering by concealing the product's true nature. A company can use these techniques to go on the offensive and transform a category by demolishing its traditional boundaries.[16] Detailed knowledge on how innovation, market performance, and competition serve as a basis for making decisions of firms is important for the firms to gain and determine the life cycle of a product. Managers should consider consumer preferences and product knowledge as significant drivers while changing market conditions.[17]

It has been observed that increasing global competition and heterogeneous markets segments together with shorter product life cycles are forcing many companies to simultaneously compete in the three marketing domains comprising products, processes, and value chains. Uncertainty in decision-making across these domains make competitive strategies of companies very complex in the marketplace. Managers should be consistent in the product attributes comprising commonality, product service platforms, product designs and values, and product modularity. This framework can be used to focus product design and product architecture dimensions that are critical for a given operational strategy. To assess advantages and limitations of operational strategies in conjunction with given product architectures, firms need to develop dynamic capabilities such as planning effective product and operation strategy combinations. Firms should understand that the process life cycle is distinct from the product life cycle that facilitates

[16] Moon, Y. (2005). Break free from the product life cycle, *Harvard Business Review*, *83*(5), 86–94.

[17] Werker, C. (2003). Innovation, market performance, and competition: lessons from a product life cycle model. *Technovation*, *23*(4) 281–290.

the strategic decisions of a firm in positioning new products with innovation and technology in the competitive marketplace. A company may seek competitive advantage in the market but should understand the implications of each move.[18]

Success of new products is a major concern of companies as it determines their standing in the marketplace. Strategies that can provide innovative combinations of products and services as "high-value integrated solutions" tailored to each consumer's needs instead of simply "moving downstream" into services are being developed by large and reputable firms in order to sustain in increasingly competitive markets. Innovative combinations of service capabilities such as operations, business consultancy, and finance are required to provide complete solutions to every consumer's needs to augment the consumer value perceived in innovative or new products. The time gap between changes in customer preferences and product mix affects the introduction of a new product and its life cycle in each market environment. The consumer product manufacturing and marketing firms observe seasonality within markets and are exposed to demand volatility for certain elements of the complex product mix. Market responsive manufacturing strategy entails adaptive and flexible production and supply capability in conjunction with real-time market interaction through profit optimization.

Challenge-Based Innovation

Successful innovation leads to customer involvement and profits, which can be achieved through co-creation by aligning consumers and market players in the innovation process. Some multinational companies have invested resources taking advantage of social media to diffuse new ideas and stimulating co-creation of innovative products and services. For many companies, developing new products does not occur as a chance or coincidence but innovative products emerge through careful attention to many important criteria. Firms should analyze their innovation practices and capabilities to become more effective in driving innovation as breakthrough and gain the competitive advantage. The contribution of employees towards innovation in products, services, or strategy signifies the value and quality of innovation portfolio of an organization

[18] Rajagopal (2014), Architecting Enterprise: Managing Innovation, Technology, and Global Competitiveness, Basingstoke, UK: Palgrave Macmillan.

and projects the innovation effectiveness curve of the company.[19] Firms may be involved in innovation process routinely understanding various perspectives in generating and managing innovative ideas.

Breakthrough innovations in markets are a continuous process, which is backed by the distribution, retailing, and services industry. Innovations leading to commercial breakthroughs demonstrate a highly skewed distribution of use value of inventions explaining that some are useless, a few are of moderate value, and there is rarely one that qualifies as a breakthrough. Those breakthroughs embed the long tail of innovation, and distribution plays a key role in the breakthrough process. It is necessary for the firms to account for the total number of inventions a company generates, the average score of the inventions, and track the number of successful breakthrough inventions. Such corporate awareness may help in developing strategic balance between individual innovation workers and teams. Greater team diversity stimulates in building higher involvement in working with breakthrough innovations. Thus, it is first and foremost requirement for the companies to introspect within the organization and identify how they want to improve their innovation process, take appropriate measures to drive the innovative products and services as breakthrough, and contrary to that address any deficiencies in the process. Such dynamism in innovation process would allow the companies to improve their competencies and capabilities to innovate in ways that make the best sense for the organization and market.[20] Innovation and enterprise integration are two compelling sources of growth in a dynamic competitive marketplace. The ability to coordinate across organizational boundaries largely appears as a critical factor in determining the speed and life cycle of a market driven innovation. Innovations need to be integrated into the larger operations of the corporation at sufficient level of scale to show a prolific impact on business and sustainability in the marketplace. Many large businesses spend resources on innovations but fail to capitalize on them. There are a variety of innovations driven by firms in global marketplace. Innovations are not limited to consumer-centric or market-oriented products and services. Categorically, most of

[19] Kandybin, A. (2009). Which innovation efforts will pay? *MIT Sloan Management Review*, *51*(1), 53–60.

[20] Farzaneh, M., Wilden, R., Afshari, L., & Mehralian, G. (2022). Dynamic capabilities and innovation ambidexterity: The roles of intellectual capital and innovation orientation. *Journal of Business Research*, *148*, 47–59.

the large firms possess trajectories of innovation and technological change in reference to the consumer requirements. While the market today is very unpredictable, small firms are thrusting more resources to increase innovation to compete with the large industries and commercial brands.[21]

Firms in many industries have immense pressure to improve their ability to innovate consumer centric products and services. However, managers know that the best ideas don't always come out of their own research and development laboratory. Hence, a growing number of companies are exploring the idea of open-market innovation, an approach that uses tools such as licensing, joint ventures, and strategic alliances to bring the benefits of free trade to the flow of new ideas.[22] Disruptive innovation is linked to reverse innovation that drives the firms back to the consumers' buying behavior in reference to 4As paradigm comprising awareness, acceptability, adaptability, and affordability. Reverse innovation refers to developing ideas in an emerging market and persuading them in the existing markets, which drives tough challenges. Such innovation requires a company to overcome the institutionalized thinking that guides its actions and acquire ideas through social media. Firms following reverse innovation develop a radically simpler and cheaper way of creating products in emerging markets and then position them in the desired consumer segments.[23,24]

The reverse innovation is driven by the cost and factors. Large companies thus roll over to the local markets to identify the customer-centric innovations developed by the local enterprises and tend to evaluate the economics of their business projects. When a company with the capability of sponsoring the reverse innovation investigates a new product opportunity, it not only defines the problem to which an innovation serves as

[21] Rajagopal (2014). *Architecting enterprise: Managing innovation, technology, and global competitiveness*, Basingstoke, UK: Palgrave Macmillan.

[22] Rigby, D. K., & Zook, C. (2001). Open-market innovation, *Harvard Business Review*, *80*(10), 80–89.

[23] Nooyi, I. K. & Govindarajan, V. (2020). *Becoming a better corporate citizen*, HBR Web Article, Harvard Business School Press, March–April Issue. https://hbr.org/2020/03/becoming-a-better-corporate-citizen.

[24] Rajagopal (2016). *Innovative business projects: Breaking complexities, building performance (Vol.2)-Financials, new insights, and project sustainability*. New York: Business Expert Press.

a solution but also lists the requirements that are needed for commercializing the innovation. The sponsor companies will then develop ways to dictate a viable solution for wider markets independently from the company's existing lines of similar products to target the adopted reverse innovation in a mass market. The reverse innovation helps companies penetrate in the entering emerging markets or aim to realize opportunities to create high-performance, high-value products and service at low cost and affordable prices that appeal to consumers with low per capita income. The primary challenge to developing innovations for emerging markets and catering to the customers therein is delivering solutions of adequate quality at a competitive price for the masses.[25]

The international innovation companies need to segment their markets—upstream and mass that fit into the innovation attributes exhibiting the price, value, for money, perceived value, performance, and product life cycle. Companies may have to deliver high performance of their products in western markets equivalents with high price, while the reverse innovation offers the opportunity for the companies to enter in the emerging markets with the same corporate and extended brand strength. Determining the performance required by a technology as in the case of generic two-wheeler motorbikes' engines in reference to emissions' reduction and longevity of engine life at the price at which it will be adopted is the critical first step in creating products for emerging markets. The commercialization of reverse innovation often gives a radical push to the product, company, and industry as well. Commercializing reverse innovation is a disruptive leap to hit a product in the target market, and it demands to develop organizational insight into how a new product could drive an impact in emerging markets. A product that delivers significantly more performance at a lower price may become the basis for a new product platform, which can have features added or removed to adjust its price and performance to the specific needs of wealthy or poor markets, which makes the reverse innovation management a success. GE Healthcare has demonstrated this idea with the customization of its low-cost ultrasound and electrocardiogram machines, which started as emerging market products and then evolved into valuable devices for North America and Europe. Companies can envision the

[25] Rajagopal (2016). *Innovative business projects: Breaking complexities, building performance (Vol. 1)-fundamentals and project environment*. New York: Business Expert Press.

process of engineering reverse innovations before any metal is cut, plastic is molded, or prototypes made. The reverse innovation products move slow in the adaptation process in the non-familiar consumer segments and face price constraints in the market. However, based on the solutions that existing technologies provide, companies can envision the reverse innovation to derive the global product line around a new technology platform by using benchmarks of other products in the marketplace to analyze the possibilities of outwitting, outperforming, and outmaneuvering competitors, while delivering the low cost and better performing solutions to consumers. By scoping onto the worldwide market opportunities and understanding the probable constraints in marketing the products across market segments and destinations, companies can engineer reverse innovations to mark impact on markets and consumers in the global marketplace.[26]

Reverse innovation offers scope to experience the innovation concept, process, and deliverables in the niche markets and scale them up for a wider market beyond the emerging markets. The start-up enterprises managing innovation need for the relatively smaller geo-demographic segments and at bottom of the pyramid may throw up immense challenges for commercializing the innovations in the international markets. However, it requires a company to follow the institutionalized thinking that guides its actions in the global marketplace. The reverse innovations that are adopted by the sponsor companies need to make design adjustments and fabricate for the mass consumers in the global markets in a radically simpler and cheaper way to serve the customer with high perceived value. Companies can develop new products in emerging markets by using a radical change from below (generic innovation design) combined with smart leadership from top (up-market strategy). The small start-up enterprises may set audacious goals to match with the new organizational structure of sponsors and adopt new design and commercialization methods. However, the start-up enterprises may also nurture the reverse innovation provided they could arrange adequate resources to upscale the innovation by shifting the gravity of business beyond emerging markets.[27]

[26] Winter, A., & Govindarajan, V. (2015). Engineering reverse innovation. *Harvard Business Review. 93*, (7–8), 81–89.

[27] Govindarajan, V. (2012). A reverse-innovation play book, *Harvard Business Review, 90*(4), 120–124.

Most international companies are getting engaged in managing the reverse innovation for global markets, in which products are designed first for consumers in low-income countries and then adapted into disruptive offerings for developed economies. But only a handful of companies have managed to do it successfully until now. International companies usually create products by following time-tested methods, struggle to overcome the constraints, and leverage the benefits of emerging markets. They tend to develop reverse innovations by matching market segments to existing products, lowering price by removing features, redesigning technical specification of generic products and upholding stakeholders value, and creating scope for penetrating into the low-income markets that could have global appeal. For example, a low-cost wheelchair initially designed in India for navigating through rugged terrain in places with poor infrastructure has been developed by a company for upstream markets upon modifying the design for Western markets, which could serve in the storm and snowfall.[28] Reengineering reverse innovation process is discussed in the phases as stated below:

Phase 1—Analyzing Local Innovation—In this phase, the local innovation is identified, and its potential is analyzed from the perspectives of process improvement, deliverables, and potential for commercialization. In the initial look-up of the reverse innovation process, sponsor companies are focusing on developing products for the in-country market with mass production possibilities. The sponsors of reverse innovations also consider the "market-back" with a zero-based assessment of customer's needs, rather than considering the demand benchmark of the generic product in the given market. Accordingly, the sponsor company adopting the reverse innovation would suggest necessary alterations to the products for upscaling its production for the redefined market. As teams develop products for the local market, the company enables them to remain connected to, and to benefit from, the global resource base.

Phase 2—Adopting Reverse Innovation—Once the generic innovation growing in the local market qualifies for upscaling model of the sponsor company, the adoption of reverse innovation qualifies from "in country–for country", to "cross-country–cross-region" base. The sponsor

[28] Winter, A., & Govindarajan, V. (2015). Engineering reverse innovations, *Harvard Business Review*, *93*(7), 80–89.

companies complete the reverse innovation process by taking the innovations originally chartered for poor countries, adapting them, and scaling them up for global markets.

Phase 3—Design to Market—In this phase, reverse innovation sponsor companies modify the product design, improve its functionality to create higher customer value, and make efforts to lower the costs of production. This strategy would drive the product to be competitive in the regional or global marketplace. Accordingly, the companies focus on winning market share by adapting global offerings and meeting local needs to stay in the home market. Innovation remains originally with home-country needs, but products and services are later modified to win in each market. However, to meet the budgets of customers at the bottom of the pyramid, they sometimes de-feature existing products.

Phase 4—Upscaling Innovation to Market—As the reverse innovations succeed in the test markets and are improved to gain higher customer values, the sponsor companies run the economies of scale on the reverse innovation projects and develop market for products and services around the world. Innovation that has been commissioned at home is driven to the new offerings and distributed everywhere.

The fundamental driver of reverse innovation is the disposable income of consumers, consumer culture, cost of innovation, and the price of delivery to the end users. As the gap in the innovation process widens across the elements of innovations, the innovative products tend to fall off the market soon that shortens the product life cycle. There is no way to design a product for the American mass market and then simply adapt it for the Chinese or Indian mass market due the elements discussed above. Buyers in emerging markets, who are price sensitive, demand solutions on an entirely different price-performance curve and turn loyal to the brand if the innovative products satisfy the consumers, uphold the value for money, and offer competitive advantage. Consumers would demand new, high-tech solutions that deliver at low costs and match their personal standards of "good enough" quality. In fact, reverse innovation is not always a prolific solution for the large companies to boost their revenue and business growth. However, the reverse innovation is bottom-up outcome of what consumers look for and hence embeds enormous potential for mass marketing. As the Darwinian effect in market evolution is seen in the global marketplace, the multinational companies are trying to uncover the remote niches of the mass market and bottom-of-the-pyramid market segments, while on the contrary local companies are seeking expansion. The reverse innovations will power the future of large companies (international) to reach consumers in the lesser-known markets. Hence, to stay noticed and sustain the market competition, multinational companies must be just as adopt reverse innovation beyond their home. Successful and long-established multinational corporations, who are seeking explosive growth in emerging economies, must now learn new tricks to succeed. Reverse innovation directs them how to make innovation in emerging markets happen and how such innovations can unlock opportunities throughout the world.[29]

Open innovation is a model that assumes that firms can and should use external ideas as well as internal ideas, and internal and external paths to market, with the advancement of technology application in developing innovative products. The concept of open innovation emphasizes that knowledge on new ideas, products, use values, and innovation are widespread in the world, and it is not possible for the companies to explore this wealth to their fullest capacity. However, business ideas, concepts, and innovation processes are licensed from other companies. In addition, firms can take internal inventions, not being used in their business, outside the company to get them licensed and earn royalty by selling them to client organizations. Most companies that intend to use open-market innovation apply tools such as licensing, joint ventures, and strategic alliances to bring the benefits of free trade to the flow of new ideas. However, eco-innovation can be environmentally motivated through social organizations and public policies along with the considerations on reducing production costs. Managing institutional changes in values, knowledge, norms, and administrative actions would attract collaborations with new stakeholders. The impact on technologies for eco-innovation depends on their social adaptation and creation of market demand. Creating demand, therefore, requires identifying a suitable market with sufficient policy support to foster their initial uptake. The mainstream market prefers to adopt new innovative technologies once they are "proven" and endorsed by the consumer.[30]

[29] Govindarajan, V., & Trimble, C. (2012). *Reverse innovation: Create far from home, win everywhere.* Cambridge: Harvard Business Review Press.

[30] Rajagopal, (2020). *Sustainable businesses in developing economies—socio-economic and governance perspectives.* New York: Palgrave Macmillan.

Sustainable Innovations

Ecological innovations have been evolving chronologically in society over the years. In traditional societies, conservation of natural resources like land and water, and agricultural production have been used with conventional wisdom in the developing countries. The concept of eco-innovation has received scientific attention after the post-World War II period, after United Nations Framework Convention Climate Change in 1992 promoted by all nations. This initiative has been followed recently by Paris on climate change in 2016, which was signed by the developed countries. Over time the ecological innovations have shifted from large companies to niche enterprises as the latter follow cost-effective and price-competitive strategies. The eco-innovations at niche markets in developing countries are aimed at the low-income consumer communities who are the big target towards contributing to social sustainability. The polyethylene terephthalate (PET) bottles have a low recycling value in the Uganda markets, which has driven people to discard PET bottles. Consequently, such public behavior has caused heaps of PET bottles, driving society to take easy action of either burning or strewing them across streets and fields as litter. The solution to such ecological issue has been proposed by a local company with a low-cost frugal innovation company—Takataka Plastics. This niche-based company has focused on the use of plastic for construction materials and innovated plastic wall tiles. The company has founded its manufacturing model with generic equipment and locally built machines as they are cheaper and easier to maintain and fix if they break. The company has used an open-source design for their machines and modified them to be adaptable to locally available parts and fabrication techniques. These machines are easy to replicate and inexpensive to scale the project up. Takataka is an emerging example of a home-grown solution to a local problem. The company is currently working on a small scale but in future, it could create a source of income not only for informal waste collectors in the country but also be able to deliver a macro-frugal solution to complex social sustainability issues in the similar economies.[31]

The initiatives of Uganda in promoting social consciousness on environmental protections as a developing nation sets new dimensions to

[31] Rajagopal, (2020). *Sustainable businesses in developing economies—socio-economic and governance perspectives*. New York: Palgrave Macmillan.

social values-led business modeling. There are several such best practices that drive butterfly effect on eco-innovation and sustainability-driven projects across countries. Strategies of firms, which emerge out of market environmental chaos, help firms in stimulating eco-innovations and sustainability-led business modeling in local markets to achieve green competitiveness in the global marketplace. Consequently, every small change emerged out of the social enterprises contributes to a long-range global and sustainable effect in the market. While large and multinational firms have historically relied on technological know-how and reliable processes, they are planning to develop competencies in external relationships for sustainability in the competitive marketplace. External relationships help firms in strengthening and extending their organizational core competencies while responding to the demands of globalization, mass customization, enhanced quality, and rapid technological change.[32]

Innovation and technology development arise from a complex set of relationships among industry, business firms, society, and consumers besides the government that intervenes through the public policies. This system is different in each country and influenced by the national policy and institutional context. Social organizations, non-governmental organizations, and government are pivotal in creating social and industrial systems that support these various relationships in the context of sustainability-led business modeling. Such convergence of social needs, industrial manufacturing, and eco-innovations encompass institutional capacity and its strength or weakness in a country as a key factor in the development and transfer of technology. In small and medium companies, institutional capacity is often weak due to resource limitations, and the development and adaptation to eco-innovation technologies are delayed. The administrative overheads and transactional inefficiencies contribute to an increase in both tangible and intangible costs for small and medium enterprises. Ineffective integration of information, policies, resources, and processes and coordination between various government departments, social needs, and corporate social responsibility initiatives may stay misaligned and ineffective in managing and implementing the sustainability projects effectively.

[32] Rajagopal , (2015). *Butterfly effect in competitive markets: Driving small change for larger differences*, Basingstoke, UK: Palgrave Macmillan.

The eco-innovations and sustainable manufacturing are intertwined. For example, the eco-innovations in air-conditioning industry have revolutionized through hot- or cold-water function through pipes to the units located on each level of the building. The amount of cold water varies according to the desired temperature relative to the outside temperature. The New Energy and Industrial Technology Development Organization (NEDO), a public organization established by the Japanese government, coordinates R&D activities in the eco-innovation process of hydro-air-conditioning system for industries. The conventional air conditioners operate at the pressure required for maximum heating—and cooling demand, while the Yokogawa Electric, a Japanese manufacturer, has developed a simple and low-cost, low-risk control mechanism that would eliminate wasteful use of energy. This innovation has been commercialized with the brand name Econo-Pilot, which controls the pumping pressure of air-conditioning systems in a sophisticated way and can reduce annual pump power consumption by up to 90%. Econo-Pilot HSP controls primary pumps and cooling water pumps for heat sources in water circulation systems such as central air-conditioning.[33]

The expansion of ecological innovation has been accompanied by the philosophy of in-home solutions with low-cost technologies and high-utilitarian values. Considering the growing global environmental concerns, such as green energy and increasing scarcity of resources, the manufacturing industries have shown more interest in sustainable production with the social business models. These models present the low-end technoscape for the consumers and are jointly implemented through the public–private partnership as corporate social responsibility (CSR) initiatives. However, the social awareness and effective implementation of public policies have improved the efficiency of sustainable consumption and growth of the emerging markets. Reduction in the emission of greenhouse gases has been considered as a priority among the governments of developing countries, and many have adopted strategic frameworks. Interestingly, the economic leverage to enterprises engaged in manufacturing green products and providing eco-conservation services developing countries have raised public interest and expectations from the environmental protection programs to achieve sustainable development. In developing

[33] Onishi, T., Miura, H., & Kobayashi, S. (2010). Econo-Pilot HSP Energy-saving system for heat source water pumps: Reducing electricity onsumption and CO2 emission in the pump. *Yokogawa Technical Report*, English Edition, *53*(1), 27–30.

countries, the green recovery public policy has attracted public investment in environmental technologies and encouraged the implementation of collaborative sustainability projects. Green recovery projects are targeted towards regenerating ecological conservation that have been affected by the community ignorance in urban-rural geo-demographic segments. The green recovery concept has geared up over time as a core part of economic stimulus measures at global–local levels.

Disruptive innovation in ecological conservation and delivering social sustainability products possess utilitarian values at competitive prices. Such products and services are designed for a new set of customers, which differentiates them from the existing stream of buying. Generally, disruptive innovations are technologically straightforward and convincing to consumers, and generate value for money. Some disruptive innovations offer more for less to customers through a different package of attributes that have higher significance to the consumers in the bottom of the pyramid market segment than to those of the mainstream market. Large firms are quick to take advantage of disruptive innovation and offer product differentiations by ways of customization, price competitiveness, desired solution to the sustainability problems, and convenience in the global–local markets. However, large companies need to develop an ethnic innovative perspective, a local business vision, prevention against disruptive and counterfeiting products in local markets, developing partnerships and alliances at the destination market, and drive a supportive consumer ambience. Most companies explore cost-effective, niche-based strategies to transform the various social consumption practices and enhance the performance social sustainability[34].

Much attention has been paid recently to innovation as a way for industry and policymakers to achieve more radical, systemic improvements in corporate environmental practices and performance. The social-ecological innovation has emerged as an important consideration in environmental governance in addition to the sectoral issues in sustainability. Eco-innovations encouraged local markets to contribute to the resilience of ecosystem services in urban socio-economic and ecological landscapes. Consequently, urban and rural areas need implementation of green recovery programs as a range of important ecosystem services. Urban centers have grown in the recent past with satellite industrial

[34] Rajagopal (2020). *Sustainable businesses in developing economies—Socio-economic and governance perspectives*. New York: Palgrave Macmillan.

production centers and have observed degradation of environmental standards over the years. These centers have become combined geo-demographic segments with industrial production centers and populous habitats. Crowdsourcing of innovative ideas, collective intelligence to improve the resources utilization, and management of green space in urban social-ecological systems have emerged as effective tools to manage sustainability projects. Such practices can drive public–private partnership to develop social-ecological innovation and provide a valuable resource in the production and adaptive management of local ecosystem services with social governance efficacy.[35]

The community-based natural resources management has been encouraged by the social organizations (self-help groups and non-governmental organizations) on the assumption that the decision-making process in natural resource management is a collective process within the communities and among stakeholders. This community approach has not only fostered knowledge and commitment among the stakeholders, but also stimulated ecological innovation in start-up enterprises at the local level. However, commercialization of frugal and reverse innovations in the green economic and industrial sector is a major challenge. The problem of commercialization of innovation is largely attributed to the interface of top-down (public policies and funding) and bottom-up approaches (social and entrepreneurial governance), which primarily involves the inter-institutional arrangements to diffuse and market the innovations.[36] Ecological innovations have become dispersed as the market is becoming increasingly demanding and the users have formed their niche. Accordingly, innovation has shifted from public technology to business models, and is more focused on marketing than social needs. Many innovations are emerging in the market that are simplified, while some are scaling up in improving the existing products or services and positioning them as innovations. However, managers may align their business strategies with competitive advantages of markets and manage innovation in emerging

[35] Dennis, M. & James, P. (2018). Urban Social-ecological innovation: Implications for adaptive natural resource management. *Ecological Economics*, *150*, 153–164.

[36] Armitage, D. (2005). Adaptive capacity and community-based natural resource management. *Environment Management*, *35*(6), 703–715.

economies to diffuse and commercialize.[37] Traditionally positioning innovation of products and services makes a company competitive which is a myth in the present state of global marketing. Consequently, firms continually reinvent in large and small ways in reference to shift in market demand and changes in the economy develop competitive marketing strategy in reference to the shifts in the product and market behavior, knowledge of innovative products, and innovation positions. Though the company may develop efficiency regarding the above strategic positions of product/market, knowledge, and innovation independently, the firms are still risk averse with the innovation.[38]

Successful innovation leads to customer involvement and profits, which can be achieved through co-creation by aligning consumers and market players in the innovation process. Some multinational companies have invested in sustainability projects by taking advantage of social media to diffuse new ideas and stimulating co-creation of innovative products and services. For example, the role of co-creation has become central to sustainability management in the social initiatives of the twenty-first century. Energy market transition, which is enabled by new affordable energy technologies and digitalization, opens novel opportunities for developing innovative energy solutions through collective intelligence and public–private co-creations. The new technologies emerging through co-creation facilitate stakeholders to buy low-cost renewable energy. The process of co-innovation is stretching the ideation process through the extensive use of digital platforms and stakeholder involvement. Co-innovation is an ecosystem-wide activity that involves multiple stakeholders, who collaborate toward a shared social goal and explore niche strategies to commercialize eco-innovations. However, in active societies like Chinese sociological and business culture, the co-innovators simultaneously compete with one another across the geo-demographic segments to market their innovative products and services.[39]

[37] De Meyer, A. (2011, September 15), Diving into the new innovation landscape, *IESE-Insight Magazine*.

[38] McDonough, E. F., Zack, M., Lin, H. E., & Berdrow, I. (2008), Integrating Innovation Style and Knowledge into Strategy, *MIT Sloan Management Review*, *50*(1), 53–58.

[39] Kotilainen, K., Saari, U.A., Mäkinen, S. J., and Ringle, C. M. (2019). Exploring the microfoundations of end-user interests toward co-creating renewable energy technology innovations. *Journal of Cleaner Production*, *229*, 203–212.

PART III

Design, Development, and Diffusion

CHAPTER 8

Technology Thrust: Design, Development, and Diffusion

Stages of Technology Development

Exponential growth of technology has moved today from conventional wisdom to the machine age, which blends collective intelligence and computer-aided solutions for the societal problems and needs at the grass-roots. Hybrid technology is propelling innovation through a powerful but cost-effective devices (smartphones), where each is equipped with an array of processors, sensors, and value-based techno-economic derivatives. Among various social service technologies, Uber and Waze became feasible in the past few years as technology-facilitating transport services because of increase in accumulated digital power, decline in technology cost, and increase in technology utilization. There are many social challenges that require machine age technology and digitization converges the social needs with accessibility and utilization of technology-based platforms.[1]

Firms face challenges in positioning new products in the target market segments and follow market-driven approach to product development as they thrive on continuous innovation. Another pertinent challenge the

[1] Brynjolfsson, E., & McAfee, A. (2015, Fall). The digitization of just about everything. *Rotman Management Magazine*, pp. 39–42.

A. Molina and Rajagopal, *Challenge-Based Learning, Research, and Innovation*, Palgrave Studies of Entrepreneurship and Social Challenges in Developing Economies,
https://doi.org/10.1007/978-3-031-29156-2_8

companies face is towards avoiding the innovator's dilemma on bringing successful technology or protecting the new products against disruptive technology. Firms engaged in product innovations and improvements should develop a set of design and technical features, strategies for consumers purchase benefits, and alliances with potential brands to sustain market competition and ensuring high market share. However, since developing consumer value and market share of firms are largely generic in nature, the core technologies on which innovations are based drive the scope of new products in the market. By focusing their efforts on generic as well as hybrid technologies, firms can be unconventionally innovative and remain sensitive to customer needs and simultaneously focus on market-driven strategies to lead the market competition. Firms that seek to develop successful and sustainable strategies for innovation must identify generic technologies with unique product designs and competitive marketing strategies.[2]

Firms can benefit from opening the new idea development process to make competitive and effective decisions by integrating the principles of continuous innovation with the *stage-gate* process. This process examines the potential opportunities of employing the principles of both inbound and outbound continuous innovation of a firm in both upstream and downstream marketplaces. The stage-gate model can exploit the advantages of openness, spot rationale, and sustainable effect of decisions that are required in the marketplace. This model would allow explicit consideration of import and export of know-how and technology through gate evaluations and enable firms to continuously assess their core capabilities and business model. The application of this model can assist firms in capturing value from both internal and external technology exploitation in increasingly open innovation processes.

A stage-gate model is a conceptual and operational road map for moving a new product project from idea to launch. This model divides the effort into distinct stages separated by management decision gates. Cross-functional teams must successfully complete a prescribed set of related cross-functional tasks in each stage prior to obtaining management approval to proceed to the next stage of product development. Stage-gate processes have a great deal of appeal to management, because, basically,

[2] Glazer, R. (2007). Meta-technologies and innovation leadership: Why there may be nothing new under the sun. *California Management Review, 50*(1), 120–143.

they restrict investment in the next stage until management is comfortable with the outcome of the current stage. The gate can be effective in controlling product quality and development expenses. Stages-and-gates in the model function as sequential phases and may run into some overlapping activities, especially when they cross the decision points. The stage grate processes may not lead towards completing tasks in earlier phases to keep them off the critical path, but they foster a mindset in which the work proceeds sequentially step by step. A newer alternative to stage-gate process is the bounding box approach, which is essentially a management by exceptions technique in which certain critical parameters of the project, such as profit margin, project budget, product performance level, and launch date, which are negotiated as the bounding box. Firms need to conduct regular checks so that the process managers remain within bounds.

The stage-gate process begins with the identification and documentation of a new idea in improving business. Tasks associated with the development of the product are then divided into a sequence of logical steps called *stages*, each of which is preceded by a *gate* where the attractiveness of the project is assessed. During each stage, a cross-functional project team carries out tasks that result in the completion of defined deliverables including those related to technical (manufacturing, R&D, quality, regulatory) and business (sales, marketing, business development) functions. The advantages of using the stage-gate process are as follows:

- To improve customer satisfaction.
- To reduce the time to market.
- To improve new product success rates.
- To improved launch management of new products.
- To ensure earlier detection of failures.
- Increasing the speed of innovation and productivity.
- Ensuring less recycling and rework.

Competitive technology-oriented decisions are strategic business initiatives that involve significant resources and managerial skills. New technology led products fail because the market tests are not elaborative to forecast their commercial success accurately. Firms need to develop systems thinking and the stage-gate process method that capitalizes on the power of the wisdom of market players by allowing managers to interact in organized markets governed by well-defined rules. Consumer-centric technologies motivate users to analyze information freely through a price and user value discovery process. Prediction markets seek information aggregation from a large group of diverse individuals by encouraging active participation.[3] The stage-gate process demonstrates the power of the decision manager to perform strategically in the competitive markets. Technological transitions are challenging in local entrepreneurship, which are important for social and economic development at the grassroots. Emerging entrepreneurs tend to adapt to new technologies, to explore opportunities to enter competitive markets early. While some established companies become early adopters of new technologies, the authors argue that they typically lack the vision and the commitment to become leaders. New technologies can open opportunities that extend well beyond the predetermined scope of legacy products.[4]

Technology has created an attractive product market, and consumers are continuously motivated to consider a new option with better value for money. Technology innovation has made emerging business firms creative think tanks. The twenty-first century is largely driven by the development of technology, and business enterprises are becoming dependable on technology not only to offer new products but also to drive consumers to more convenience bound behavior. Technology growth in society affects people (including consumers), products, operations, materials, manufacturing and marketing processes, and the state of consumer preferences. Before employing any new technology firms, we need to assess its social, economic, and legal perspectives.

Firms can create awareness by adequately sharing the idea of new technology development with the employees, stakeholders, and market players to gain the workplace confidence and build a favorable environment within the organization to carry out technology in new product manufacturing and marketing process. Firms need to employ a systematic multi-functional audit to adopt new technology and ensure the

[3] Roy, S. K., Singh, G., Hope, M., Nguyen, B., & Harrigan, P. (2019). The rise of smart consumers: Role of smart servicescape and smart consumer experience co-creation. *Journal of Marketing Management, 35*(15–16), 1480–1513.

[4] Suarez, F. F., Utterback, J. M., von Gruben, P., & Kang, H. Y. (2018). The hybrid trap: Why most efforts to bridge old and new technology miss the mark. *MIT Sloan Management Review, 59*(3), 52–57.

technological development process to meet their predetermined manufacturing and marketing goals of new products. Firms should also ensure the availability of the required production infrastructure for using the new technology. Therefore, carrying out periodical audit of the social technology understands shifts in PNS factors and stakeholder preferences. It is also necessary for the firms to develop adequate knowledge and skills on transfer of technology to the new product development process. Managers, employees, and the principal technology team should be given the required training to deploy quality and cost efficiency in carrying technology to new product development process. However, a major challenge in developing acceptable social technology platforms is to transform the conventional wisdom with innovative technology skills. Training on transforming knowledge should be offered vertically in the concerned departments to all levels of employees and horizontally across functional departments including engineering, production, operations, and marketing. Besides developing all backward linkages necessary for developing new technology, employees of a firm need significant motivational push to perform. Substantial time and resources need to be invested in growing the capabilities and competencies of the employees and the managers to identify the key drivers in developing new technologies and successfully executing strategy. Business organizations also need to align the employee's individual goals with technology development and implementation strategy. Those organizations that have successfully done so, however, enjoy breakthrough results. Organizations should ensure rendering timely and efficient technical support for employees during the process of developing new technology as well as technical support to customers in resolving product-related issues.

Managers responsible for developing new technology products begin the development process with the consumers but not with the predetermined technology idea and prioritize concepts using sharply defined business criteria instead of personal or social impulse. Technology-based new product design should be integrated in the business model along with the service features and functionality. It is important for firms to conduct rigorous ground-breaking tests for launching new technology-led products with consumers and market players. To make the technology-led new product a success in the market, firms need to develop efficient backward and forward linkage. A quality-deployed backward linkages and customer-driven forward linkages would help the new technology to sustain in the market as well as attract desired business. One of the major tasks in introducing new technology in the marketplace is its proper implementation. Managers engaged in implementing the new technology should bridge the gap between the designers and the users of the innovation and develop a smooth transition in the convergence process. Often this task is difficult if the employees, market players, and/or consumers show incongruity and resistance. Implementation managers must learn how to guide the innovation from the laboratory to the workplace and meet both developer and user needs on the merits of its use values market by market. Simultaneously, operational managers in association with top management and business leaders should prepare the market to receive the technology.[5]

Companies have become increasingly aware of the social and environmental pressures on developing new technologies in business. Often market demand for developing new technologies offers opportunities for emerging companies and motivate them to drive organizational impetus for innovation to achieve sustainable growth. However, complying with technology needs and market demand has considerable difficulty in making the efforts to sustainable development. Such intricacies in business organizations arise when innovation strategies are often inadequate to accommodate the highly complex and uncertain nature of these new demands. However, sustainable development innovation is more intricate than market-driven innovation because it typically has a wider range of stakeholders and long-term demands driven by the societal and environmental needs. Organizations that fail to understand such issues may pile up sunk costs in bringing new technologies to market.[6] Growing firms in the global marketplace tend to involve suppliers in product/process/service development with new technology to gain significant results. It has been observed reviewing the best practices of multinational companies that supplier participation in product development technologies can help reduce cost, reduce concept-to-customer development time, improve quality, and provide innovative technologies that can help capture market share. Supplier integration is most successful by enhancing supplier capabilities, managing the level of complexity of

[5] Barton, D. L., & Kraus, W. A. (1985). Implementing new technology. *Harvard Business Review, 63*(6), 102–110.

[6] Hall, J., & Vredenburg, H. (2003). Challenges of innovating for sustainable development. *Sloan Management Review, 45*(1), 61–68.

the technology at the bottom line of market, and minimizing degree of market and consumer risk.[7]

Social Technology

Design thinking can be a critical facilitator of new technologies, but it is also a technology in its own right social technology that encourages more productive innovation conversations that are strategically valuable for dynamic capability building. By overcoming social and psychological barriers in innovation processes, design thinking accelerates progress on critical imperatives: allowing innovators at all levels to sense new opportunities; seize them by overcoming cognitive biases and aligning stakeholders; and transform and reconfigure resources. It accomplishes this through a set of well-recognized practices. In fact, recognizing and responding to human irrationality underlies many popular management approaches, from design thinking to agile software development, lean start-up, and choice architecture. In the strategy field, behavioral strategy and strategy as practice perspectives call attention to the essential role of human actors in capability building. A shared premise of these approaches is that while attempting to predict or control human conduct is hazardous, behavior can be anticipated and shaped to the mutual advantage of humans, their organizations, and society.

Technology development to meet social challenges in developing economies is largely based on the collective design thinking process, which has six principal domains comprising inspiration, stakeholders' involvement, alignment, co-creation, articulation to facilitate technology operations, and social visualization towards sustainability as illustrated in the Fig. 8.1. The social challenges broadly include technologies to support low-cost renewable energy, green housing, faming operations, and public health management. The social connectivity and collective intelligence-driven technology development support innovations to be used at community commons to meet social challenges. The involvement of technology developers with society is an important consideration to understand the problems, needs, and probable solutions for the stakeholders within the given demographic attributes. The stakeholder preferences on technology-based solutions help in designing and

[7] Rajagopal. (2014). *Architecting enterprise: Managing innovation, technology, and global competitiveness*. Basingstoke, UK: Palgrave Macmillan.

development affordable technologies at the grassroots. The involvement of stakeholders, therefore, strengthens the process of design thinking through user insights. Community involvement, technology co-creation, and user insights foster the social acceptance of technology through perceived use value and ease of use perceptions of stakeholders. The user insights in technology transfer to the stakeholder inspire all categories of users including lead users, early adapters, early majority, and late majority, except laggards. However, the technological attributes determine the cost of technology and its life cycle, which affect the social entrepreneurship and stakeholder engagement. Commonly social technologies address the triple bottom line embedding people (stakeholders), planet (sustainability), and profit (social payoff). The governance of social technology can be well managed by the stakeholders with adequate knowledge and experience. Therefore, adequate knowledge and skills should be imparted to the technology governance teams. Transfer of social technologies requires need-based user alignment and articulation to manage its applications, which will help diffusion and adaptation of technology. Co-creation helps design thinking to develop social technologies through consortiums supported by the government and public–private partnership programs. Converging the divergent factors as discussed above, the quadruple domains of involvement, inspiration, alignment, and co-creation help in developing technologies contextual to ecological engineering and socioeconomic development. The major concern of challenge-based research is to manage the uninterrupted technology transition and generation effects by ensuring continuous improvement. The prototype development and experimentation widely support the process of social visualization of technology, which not only delivers experience but stimulates social actions through continuous learning. The Four A's comprising awareness (PNS factors of stakeholders), attributes (preferred solutions), affordability (cost of technology), and adaptability (technology acceptance) remain central to the development of social technology.

Broadly, social technology addresses the social and psychological aspects of innovation, which helps decision makers often to make choices driven primarily by analyzing the prevailing problems, needs, and expected solutions. Since start-up technologies possess a mindset that prefers to develop low-cost technology platforms to seize opportunity, they tend to drive social action by understanding the PNS factors of stakeholders. Thus, significant collective intelligence and participatory research

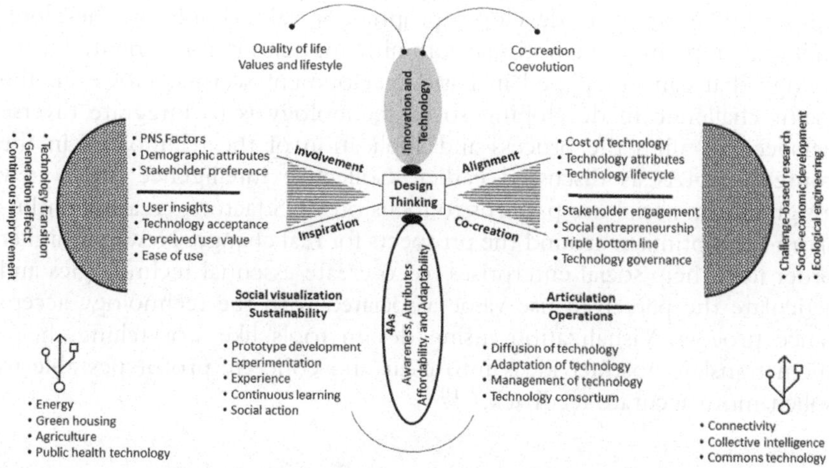

Fig. 8.1 Technology evolution, experiment, and experience (*Source* Author [Rajagopal])

in the community are encouraging tools to undertake experimentation-based learning in action. Increasing confidence and sense of economic growth within the communities by adapting to new technologies has significantly encouraged the social innovation process and has fostered new mindsets and behaviors. Therefore, social technology today provides a set of knowledge to drive entrepreneurship, scalable tools, and methods to expedite, in a human-centered way to drive continuous innovation. Digital technology also brings a social technology capable of facilitating the development of dynamic capabilities needed to meet the challenges of adaptation and innovation in a VUCA (volatility, uncertainty, complexity, and ambiguity) environment, where both innovation and technology demands continuous improvement.[8]

Co-creation drives social innovation, and technology improves social and economic conditions to help perform each entrepreneurial activity successfully. It also resets entrepreneurial mindsets and processes to develop affordable innovation and technology. The PNS factors within society can be explored by ethnography, which provides insights to the

[8] Liedtka, J. (2020). Putting technology in its place: Design thinking's social technology at work. *California Management Review*, *62*(2), 53–83.

innovators' mindsets to develop appropriate social technology. Therefore, building empathy and emotional commitment helps in user-oriented technology that can be applied in basic development sectors. However, the major challenge in developing social technology is to integrate diverse perspectives align the process and application of the technology in the context of 4As as discussed earlier. Collective intelligence offers new insights from social use patterns to focus on PNS factors, creating enthusiasm and optimism around the prospects for real change. New and higher order ideas help social enterprises to co-create essential technologies and articulate the perceived use value associated with the technology acceptance process. Visualization, using design tools like storytelling, helps them translate abstract ideas into clear and concrete prototypes able to solicit more accurate feedback.[9,10]

Social Adoption of Technology

Diffusion of innovation is the process that disseminates knowledge on an innovation to make the consumers, suppliers, and other players to acquire knowledge on the new products and technology and perceive their use value against the existing and substitute products available in the market. Effective diffusion of innovation prepares consumers in adopting the new technology-led innovation to drive success of the products. The following factors influence adoption of an innovation[11]:

- Attributes of innovation,
- Communication channels involved in diffusion of innovation,
- Time of launching the innovation, and
- The market segment and society where new technology is introduced.

The innovation-decision process theory, the individual innovativeness theory, the rate of adoption theory, and the theory of perceived attributes

[9] Beckman, S., Scott, S., & Wymore, L. (2018). Collaborative innovation: Exploring the intersections among theater, art and business in the classroom. *Journal of Open Innovation: Technology, Market, and Complexity, 4*(4), 52. https://doi.org/10.3390/joitmc4040052

[10] Schoemaker, P., Heaton, S., & Teece, D. (2018). Innovation, dynamic capabilities, and leadership. *California Management Review, 61*(1), 15–42.

[11] Rogers, E. M. (2003). *Diffusion of innovations* (5th ed.). New York: Free Press.

explain the diffusion of technology process. The innovation-decision process theory is based on cause and effect of time spread across five distinct stages. The first stage is knowledge in which potential adopters learn *prima facie* about the innovation based on new technology and product design and move to the second stage persuading the merits of the innovation. In the third stage, firms decide to adopt the innovation into the business stream and develop plans to implement it, and in the following, stage the innovation project is analyzed in terms of the innovation life cycle in the market and anticipated consumer value that can be generated. In the fifth and last stage of innovation-decision process, firms confirm that their decision to adopt was the appropriate decision (Rogers, 2003). Once these stages are achieved, diffusion shows the results on the ACCA cognitive variables comprising awareness, comprehension, conviction, and action among users as detailed below:

- New technology generates awareness.
- Diffusion drives comprehension on the innovation.
- Awareness on innovation develops conviction (inclination) to adopt among users.
- Users take action to accept and adopt the innovation driven by new technology.

ACCA paradigm of consumer behavior argues that awareness on the sales promotions in convergence with the contents of advertisements generates conviction among the consumers which leans towards action resulting in the store choice and buying decision. It is believed by the consumers that a strong conviction towards buying decision can effectively influence the action of buying decision.[12] Individuals experience five stages of accepting an innovation comprising knowledge, persuasion, decision, implementation, and confirmation. As the innovation is accepted by society, it spreads through various communication channels. During communication, the core idea is rarely evaluated from a scientific standpoint rather, subjective perceptions of the innovation influence diffusion. Finally, social systems determine the contents, reach, and frequency of technological or innovation diffusion. The social platforms also set the

[12] Rajagopal. (2011). The symphony paradigm: Strategy for managing market competition. *Journal of Transnational Management, 16*(3), 181–199.

norms on diffusion and determine the roles of opinion leaders and change agents, types of innovation decisions, and evaluate the cause and effects of innovation and technological change. Diffusion of innovations is a theory that seeks to explain how, why, and at what rate new ideas and technology spread through cultures. Diffusion is the process by which an innovation is communicated through certain channels over time among the members of a social system. The origins of the diffusion of innovations theory are varied and span multiple disciplines that envelop innovation, communication channels, time, and a social system involving enormous human capital. The innovation must be widely adopted to self-sustain. Within the rate of adoption, there is a point at which an innovation reaches critical mass. Diffusion of Innovations manifests itself in different ways in various cultures and fields and is highly subject to the type of adopters and innovation-decision process.[13] As new computer technologies emerge for the design and development of innovative product platforms, applied theories of innovation diffusion and technology acceptance will become increasingly important. Firms engaged in product innovation thrive in the industry as well as marketplace for securing user cooperation with an information management system for sustaining the new product families. Effectively engaging human resources in the new technology led innovation, and diffusion process will shorten the time required to reach return on investment and increase the reach and analytics of information. The history of innovation adoption theories are explored and extended to the product family infrastructure managed by the large firms.[14] The multi-disciplinary approach had led to the creation of new attribute of technology-led innovations, and often the product line of companies is overlapped with similar or identical new products that tend to compete with the products within the product line and lower the rate of success of new products. Although some products exceed the targets in the market compensating performance of other products, there are numerous individual, organizational, and technological variables that measure the key determinants of user acceptance. Diffusion of an innovation occurs

[13] Moores, T. T. (2010). Organizational performance under conditions of vulnerability: A multi-agent perspective. *Expert Systems with Applications*, 37 (4), 3111–3117.

[14] Byron, B. M., & Shooter, S. B. (2005). *An introduction to innovation adoption theories for the design of a product family information management infrastructure*. Proceedings of IMECE, ASME International Mechanical Engineering Congress and Exposition, November 5–11, 2005, Orlando, Florida, USA.

through the decision process induced by knowledge, persuasion, decision, implementation, and confirmation. An individual might reject an innovation at any time during or after the adoption process. These stages of the adoption process are as discussed below[15]:

- Knowledge: In this stage, users of innovation and new technology are open to multidimensional application of the innovative products, but most users face paucity of information about the chronology of innovation and its concealed values. During this stage of the process, users also get demotivated in searching for relevant information on innovation and new technology.
- Persuasion: In this stage the users find comprehensive information on innovative products and the application of technology. They express interest in innovation and actively seek peer evaluation on the products.
- Decision: Users perceive the change and evaluate the advantages/disadvantages of using the innovation and decide whether to adopt or reject the innovation.
- Implementation: Firms employ various strategies to implement innovation by boosting user awareness, promotions, and enhancing the use value of innovation. During this stage, the users determine the application and perceived use value of the innovation and acquire further information about it.
- Confirmation: Users determine their decision to continue using the innovation. In this stage both introspective (may also cause cognitive dissonance) and interpersonal confirmation is sought by the users to affirm that the user has made the right decision.

There are several complex attributes of innovations that influence users' decision towards adopting or rejecting an innovation led with the new technology. The individual innovativeness theory is based on who adopts the innovation and when. While imparting knowledge on new

[15] Rajagopal. (2014). *Architecting enterprise: Managing innovation, technology, and global competitiveness*. Basingstoke, UK: Palgrave Macmillan.

technology and innovation, firms should focus user-oriented instructional development process through the following phases[16]:

- Identifying the consumers segments,
- Measuring perceived use value of consumers on innovation and new technology integrated with the innovation,
- Develop a user-friendly product or customize the existing products,
- Diffuse adequate knowledge about the consumer-oriented innovation, and
- Provide adequate services support to the consumers on the innovative products and technology.

Though there are various theories supporting the adoption process of new products and technology among potential users, the Technology Acceptance Model suggests how various factors influence the decision process of users in accepting the technology. Firms should understand that the individual user's decision to use technology and new products is influenced by their perceptions of inputs against expected outcomes. The cognitive effects on consumer perception about the new technology and products can be measured by considering how satisfied the user is with the experience and how the new products and technology would provide competitive advantage and sustainable value for money. A consumer's intent to use new technology may also be impacted by the subjective norms in reference to social pressures to use (or not use) the newly introduced technology. Such pressures may come from peers and corporates employees. There are various factors that influence consumer preferences in adopting new products and technology:

- Relative Advantage: The extent of advantage the new or improved products delivers over the previous generation.
- Compatibility: The level of compatibility that an innovation assimilates into user's needs, and socio-cultural and economic values.
- Complexity vs. Simplicity: If the innovation is perceived as complicated or difficult to use, an individual is unlikely to adopt it. Most consumers like simple and user-friendly new products.

[16] Rajagopal. (2014). *Architecting Enterprise: Managing innovation, technology, and global competitiveness*. Basingstoke, UK: Palgrave Macmillan.

- Trial: How easily an innovation may be experimented. If a user is able to test an innovation and perceive economic and personal advantages, consumers will be more likely to adopt it.
- Observation: This factor indicates to what extent that an innovation is visible to others. If an innovation is more visible, it will drive communication among the peers and will in turn creates more positive or negative reactions.

Consumers are more likely to adopt an innovation if it offers high relative advantage and compatibility with the consumers' values, beliefs, and needs. Perceived attributes are important because they show that users derive a variety of attributes of an innovation over the relative advantages. A successful innovation will have an initial slow adoption before experiencing a rapid change and then a gradual leveling off. The period of rapid expansion, for most successful innovations, occurs when social and technical factors combine to permit the innovation to experience dramatic growth.[17]

Growth of Social Technology

The ethnographic factors are broadly considered to develop user-driven design criteria through collective ideation process. Social insights and stakeholder values serve as stimulants to drive idea generation. The digital technology (DT) has been helpful to innovators and technology developers to embed new ways to augment the perceived use of technology and produce higher quality solutions more likely to receive user acceptance. The emphasis on co-creation of innovation and managing innovation business projects in partnership with the local companies is gradually generating technological breakthroughs, allowing emerging companies to reduce the time to bring innovative products and services to market. The recent trend of carrying out innovation in the business-to-consumer and business-to-business segments by companies exhibits different ways of deploying price and volume advantages in global competition. Large companies practice outsourcing innovation, collaborating with start-up enterprises, investing in open innovation, and engaging in driving public–private partnerships. Figure 8.2 exhibits the elements influencing the

[17] Rogers, E. M. (2003). *Diffusion of innovations* (5th ed.). New York: Free Press.

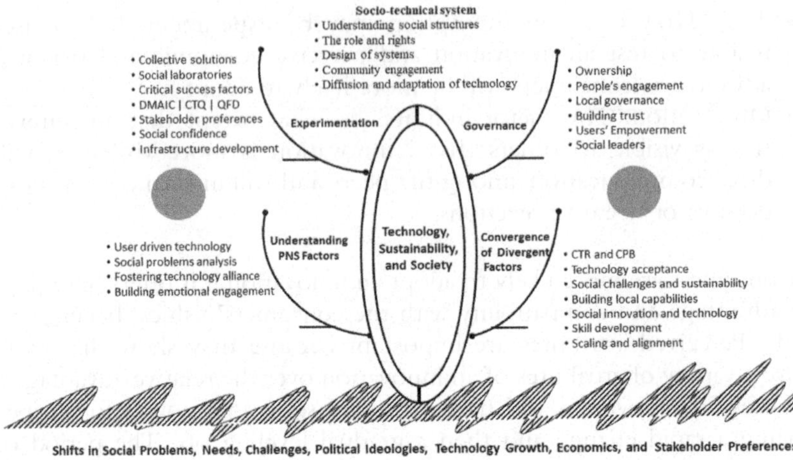

Fig. 8.2 Technology, sustainability, and society (*Source* Author [Rajagopal])

convergence of divergent perspectives of technology, sustainability, and social systems towards developing social technologies for commons.

Technology, sustainability, and society are intertwined and interrelated that influence the social and economic development in a region. As shifts in social problems, needs, and social and economic challenges are often abrupt due to global–local disruptions, the political ideologies significantly influence the economics, technology growth, and stakeholder preferences. Consequently, technology and society can be well integrated from the perspectives of social development by understanding the PNS factors, experimentation, and governance modalities as exhibited in Fig. 8.2. However, the higher challenge is experienced in converging the divergent factors associated with the human elements in operationalizing technology for social development. The concept of social technology describes a system of conscious and purposeful people's organization engaged in collective development of the society. Social technology has now been adopted for various challenge-based development activities with a project approach, which encourages systematic learning and work breakdown structure towards delivering predetermined social solutions.[18] The user-driven technology developed by appropriately analyzing social problems and determining contextual needs serves stakeholders as congruent with the PNS factors. Often social technologies are developed under public policy programs in developing countries and are fostered by technological alliances with large companies. Global–local alliances have been effective in developing countries for the development of specific sectors such as health, housing, and farming. Social technologies are tested commonly tested for collective solutions in the social laboratories. Most social technologies are developed through the project management approach using DMAIC (define, measure, analyze, implement, and control), CTQ (critical to quality), and QFD (quality function deployment) tools. Such technologies and supporting infrastructure are developed in congruence with the stakeholder preferences to gain confidence in society. In delivering social technologies one of the major challenges is determining the ownership and local governance. It requires social leaders to ensure people's engagement in the technology development process and building trust among the stakeholders. The economics of social technology is largely determined by analyzing the proportionate triadic effects of CTR (cost, time, and risk) and CBP (cost, benefit, and profit). Accordingly, the socio-technical system plays a critical role in developing and delivering social technologies by understanding the social structures, design of systems, and applications thereof.

As technology grows sophisticated, the stakeholders' expectations also swell exponentially. In fact, the convergence of a few key technologies is enabling that change. Sustainable technology has driven a new revolution in social technology and has not only helped to increase the quick social development prospects but has also attracted economic growth at the niche demographic segments. Social technologies have offered a wide variety of applications that could revolutionize activities and reduce costs. Despite the benefits of the digital revolution in services, several issues inhibit their widespread use, especially in open systems. There has been a significant change in social development perspectives over the years. Modernization, systematization, and techno-innovations are the catch phrases and keys to understanding the PNS factors and social challenges. In increasing global competition, social technologies refer to superior

[18] Organ, J., O'Neill, S., & Shanahan, B. W. (2022). Development of social technology entrepreneurial ventures: A challenge project-based learning approach. *IFAC-Papers Online, 55*(39), 181–186.

solutions through self-services among stakeholders. The technological platforms are shifting to a 3-D web space. It is found that self-service technologies, which can be customized by the users, build a higher sense of belongingness and safety in utilizing solutions for social and economic challenges.

Drivers of Technology and Social Consumption

Technology is associated as one of the principal factors of production and economic growth of a country or development sector as an agent of growth and prosperity. However, consumer sector which is part of the distribution side of the economy has also contributed significantly to advances in technology, economic growth, and betterment of the society. Technology and retailing have been inextricably linked both in terms of their development and their ability to deliver unique benefits to consumers.[19] Increasing globalization and competitiveness in the retail environment is thrusting retail firms to reach high levels of consistent experimentation of new technology in store management, product information, and customer services. Technology management can be used to help retailers test new ideas and implement the most successful ones. However, human behavior is particularly important in the retail setting, where projects are generally focused on testing new concepts, increasing collaboration, and implementing new technologies.[20]

Information and internet-based technologies have fostered new supply chain initiatives in food retailing which have significantly contributed towards enhancing the efficiency of store format, membership in a chain, unionization, and adoption of variety of information diffusion tools. The breakthrough has emerged in supply chain management in the fields of data sharing, decision sharing, and technologies that support product assortment, pricing, and merchandising decisions. Among many innovative technological processes, radio frequency identification (RFID) is gaining popularity among retail firms for managing the inventory and

[19] Tamilia, R. D., & Reid, S. E. (2007). Technological innovation and the rise of the department store in the nineteenth century. *International Journal of Technology Marketing*, *2*(2), 119–139.

[20] Thomas, R., Tillmann, W., & Fawcett, S. (2008), Project management in retailing: Integrating the behavioral dimension. *International Review of Retail Distribution and Consumer Research*, 18 (3), 325–341.

just-in-time supplies. RFID tag has the potential to significantly reduce costs in retailing. Although this technology is still not cost-effective for all manufacturers, it may soon become mainstreamed as its advantages outweigh its initial investment.[21] With many manufacturers and vendors becoming early adopters, the cost barrier for RFID will quickly be eliminated. It is unlikely, however, that RFID tags will replace bar codes soon because of the start-up cost to retailers and suppliers. RFID tags enhance the operational efficiency as the retailers can store much more information about products than bar codes can, and unlike bar codes they don't have to be seen by a scanner to be recorded. In fact, RFID tags can signal their presence to scanners a few yards away even when obscured by packaging, so the contents of a closed container can be quickly scanned and recorded.[22] In the scenario of growing competition, retailer firms can also establish how a customer relationship management and monitoring system ensures the buying decision-making process through the use of joint project teams and facilitating technology. Development and innovative applications of e-commerce transactions, as well as the integration of available technology, can provide an organization with a unique opportunity to remain competitive within today's global business environment. Although technology plays an important role in gaining a competitive advantage for organizations worldwide, information technology professionals, consumers, and e-retailers ensure proper security measures to overcome harmful impact of the misuse of these same technologies.[23]

The market drivers of technology comprise the needs of common customers, global customers, global channels, and transferable marketing. The customers' needs become a compelling factor for the multinational companies when customers of the different countries have the same needs in a product category. The free trade and unrestricted travel have created homogenous groups of customers across the countries in reference to specific industries. However, some markets that typically deal with the culture bound behavior and resistant towards adoption of new

[21] Timothy, P., & Robert, K. (2007), Evaluating food retailing efficiency: The role of information technology. *Journal of Productivity Analysis, 27*(2), 101–113.

[22] Pate, S. S., Blaylock, K., & Southward, L. (2007). RFID: An interface survey between students and retailers. *The Marketing Review, 7*(3), 273–281.

[23] Medlin, B. D., & Romaniello, A. (2008). The cost of electronic retailing: Prevalent security threats and their results. *International Journal of Electronic Marketing and Retailing, 2*(1), 80–96.

technologies prefer to offer customize products to consumers within niche. The global channels, distribution, and logistics companies offer seamless transport, storage, and delivery services. Companies can expand internationally provided the channel infrastructure is met with the distribution needs of the company. Transferability in technology marketing is applied in congruence with the marketing ideas on brand names, packaging, advertising, and other components of marketing-mix in the different countries. The competitive drivers of technology support the companies for matching their technology development and marketing strategies in accordance with the consumer preferences. The existence of global competitors indicates whether a new technology or product is ready for international business operations. The firms need to develop market infrastructure for the new technologies and products to enable the domestic company to explore the scope of expansion. The competitive efforts put pressure on companies to globalize their marketing activities to derive optimum performance of the new products by interpreting appropriately the competitor signals.

The cost drivers of technology and new products are largely based on the scale of economies that involve the cost of production functions in large and complex industries, cost of outsourcing, diffusion and adaptation of technology, tariffs, and taxes and costs associated with the basic and advanced marketing functions. The macroeconomic factors of the neighboring countries also govern the cost drivers. When a new automobile plant is set up, it aims at designing, manufacturing, or assembling and delivering a particular model by penetrating into the neighboring markets to gain the advantages of economies of scale. The high market shares multi-domestic companies derive gain from spreading their production activities across multiple product lines or diversified business lines to achieve advantage through the scope of economies. The other cost drivers include global sourcing advantages, low global communications, and automation processes. The location of strategic resources to the production plants, cost differences across the countries, and transport costs are also some important considerations of the cost drivers.

The lowering of trade barriers made globalization of markets and production a theoretical possibility, and technological change has made it a tangible reality. Since the end of World War II, the world has seen major advances in communications, information processing, and transportation technology including, most recently, the explosive emergence of the Internet and World Wide Web. Technology drivers play a significant role in global business. Global expansion of multinational companies has been highly stimulated by the technological advancements in the designing, manufacturing, and marketing of consumer and industrial products. The services were also improved by many technological breakthroughs. The internet revolution has triggered e-commerce as an open access channel that acts as strong driving forces for the global business in the consumer and industry segments. Improved transport and communication now make it possible to be in continuous contact with producers anywhere in the world. This makes it easier for companies to split production of a single good over any distance. Storage and preservation techniques have revolutionized the food industry, for example, so that the idea of seasonal vegetables is no longer relevant today as anything can be exported all the year round from anywhere.

In addition, the IT revolution has made the movement of investment capital around the globe an almost immediate process ensuring that financing opportunities across the developed and developing world have both expanded and become more flexible. Technological upgrading, in the form of introduction of new machinery and improvement of technological capabilities, provides a firm with the means to be successful in competition. In the process of introducing better technologies, new lower-cost methods become available, which allow the firm to increase labor productivity, i.e., the efficiency with which it converts resources into value. Firms adopt these newer methods of production if they are more profitable than the older ones. The ability of a firm to take advantage of technical progress is also enhanced if the firm improves its entrepreneurial and technological capabilities through two competitive strategies, namely learning and adaptation, and innovation strategies. The latter is a process of searching for finding, developing, imitating, adapting, and adopting new products, new processes, and new organizational arrangements. Because rivals do not stand still, the firm's capacity to develop these capabilities, as well as its ability to compete depends on the firm's maintaining a steady pace of innovation. Containerization has revolutionized the transportation business, significantly lowering the costs of shipping goods over long distances. Before the advent of containerization, moving goods from one mode of transport to another was very labor intensive, lengthy, and costly. It could take days to unload a ship and reload goods onto trucks and trains. The efficiency gains associated with containerization and transportation costs have plummeted, making it much more economical to ship goods around the world, thereby helping to drive the globalization of markets and production.

Communication is another important driver of innovation and technology. Mass media channels are the most rapid and efficient means of communicating to many potential adopters, but interpersonal communication is more effective in persuading potential adopters to accept a new idea. Direct communication among users of the same socio-economic segment and educational level increases the potential of acceptance even more. Although scholarly writings and curriculum resources provide an abundance of information about the effectiveness and benefits of media literacy training, most potential adopters will be more influenced by conversations with their peers.

The most evident reason to drive companies to go global is the market potential in the developing countries that act as major players in the world market. The companies such as Nintendo, Disney, and the Japanese Motorcycle industries have been greatly benefited from exploiting the markets of the developing countries and reassuring their growth in the world market to harness the promising market potential. The emerging scope of spatial diversification has also been one of the drivers for enhancing the global business utilizing the additional production capacity at the economies of scale and low-cost outsourcing. The saturation of the demand for the products and services of a company in the domestic market may also be an effective driver to globalization wherein the company looks to build value for its brand across the boundaries. A product, which is near to the end of its life cycle in the domestic market, begins to generate growth abroad. Sometimes the cross-culture attributes of overseas markets become the source of new product ideation. Such backward sourcing of technology insights may also be considered as one of the potential drivers for globalization of business and explore the strategic alliances with prominent regional or multinational brands thereof. Information and communication technologies, optical technologies, production technologies, materials technologies, biotechnologies, nanotechnologies, microsystems technologies, and innovative services are the drivers of innovations—above all in the areas of application such as automotive engineering, medical technology, mechanical engineering, and logistics. Developments in these key technologies provide solutions for the challenges of our time.

The dynamic growth of technology and product innovations has created a huge web-based nebulous mass that facilitates connectivity globally. Wireless, Internet, and mobile technologies are all converging and creating connectivity with consumer infrastructure and technology application levels in the global marketplace. Increased involvement of information technology in new product development has led to the demand for intelligent products and services. Flexible technology architectures and application frameworks tie all new products, technologies, and users together. Rapidly changing technology markets in many industries have called for strategies to expedite support services for technologies and product development. However, unplanned or ad hoc technology in the market makes the managerial tasks of forecasting, marketing, and its user values indistinct and erratic. Fast-cycle decision-making for induction of new technology and products should be based on rethinking of the decision-making model, where managerial intuition replaces extensive analysis as the main driver of decisions.[24]

Performance of a business organization can be viewed from many perspectives. However, not necessarily the performance endorses growth of business in a competitive marketplace. Financial performance of a firm may unveil a different scenario of growth as compared to the performance of various brands with a product category in the overall product-mix. Achieving good organizational performance requires more than the will of a single person; indeed, it requires the united commitment of an organization's members. This commitment must also move beyond mere talk and encompass concrete action. The top management of the firm needs to evolve the true definition of performance and its relevance in the competitive market environment. Performance expectations, which are fundamentally a manager's expectations envisaging the competitive stand of the firm in a marketplace, have a big impact on decision-making in firms, particularly in relation to investment decisions. The strategists may contribute towards improving the performance of the firm by linking expectations to the capability and competence of managers and employees of the firm and providing necessary support to improve the capability and competency at the first stance.[25]

Successful technological products in the competitive marketplace always try to gain a distinct place among competing firms and focus

[24] Rajagopal. (2014). *Architecting enterprise: Managing innovation, technology, and global competitiveness*. Basingstoke, UK: Palgrave Macmillan.

[25] Adler, R. (2010). Enhancing business success: The role of performance management, *Business Horizons, 53*(4), 331–333.

on acquiring new customers and retaining the existing ones. The repeat buying behavior of customers is largely determined by the values acquired on the product. The attributes, awareness, trial, availability, and repeat (AATAR) factors influence the customers towards making re-buying decisions in reference to the marketing strategies of the firm. The perception of repeat buying is affected by the level of satisfaction derived from the buying experience of customers.[26] Among growing competition in retailing consumer products, innovative point of sales promotions offered by supermarkets are aimed at boosting sales and augmenting the store brand value. Purchase acceleration and product trial are found to be the two most influential variables of retail point of sales promotions. Analysis of five essential qualities of customer value judgment in terms of *interest, subjectivity, exclusivity, thoughtfulness, and internality,* need to be carried out to make the firm customer-centric and its strategies touching bottom of the pyramid.[27] Dynamic complexity in business may arise in oligopolistic market systems with high risk in investment, brand development, and generative customer loyalty. It may be observed in a beer distribution that exhibits the switching behavior of consumers when distribution of product of a company is weak in the market. In many cases companies are not able to carry out controlled experiments on implementing business strategies due to cost-related and ethical reasons. Hence, dynamic complexity not only slows the learning loop but also reduces the learning gained on each cycle. Developing right business strategies in a right market situation is a growing challenge among the systems thinkers and business strategists. Delays in developing appropriate strategies create instability in market dynamic systems. Adding time delays to risk and negative feedback loops increases the tendency for the system to be non-sustainable.

Social Entrepreneurship

Social enterprises are community-conscious organizations evolved within the social framework, which address co-creation of solutions to a predetermined social need or a problem. Among many social problems in

[26] Rajagopal. (2008). Outsourcing salespeople in building arousal towards retail buying. *Journal of Database Marketing and Customer Strategy Management, 15*(2), 106–118.

[27] Dobson, J. (2007). Aesthetics as a foundation for business activity. *Journal of Business Ethics, 72*(1), 41–46.

the urban-rural environment, sustainable housing, green energy, natural resources management, transportation and logistics, and poverty alleviation are some primary areas for social enterprises to work with. Social enterprises are evolved with stakeholders to serve the urban and rural demographics, which also serve the underprivileged consumers in a weak regulatory framework. In emerging markets, customers and members of social enterprises at the bottom of the pyramid are targeted for the basic benefits and services such as healthcare, education, and farm and non-farm activities. Social entrepreneurs use innovative business models to build solutions with the available resources and offer basic services to the stakeholders in a sustainable way. The principal objective of social enterprises is to create social impact and generate economic and social values in a sustainable manner.[28] Social entrepreneurship is emerging as a principal move towards sustainable development through volunteerism and civic commitment. The critical difference between social and traditional entrepreneurship can be seen in delineating the social mission and the market. Social entrepreneurs emphasize ways to produce progressive social business or public properties.[29] Social entrepreneurship has high-value proposition and intended to drive societal transformations. Such entrepreneurs address social issues and problems and empower transformational progress throughout the system. The dominant factor for the rise of social entrepreneurship is the societal pressure on green recovery and sustainability governance.[30]

The entrepreneurial marketing approach involves cost-effective activities by avoiding formal market research or involving mass promotions strategies to promote business. However, entrepreneurs of small and medium business segments significantly depend on their personal networks to collect information about consumers and the market. These entrepreneurs heavily use consumer psychodynamics and interpersonal communication such as word of mouth to promote their products and

[28] Mair, J., Martí, I., & Ganly, K. (2007). Institutional voids as spaces of opportunity. *European Business Forum, 31*(1), 34–39.

[29] Heeks, R., Foster, C., & Nugroho, Y. (2014). New models of inclusive innovation for development. *Innovation and Development, 4*(2), 175–185.

[30] Gandhi, T., & Raina, R. (2018). Social entrepreneurship: the need, relevance, facets, and constraints. *Journal of Global Entrepreneurship Research, 8*, Art. 9, 1–13 https://doi.org/10.1186/s40497-018-0094-6.

services.[31] The social facet of entrepreneurship education has closer proximity to innovation diffusion and business modeling than the formal teaching pedagogy or regulatory education to entrepreneurs. Though regulatory and social environment resources are external to entrepreneurship education, they can be purposely integrated and aligned with the entrepreneurial touchpoints to expand and enhance customers' journeys, customer experience, and marketability of their products or services in the emerging markets.[32] Traditional approaches to social enterprise strategy of both start-up enterprises and large companies assume that the social behavior and values are relatively stable and predictable. However, new technologies and greater transparency have combined to achieve the social business goals on sustainability. Such a shift in the business environment has generated more risk and vulnerability among social enterprises in engaging with new innovative projects. Social enterprises that thrive to follow the integrated innovation strategies, as discussed above, can alter the consumer behavior quickly and manage the market demand. These enterprises experiment rapidly and frequently with products and services as well as business models, processes, and strategies, to achieve a sustainable market for innovative products.

Innovation entrepreneurship is a convergence of start-up enterprises and the sponsoring companies, which moves from the stage of initiation to the systematic project management to commercialization, and finally developing sustainable innovation through incremental innovations. Companies need to invest substantial resources towards consumer education in order to create consumer demand. Besides, they also must carry out product demonstrations such as 'do-it-yourself' and adaptive customization by allowing consumers to use the new products for a reasonable period and perceive value for money associated with the products. However, the opportunities for open innovation, incremental innovation, and enhancement of the use value of innovative products over the stages of product life cycle finally take the innovation business projects to the initiation stage of the next-generation innovative products. Incubation of innovations has emerged as a new model of start-up facilitation

[31] Copley, P. (2013). The need to deliver higher-order skills in the context of marketing in SMEs. *Industry and Higher Education*, 27 (6), 465-476.

[32] Homburg, C., Jozić, D., & Kuehnl, C. (2017). Customer experience management: Toward implementing an evolving marketing concept. *Journal of the Academy of Marketing Science, 45*(3), 377–401.

in most developing economies. Venture capitalists review the incubators and assess the projected growth and profitability in businesses to invest. They review the incubators to diversify risky investment portfolios, while the prospective entrepreneurs approach the incubators to review the economically viable and technologically feasible support for start-up projects. Entrepreneurial incubators face both challenges and opportunities to grow into competitive enterprises considering the embedded investment and entrepreneurial risks. Broadly, there are five incubator archetypes such as the university incubator, the independent commercial incubator, the regional business incubator, the company-internal incubator, and the virtual incubator.[33] An innovation breakthrough in firms can deliver a strong advantage to the overall posture of the company in the marketplace and drive a major shift in industry leadership. However, not all companies show the ability to foster management innovation due to lack of generating unique ideas. A management innovation creates long-lasting advantage if it is based on a novel principle that challenges the traditional wisdom, is systemic in processes and methods, and is supported by a program of the company to carry out innovation.[34]

Innovation in small and micro enterprises are explored at all levels in the marketplace by generating consumer involvement in the projects of new product or services development. In view of the fast-growing market competition, more and more companies are recognizing innovation as a business opportunity. Such a shift in thinking in many companies and industries, where learning-organization principles are being applied to create sustainable business models, has evidenced change in organizational culture and improvement in the core competencies. Small firms differ in assessing the cost, benefits, and risks (CBR) effects during the manufacturing to marketing process as compared to large partnering firms engaged in innovation across destinations. However, strategic alliances between small and large companies towards innovation sharing, and coopetition in building marketing strategies can provide these firms an appropriate CBR measures. In this process, small and

[33] Carayannis, E. G., & von Zedtwitz, M. (2005). Architecting gloCal (global–local), real-virtual incubator networks (G-RVINs) as catalysts and accelerators of entrepreneurship in transitioning and developing economies: Lessons learned and best practices from current development and business incubation practices. *Technovation, 25*(2), 95–110.

[34] Hamel, G. (2006). Why, what, and how of management innovation, *Harvard Business Review, 84*(2), 72–84.

large firms evaluate benefits and risks associated in developing strategic alliances for acquisition and commercialization of innovations of small firms. It has been observed in previous research studies that small firms are less reluctant on alliance project than large firms, especially if the cooperation for managing competition (coopetition) allows them to reduce their costs and optimize long-term benefits. The innovation alliances between small and large companies help in developing design-to-market and time-to-market strategies. Small innovation-led firms grow as learning organizations. They become inspirational, energetic places to work, where even relationships with customers and suppliers improve. However, a more integrated view will enable companies to innovate for long-term profitability and sustainability. There are three core competencies that learning organizations must master to profit from sustainability: encourage systemic thinking; convene strategic market players and customers towards changing conventional thinking; and take the lead in reshaping economic, political, and societal forces that baffle change.[35]

[35] Rajagopal. (2020). *Sustainable businesses in developing economies—Socio-economic and governance perspectives*. New York: Palgrave Macmillan.

CHAPTER 9

Social Innovation and Technology: The Road Ahead

In the dynamic social and industrial blend, research is oriented towards exploring new socio-economic and technology-driven challenges to optimize the triadic leverage among social development, role of industry, and public policies. Cutting-edge technologies significantly affect social and industrial development in transitional economies. The prominent technology edges that drive challenge-based research include artificial intelligence, augmented reality, virtual reality, wearable technology, robotics, and big data analytics.[1] The convergence of challenge-based research with learning continuum and innovation has emerged as the new trend of business modeling by integrating the concepts of knowing, doing, and being. Interactions in the global society have become an increasing requirement for the researchers to use creative thinking skills to meet the social, ecological, and industrial challenges. There is a positive relationship between development perspectives and challenge-based research, which leads to the economy-wide impacts of different types of research and development, and educational investments portfolios. Previous studies

[1] Ameen, N., Hosany, S., & Tarhini, A. (2021). Consumer interaction with cutting-edge technologies: Implications for future research. *Computers in Human Behavior*, 120 (*in press*). https://doi.org/10.1016/j.chb.2021.106761.

A. Molina and Rajagopal, *Challenge-Based Learning, Research, and Innovation*, Palgrave Studies of Entrepreneurship and Social Challenges in Developing Economies,
https://doi.org/10.1007/978-3-031-29156-2_9

have revealed that there is complementarity between research, knowledge, and human capital formation that drives balanced growth among industries.[2] The growing environmental concerns, public policies, and scientific communities describe the efforts that utilize ecosystem processes to boost challenge-based research in engineering and technology to address societal challenges. The challenged-based research outputs have significantly contributed to the development of farm- and non-farm sector economy.[3] Contributing research for the development of low-cost technology to explore nature-based solutions through native enterprises can alleviate societal challenges. Research on meeting societal challenges concerns effectiveness, co-design approaches, and implementation of research output to drive social, economic, and business growth.[4] To ensure the research-based learnings in improving the sustainable industrial growth to leverage social and economic values in the modern society, the challenge-based research has become relevant across many areas of industrial growth with the intrinsic and extrinsic factor affecting knowledge repositories.

Social Entrepreneurship and Business Modeling

Business modeling trends have been rapidly changing from supply-led (manufacture oriented) to demand-driven (innovation-based) to challenge-based research (solution driven) since the mid-twentieth century. Such change has been a global phenomenon, which has seeded the concept of challenge-based research, learning, and innovation through agile knowledge modeling. Agility in managing social and technology-based challenges is required to conduct challenge-based research, implement its outcomes, and measure the industry responsiveness in innovation

[2] Yeo, Y., & Lee, J. D. (2020). Revitalizing the race between technology and education: Investigating the growth strategy for the knowledge-based economy based on a CGE analysis. *Technology in Society*, 62 (*in press*).
https://doi.org/10.1016/j.techsoc.2020.101295

[3] Gilvear, D. J., Spray, C. J., & Casas-Mulet, R. (2013). River rehabilitation for the delivery of multiple ecosystem services at the river network scale. *Journal of Environmental Management*, 126, 30–43.

[4] Albert, C., Schröter, B., Haase, D., Brillinger, M., Henze, J., Herrmann, S., Gottwald, S., Guerrero, P., Nicolas, C., & Matzdorf, B. (2019). Addressing societal challenges through nature-based solutions: How can landscape planning and governance research contribute? *Landscape and Urban Planning*, *182*, 12–21.

and technology derived from the research.[5] This necessity of agility can be achieved through a knowledge-based system. Companies face various organizational and operational challenges while transforming the research challenges and learning the market-induced innovations. Among many complexities, identifying and driving the business units to adapt to the challenge—based research by engineering multidimensional learning and developing innovations compatible with a sustainable social and economic growth,[6] a multidimensional knowledge framework helps in implementing the design-to-society innovation and technologies and supports ubiquitous learning (u-learning). Ubiquitous learning can be defined as an everyday learning environment supported by mobile and embedded technologies, digital platforms, and wireless networks.[7] The challenge-based research is an outgrowth of multidimensional learning on societal and environmental problems with focus on ontological reasoning that helps in u-learning with the society and industry. The ontology-based context management drives innovation and technology as a situation-aware system and orients the challenge-based research to serve as an applied engine for societal and industrial development. Exploring societal and industrial challenges is, therefore, a semantic approach to the varied situations within adaptive and ubiquitous learning systems.[8] In view of the above fundamental concerns, the role of challenge-based research is being promoted in socially responsible business, engineering, and technology schools. Such research learning has been adopted by many companies and has received increased attention in academic research. There are various dimensions of challenge-based research that affect the

[5] Llamas, V., Coudert, T., Geneste, L., Romero-Bejarano, J. C., de Valroger, A. (2016). Proposition of an agile knowledge-based process model. *IFAC-Papers On-Line*, *49*(12), 1092–1097.

[6] Chen, R., Ravichandar, R., and Proctor, D. (2016). Managing the transition to the new agile business and product development model: Lessons from Cisco Systems. *Business Horizons*, *59*(6), 635–644.

[7] Ogata, H., Matsuka, Y., El-Bishouty, M. M., & Yano, Y. (2009). LORAMS: Linking physical objects and videos for capturing and sharing learning experiences towards ubiquitous learning. *International Journal of Mobile Learning and Organisation*, *3*(4), 337–350.

[8] Souabni, R., Saâdi, I. B. & Ghezala, H.B. (2018). Context weighting for ubiquitous learning situation description: Approach based on combination of weighted experts' opinions. *International Journal of Information Technology and Decision Making*, *17*, 247–309.

performance of society in general. As people are connected to both societal and industrial advancements, digital technologies have increasingly encouraged the challenge-based research in agriculture, non-farm entrepreneurship, housing, energy, and sustainability.[9]

Entrepreneurship and regional development essentially converge with effective resource planning to highlight ambidextrous growth at micro— and macroeconomic levels. Planning for entrepreneurial resources encompasses areas from finance to human resources and extends further from knowledge management to transfer of technology. The social capital and government financial programs in the destination countries promote, deliver, and manage entrepreneurial resources as regional development measures. Besides allocating appropriate financial, technological, and human resources, effective regional planning requires accurate and spatially explicit information within the framework of changing natural resources. Natural resources have high pressure of land use patterns in urban and rural areas apart from the significance of diverse disciplines including hydrology, soil science, geology, biology, biogeochemistry, geography, and engineering ergonomics.

Leading companies today have adapted to research-driven business model, which is an outgrowth of crowdsourcing and understanding customer perceptions and emotions. Working with such business models encourages social and consumer research to explore latent problems and connect them to the industrial, social, or consumer products. Analyzing social emotions and research outcomes on product experiences contributes to the co-creation of innovation. The challenge-based research and learning guide companies to develop frugal innovations and technology, which leads to superior value propositions within society and industry.[10] Low-cost and ecological housing using the recycled polyethylene bottles, intelligent green house to support organic cultivation, and renewable energy-based household products including water heating systems, domestic and street lighting, and consumer energy products are some examples to be cited in this context. Energy intensity and green

[9] Von Haaren, C. & Albert, C. (2011). Integrating ecosystem services and environmental planning: Limitations and synergies. International journal of biodiversity science, *Ecosystem Services & Management*, *7*(3), 150–167.

[10] Verhagen, W. J. C., Bermell-Garcia, P., van Dijk, R. E. C., & Curran, R. (2012). A critical review of knowledge-based engineering: An identification of research challenges. *Advanced Engineering Informatics*, *26*(1), 5–15.

innovation techniques share a complicated political, economic, social, technological, environmental, and legal relationship. Consequently, the adaptation of green technologies needs to be pushed in society through the organized efforts involving public–private-political-partnership (4Ps) matrix. Green energy consumption has high potential in the domestic and sectoral production including agricultural and rural industries, and small and large industries. The inner ecosystem that affects the business modeling of renewable energy products focuses on exploring new opportunities for expanding to new markets by investing in high-return green energy production projects.[11] The integration of challenge-based research and learning framework that allows flexibility and customization leads to the following effects[12]:

- Developing new knowledge,
- Offering feasible technological solutions,
- Generating value for enterprise and society,
- Technology Transfer to micro, small, and medium enterprises, and
- Building technology-based enterprises.

With the advancement of technology-led business models, manufacturing today is experiencing a transition from conventional paradigm to research-based business models with a view to fostering new opportunities and issues in the control engineering field. Emerging new approaches are enabled by Industrial Internet of Things (IoT) and Cyber Physical Systems (CPS) technologies and methods.[13] Challenge-based research addresses the clear manifestation of problems in society and helps in developing common goals among diverse stakeholders. Such research largely transcends the specific social challenges and transfers knowledge and technology in society. Accordingly, challenge-based research can create social

[11] Rajagopal, (2020). *Sustainable businesses in developing economies—Socio-economic and governance perspectives*. New York: Palgrave Macmillan.

[12] Ponce, P., Mendez, E., & Molina, A. (2021). Teaching fuzzy controllers through a V-model based methodology,

Computers & Electrical Engineering. 94, (*in press*) https://doi.org/10.1016/j.compeleceng.2021.107267

[13] Panetto, H., Gutiérrez, A. M., Weichhart, P. D. G., & Macchi, M. (2021). Control issues in the cyber-physical manufacturing enterprise. *Annual Reviews in Control*, *51*, 344–345.

value and leverage industrial needs as well by finding solutions though actionable research, analyzing research inputs, and acting on results. Such research is central to the systematic exploration on a selected social indicator and focus on exploring applied solutions to create consistent social values.·[14]

Society today is largely founded on the business environment, which integrates industrial values with societal values from developed to emerging market segments. Changes in the international business governance not only affect the societal and economic development of the region, but also develop new mindsets and behaviors among emerging entrepreneurs, collaborators, and stakeholders at the grassroots level. Many start-up industries are aiming to grow along with large industries as their ancillary suppliers to meet the Industry 4.0 challenges. Local enterprises, along with large industries, play a significant role in social and economic development of the region by providing backward linkages. However, due to resource limitations and lack of adaptation to appropriate technology, they often contribute marginally to the growth of local developmental economics. The emphasis on co-creation of innovation and managing innovation business projects in partnership with the local companies is gradually generating technological breakthroughs, allowing emerging companies to reduce the time to bring innovative products and services to market. The entrepreneurial revolution has driven the challenge towards unifying human elements and digitization for achieving the new-generation business growth and economic development in the region. Local enterprises contribute to the new trends in manufacturing, finance, management, marketing, and supply chain management, which induces drastic drift in business practices across the global and local markets. Small innovation-led firms grow as learning organizations. They become inspirational, energetic places to work, where even relationships with customers and suppliers improve. However, a more integrated view can enable companies to innovate for long-term profitability and sustainability.

The challenge-based research has been adopted by many customer-centric companies like LEGO using collective intelligence generated

[14] Ponce, P., Mendez, E., & Molina, A. (2021). Teaching fuzzy controllers through a V-model based methodology,

Computers & Electrical Engineering. 94, (*in press*) https://doi.org/10.1016/j.compeleceng.2021.107267

by the crowd. The company has grown over the philosophy of low-cost alternative to creative wooden building blocks to technology-driven mechanical building-blocks' giant. The growth of the company relied on customer input and analysis of their personality and behavior in transforming its business. The company has built effective systems to engage and use the crowd contents to review and update its product portfolios constantly.[15] The crowd's value to the firm is represented as the concept of crowd capital, which embeds customer perceptions and emotions. The crowd capital has been defined as organizational resources acquired through crowdsourcing in the form of collective intelligence. Similarly, at Netflix, executives are committed to share information with people who are engaged in creative work and ensure that the information flows to everyone who needs it. Such strategy supports business agility and customer-centric management processes that need to be designed and implemented in need-based planning.[16] Most companies have experimented radical shifts in business strategies over the conventional wisdom to gain sustainable competitive advantage. Some of these strategies are people-centric and crowd-based, which have encouraged customer engagement in today's heterogeneous and hypercompetitive global business environment. The strategic agility, therefore, is a meta-capability of companies that enables them to create customer- and stakeholder values and deploy dynamic competitive strategies in a balance over time.[17]

Challenge-based research is a systematic journey to explore solutions for the social and industrial problems. The futuristic outlook of the industry in the context of society and sustainability may be towards achieving net-zero carbon economy in a net-zero industry with net-zero products, services, processes, and production systems. To achieve these goals, the challenges at the foreground include obtaining solutions to green energy, water conservation, zero-emission, waste reduction to zero level, and managing cradle-to-cradle approach in product designing and resource utilization. The cradle-to-cradle philosophy addresses positive

[15] Robertson, D., & Hjuler, P. (2009). Innovating a Turnaround at LEGO. *Harvard Business Review, 87*(9), 20–21.

[16] Worley, C. G., Williams, T., &Lawler, E. (2016). Creating management processes built for change. *MIT Sloan Management Review, 58*(1), 77–82.

[17] Fourne, S. P. L., Jansen, J. J. P., & Mom T. J. M. (2014). Strategic agility in MNEs: Managing tensions to capture opportunities across emerging and established markets. *California Management Review, 56*(3), 13–38.

ecological impacts in the built environment.[18] Companies of the twentieth century have long used teams to solve problems, take decisions, and develop business models. Market research organizations have heavily focused on investigating groups to explore customer needs and conducted consumer surveys to understand the market, while managers have kept themselves busy in attending business meetings to listen to shareholders in the past. But the words that need more comprehension such as *solve*, *explore*, *understand*, and *listen* have now taken on a whole new meaning through the technology platforms to acquire and analyze collective (crowdsourced) opinions on a larger scale. Indeed, the increasing use of information markets, free encyclopedias, crowdsourcing tools, the *wisdom of crowd* concepts, social networks, collaborative software, and other web-based tools push a paradigm shift for companies in making customer-centric decisions.[19] Crowdsourcing has emerged as a creative tool for companies today to expand their outreach to customers, map their perceptions, and understand behavioral implications of customers in business. Thus, this tool has led to delivering collective intelligence, which helps the companies in building the business design cube by integrating the concepts of design-to-market, design-to-society, and design-to-value in business modeling process.[20] Co-creation allows companies to continually tap the skills and insights of stakeholders and develop new ways of building value chain. Crowdsourcing platforms (physical and digital forums) are largely interactive for exploring new experiences and connections. The crowd-based collective intelligence process grows organically over time in the organization as a system.[21]

Entrepreneurs tend to diversify the product line periodically to increase market competitiveness. Overtime entrepreneurs develop industry networks to develop strategic alliances. Entrepreneurs draw up business plans for new ventures to make marketing, pricing, financial, and other projections. More often, their estimates bear little relationship to

[18] Ankrah, N. A., Manu, E., & Booth,C. (2015). Cradle to cradle implementation in business sites and the perspectives of tenant stakeholders. *Energy Procedia*, *83*, 31–40.

[19] Bonabeau, E. (2008). Decisions 2.0: The power of collective intelligence. *MIT Sloan Management Review*, *50*(2), 45–52.

[20] Rajagopal, (2021). *The business design cube: Converging markets, society, and customer values to grow competitive in business*. New York: Business Expert Press.

[21] Gouillart, F., & Billings, D. (2013). Community-powered problem solving. *Harvard Business Review*, *91*(4), 70–77.

reality. Planning for new enterprises differs fundamentally from planning for existing companies, given the inherent instability of start-ups. The major challenges with the start-up enterprises (SUE) in emerging markets are to explore right opportunities, co-create value, and identify suitable marketing strategies for sustainable growth. Understanding the business ecosystem of SUE is essential to analyze the performance of start-ups in reference to marketing metrics. The metrics constitute various performance indicators, which can be explained in a marketing-mix. These indicators help the SUEs in identifying the attributes of consumers and earmarking the potential consumer segments.

Diffusion and Adaption

One of the major concerns with challenge-based research is to effectively manage the transfer of technology to industry and end-users of innovation. Transferring the product and processes technology in accordance with the market demand and inculcating user experiences are complex. Knowledge transfer on innovation and technology explored through the challenge-based research is largely based on the exchange of individuals' experiences and work-related knowledge of the research team.[22] Therefore, product designing and commercialization of innovative products are closely associated with the co-creation process through customer/user engagement. Such co-created and coevolved technologies are easy to transfer through digital platforms and social applications. Most research studies rely on the seminal socialization, externalization, combination, and internalization (SECI) model of Nonaka and Takeuchi[23] to implement knowledge co-creation process through users, consumers, and stakeholders. Co-developed innovative projects are important for the high-tech industries, where research-based and core knowledge is often integrated with applied skills and performances at the macro level. Sharing specific knowledge is derived from the collective intelligence, and collaborative research with partnered companies lead to an accelerated transfer of

[22] Ibidunni, A. S., Kolawole, A. I., Olokundun, M. A., & Ogbari, M. E. (2020). Knowledge transfer and innovation performance of small and medium enterprises (SMEs): An informal economy analysis. *Heliyon*, *6*(8), (in press). https://doi.org/10.1016/j.heliyon.2020.e04740

[23] Nonaka, I. & Takeuchi, H. (1995). *The Knowledge-creating company*. Oxford, UK: Oxford University Press.

technology process in diffusing innovations among target users, industry, and market.[24]

Emerging companies grow with the fundamental resources, as its people, teams, technologies, social assets, brands, suppliers, employees, and business leaders help in deciding the growth strategies in competitive markets. As the firms become tensile against the business uncertainties and predicable risks, their abilities stem out of collective intelligence[25] and customer engagement in categorical business processes of product development, manufacturing, marketing, advertising, and customer communication. In the largest companies, customer values are largely determined by shared customer perceptions, experience, and potential business ideas. The analysis of collective intelligence not only opens a new range of business opportunities for companies, but also helps in exploring reverse innovations (evolved in niche or remote destinations) that have the potential for commercialization. Commercializing a reverse innovation is a disruptive leap to hit a commercially established product in the target market. Reverse innovations demand to develop organizational insights into how a new product could drive an impact in emerging markets.[26] Customer engagement in the emerging firms today is instrumental to value-based business modeling and exploring customer-centric business opportunities. Consequently, customers, stakeholders, and leaders hold the power to respond to major market shifts and let firms grow with the collective intelligence and necessary social interventions.[27]

Agility and agile transformation are the two facets of business, and both are correlated to business performance. Besides design-driven and technology-oriented marketing strategies, the market competition of the twenty-first century is largely driven by social stimuli, behavioral shifts in consumption, and crowd intervention. Therefore, the cutting-edge of

[24] De Alwis, R. S., & Hartmann, E. (2008). The use of tacit knowledge within innovative companies: knowledge management in innovative enterprises. *Journal of Knowledge Management*, *12*(1), 133–147.

[25] Boder, A. (2006). Collective intelligence: A keystone in knowledge management. *Journal of Knowledge Management*, *10*(1), 81–93.

[26] Rajagopal, (2016), *Innovative business projects: Breaking complexities, building performance (Vol.2)-Financials, new insights, and project sustainability*, New York: Business Expert Press.

[27] Christensen, C. M., & Overdorf, M. (2000). Meeting the challenge of disruptive change. *Harvard Business Review*, *78*(2), 65–76.

marketing strategies across the geo-demographic segments is widely influenced by the individual and group behavior, collective intelligence, and neuro-centric emotions. People (crowd) tend to disseminate persuasive messages, which aim to alter the attitude of consumers and the overall consumption behavior. Besides many operational elements, agility in business is primarily linked to the social and economic postulates of consumer behavior. The change of mind among consumers is induced by self- and social concepts that govern the business strategies, technologies, and end user values to leverage market competition. In addition to customer satisfaction, a majority of business operating models are mainly driven by corporate values by *putting the people first* and agility to adopt the revised norms quickly.[28]

Challenge-based research is used in product innovation and design of equipment. The higher education on engineering and technology has significantly contributed to providing basic and managerial education to stakeholders which helps in exploring right opportunities. While coevolving with academics and stakeholders, firms can identify appropriate technologies, carry out innovations, and prepare for effective technology transfer through training programs on face-to-face and digital platforms. Such integrated efforts leverage the social and industrial consciousness for developing new products in renewable energy, sustainability, and meeting the social challenges like poverty alleviation, housing, and community health. The technological revolution has driven the digital transformation as firms are engaged in co-creating value in industrial markets. Among the many forms of technology development, digital technologies have encouraged artificial intelligence which has the strongest pervasive impact.[29] By mobilizing resources, knowledge, and skills of different players in product-designing process, co-creation leads to the improvement of the effectiveness and quality of public services while lowering

[28] Nath, U. K., Jagadev, A. K., & Pattnaik, P.K. (2021). Agile transformation for better business values using orchestration model. *Materials Today: Proceedings* (in press). https://doi.org/10.1016/j.matpr.2021.02.177

[29] Leone, D., Schiavone, F., Appio, F. P., & Chiao, B. (2021). How does artificial intelligence enable and enhance value co-creation in industrial markets? An exploratory case study in the healthcare ecosystem. *Journal of Business Research, 129*, 849–859.

costs and ensures higher satisfaction in the socio-economic development and fulfillment of their social needs.[30]

Most manufacturing companies design for the recovery value in their products at the outset. For example, synthetic fiber manufacturing companies recycle nylon (Polyamide) fiber from polyester waste. A large part of the recycled nylon is manufactured from old fishing nets. This is a sustainable solution to divert garbage from the ocean to manufacture nylon carpets and tiles. In the recent trend, the sustainable industries include biosphere-based industries.[31] The biosphere accounts for a global ecosystem composed of living organisms (biota) and nonliving (abiotic) factors from which they derive energy and nutrients. Mostly sustainable manufacturing starts with a small group of key organizations, which brings in project management expertise, links self-interest to shared interest, encourages productive competition, and creates quick wins. Systematically developed sustainable technology and development projects build and maintain trust among the consumers, stakeholders, and society.[32]

Evaluating human behavioral traits is getting complex today. Society, people, leaders of both social and business forums, and political personalities constitute the external ecosystem of the consumers, which influences personality and behavioral traits. The social phenotype (William's Syndrome) is related to the personality, social attention, and hypersociability of individuals, and drives crowd-led influences, dynamic shifts, perceptual inconsistency, and social autism.[33] The social phenotype behavior of consumers triggers incongruency among corporate assumptions and predictions affecting the consumer personality. Such mismatch leads to the failure of predetermined customer-centric strategies. The social phenotype can be explained as the functional behavior of people,

[30] Osborne, S.P., Radnor, Z., & Strokosch, K. (2016). Co-production and the co-creation of value in public services: A suitable case for treatment? *Public Management Review*, *18*(5), 639–653.

[31] Rajagopa,l (2020). *Sustainable businesses in developing economies—Socio-economic and governance perspectives*. New York: Palgrave Macmillan.

[32] Nidumolu, R., Ellison, J., Whalen, J., & Billman, E. (2014). The collaboration imperative, *Harvard Business Review*, *92*(4), 76–84.

[33] Thurman, A. J. & Fisher, M. H. (2015). , In Hodapp, R. M. & Fidler, D. J. (Eds), *The Williams syndrome social phenotype: Disentangling the contributions of social interest and social difficulties* International Review of Research in Developmental Disabilities, Amsterdam: Academic Press, 191–227.

which integrates with the neurological functions and alters neurobehavioral traits of people. Consequently, consumers tend to build their consumption behavior on sensitive social moves and neuro-physiologically integrated endpoints. Social phenotypes are sensitive to consumption behavior, choices, and loyalty, which influences social intuitive behavior. Firms need to analyze such behavior through psychometric tools to understand consumer perceptions and develop customer-centric strategies.[34]

Entrepreneurship and hybrid firms have evolved over the growing competitive dynamics in the regional and global markets since the mid-twentieth century. Entrepreneurial firms in emerging markets are engaged in diversified business projects to drive high performance, collaborate with large firms, and gain competitive advantage in the market. Entrepreneurship over the years has developed to manage multiple business projects growing from start-up enterprises to large companies. Micro enterprises are growing rapidly as new growth models and local markets are encouraging smart enterprises. Enterprise modeling in reference to innovation and technology constitutes the core focus of enterprise management today, irrespective of its organizational size, investment, and revenue. The new trends in enterprise modeling constitute high-cost implications in digitization, computing systems, and risk management.

Challenge-Based Innovation

Incubation of innovations has emerged as a new model of start-up facilitation in most developing economies. Venture capitalists review the incubators and assess the projected growth and profitability in businesses to invest. The venture capitalists review the incubators to diversify risky investment portfolios, while the prospective entrepreneurs approach the incubators to review the economically viable and technologically feasible support for start-up projects. Entrepreneurial incubators face both challenges and the opportunities to grow competitive enterprises considering the embedded investment and entrepreneurial risks. Innovations of local origin are attracted to the global companies as they plan to bring back the local innovation, which is largely frugal in nature, to the mass market. Therefore, the relational embeddedness of large companies with the

[34] Tylka, T. L. (2006). Development and psychometric evaluation of a measure of intuitive eating. *Journal of Consumer Psychology*, *53*, 226–240.

external MSMEs appears to be essential for the evolution of local innovations to the global scale. Turning local innovations into global brands can be identified as innovativeness evoked by the large companies or their subsidiaries at the bottom of the pyramid. However, in this process, transfer of reverse knowledge in the functional areas is a critical perspective.[35] Contemporary research has revealed that information collection techniques with reference to business analytics towards backward and forward linking elements of a business influence the performance of a company. Progressive entrepreneurs reveal positive impact of web-based competitive intelligence, which is embedded in the business models to gain higher business performance within industry.[36]

Most enterprises rely on social intelligence and business analytics for developing appropriate strategies for risk management and towards building a base for decision support. A large numbers of customer-generated product reviews often contain information about competitors and have become a new source of mining competitive intelligence. Firms engaged in developing social and sustainable technologies learn the relative weaknesses and strengths of their own products, and design competitive products and campaigns.[37] Comparison of stakeholder opinions is precious information sources for the enterprises to identify the relative strengths and weaknesses of their products and services. The enterprise risk and threats of competitors need to be analyzed by the small and medium enterprises to develop design-to-market business strategies for their products and services. Mining such comparative opinions needs qualitative analysis due to the large amount of customer reviews and their informal style of opinion documentation. Most firms in the global marketplace tend to adopt a more focused business strategy and focus on realizing how the effect of interplay between premium, and low-cost rivals on achieving market share and profit can be minimized. Companies today must learn how to take on low-cost competitors in

[35] Isaac, V. R., Borini, F. M., Raziq, M. M., & Benito, G. R. G. (2019). From local to global innovation: The role of subsidiaries' external relational embeddedness in an emerging market. *International Business Review*, *28*(4), 638–646.

[36] Markovich, A., Efrat, K., Raban, D. R. 6 Souchon, A. L. (2019). Competitive intelligence embeddedness: Drivers and performance consequences. *European Management Journal*, *37*(6), 708–718.

[37] Xu, K., Liao, S. S., Li, J., & Song, Y. (2011). Mining comparative opinions from customer reviews for Competitive Intelligence. *Decision Support Systems*, *50*(4), 743–754.

the large consumer segments, develop inimitable market tools, develop organizational leadership, and build sustainable stakeholders.[38]

Broadly, the shift from conventional- to new-generation socio-technological structure and development modeling can be delineated as the helix effect in business. The core of the helix lies in disaggregating the traditional management hierarchy into two separate, parallel lines of accountability—equal in power and authority, but philosophically holding a new perspective. Successfully adopting the helix requires a transformational leadership, customer-centric business philosophy, and co-designing business models. The convergence of the shifts in management of mind-sets and a talent infrastructure lays the foundation of helix, which emerges out of entrepreneurship education and bottom-up business economy that many businesses do not currently possess. The helix concept has been managed discreetly in some social technology enterprises, which serve as feeder companies to the large industries. It is often challenging for small companies to adapt to a structural business model over the traditional family-based organizational structure. Relatively larger companies also tend to replace complex matrix structures, and redesign organizations and their decision-making processes. The helix effect helps the enterprises move ahead quickly to exploit new market opportunities. In the helix process, transformative leadership drives value creation and augments objectives, discusses business priorities, and improves performance against the goals and targets.[39] The clear distinction of enterprise management and leadership helps in constructing the helix with agile structures. However, organizational and business transformations in small companies are more challenging as compared to the large corporations due to *command and culture* disintegration. Moreover, the complex nature of the transformational necessitates in an organization often increases its overhead costs and administration process.

Most companies in the emerging markets are transforming their global value chains and planning to coevolve domestic enterprises with advanced economy multinational enterprises (AMNE) as a helix effect. Strategies like enhancing the capability and competence; investment in internal research and development; and globalization through strategic alliances;

[38] Ryans, A. (2010), The high stakes of low-cost competition, *IESE-Insight Magazine*, 4, 21–28.

[39] Smet,A. D., Kleinman, S.,& Weerda, K. (2019). *The helix organization*, New York: McKinsey & Co.

and mergers and acquisitions push local enterprises towards helix effect. These enterprises not only succeed in local markets over time but can also build global value chains. The helix effect is visible to the companies as vertical partnerships with large firms while horizontal collaborations with local network are jointly orchestrated.[40] Convergence of technology, entrepreneurship education, and public policies including the skill development programs and financial incentive to promote small entrepreneurs are the active elements in the entrepreneurial helix process. Exploring new opportunities; right decision-making in business; and developing a design-to-market strategy by building alliances with large companies have been the major focus of double helix approach of the small enterprises. Social technology firms seek the patronage of large companies to lower the cost-risk ratio and augment profit. The success of double helix approach needs a transformational leadership at both business organizations to help in redesigning organization, creating value chain, developing global standards, investing in business process improvement, and strengthening the backward and forward business linkages. The coevolution of small and big companies enhances investment in innovation, technology, and research and development. Such mergers or acquisitions in the double helix approach help companies strengthen their marketing strategies by developing customer-centric branding and promotion strategies. The convergence of technology, entrepreneurship education, and public policies on entrepreneurship development programs promote hybridization, business performance, and corporate citizenship behavior ambidextrously between small and large enterprises.[41]

The technology transformation process in social enterprises appears to be a difficult proposition due to the limitation of resources and lack of leadership drive. As this process continues, business leaders, along with the public policy implementers, begin to approach global standards of manufacturing, marketing, and services. However, in any industry, there are a few laggards, who remain moored in the old ways, although most domestic firms tend to make some progress and exhibit new business

[40] Saranga, H., Schotter, A. P. J., &Mudambi, R. (2019). The double helix effect: Catch-up and local-foreign co-evolution in the Indian and Chinese automotive industries. *International Business Review*, *28*(5), 1–18.

[41] Rajagopal & Ramesh, B. (2020). *Entrepreneurship and regional development: Analyzing growth models in emerging markets*. New York: Palgrave Macmillan.

opportunities.[42] These firms develop sophisticated backward and forward networks using technology-led supply and retailing operations. Transformation of business model of small companies include technology-driven customer services with focus on reducing the tangible and intangible cost to customer, provide convenience, lower conflicts, and disseminate effective communications (4Cs). The helix effect is an integration of business operations of small and large firms encompassing strategic alliances and processes improvements and adapting to customer-centric management with a view to explore new markets and achieve competitiveness in existing marketing.[43] The forward helix concept indicates that the local companies with standardization aim to develop alliances with external companies to reach global markets. The reverse helix interprets the association of international companies with local firms to explore reverse innovations at a global scale. The support of public policies and economic incentives to promote local firms in the emerging markets like China, India, and Brazil have upgraded their process technologies and manufacturing capabilities for developing alliances with large companies. The small enterprises adopt the latest production and management technique to improve their business performance.

The technology space in the triple helix helps entrepreneurs and government institutions to draw relevant players from different organizational sizes, destinations, and various levels of business performance. The purpose of this helix is to formulate new strategies and ideas to achieve out-of-the-niche business performance. An innovation space emerges as combined outcome of the triadic factors of triple helix.[44] The triple-helix system focuses on promoting innovation though homegrown (intermediate) technology, entrepreneurship education, and support of public policies. The triadic factors promote frugal innovations among the small enterprises, while this system has been most frequently used as a technological incubator. The triple-helix model and its indicators have been

[42] Kumaraswamy, A., Mudambi, R., Saranga, H., & Tripathy, A. (2012). Catch-up strategies in the Indian auto components industry: Domestic firms' responses to market liberalization. *Journal of International Business Studies*, *43*(4), 368–395.

[43] Jonnalagedda, S. & Saranga, H. (2017). Commonality decisions when designing for multiple markets. *European Journal of Operational Research*, *258*(3), 902–911.

[44] Kim, J. Y. & Lee, M. J. (2016). Living with casinos: The triple-helix approach, innovative solutions, and big data, *Technological Forecasting and Social Change*, *110*(1), 33–41.

used to stimulate social innovations to improve the attributes of corporate citizenship and carry out the need-based corporate social responsibility.[45]

Business Modeling in Economic Turbulence

Doing business in political and economic disruptions has been challenging which has been evident in the business shutdown during the COVID-19 pandemic occurred since early 2020. The challenge-based research focuses on evaluating the production and business alternatives through digitalization and network channels. Businesses have diversified their manufacturing and marketing activities through consortium strategies and social media channels. The paradigm shift in the business model during the turbulent socio-economic situations has focused fragmented markets encouraging customized services to customers, low-cost manufacturing, and connecting business functions (backward and forward linkages) with the local firms. The reverse business modeling during the turbulent economic situations focuses on developing scenario-based damage management strategies to handle alike pandemic-led consequences. Such business models implement the scenario drivers on both economic and social facets of businesses.[46] In the COVID-19 pandemic, business shutdown in across regions have given a new impetus among business to reorient on e-commerce using social networks to stimulate social behavior towards adapting to the alternate ways of business. Firms of all sizes have analyzed the social behavior on social networks to improve e-business accordingly. Social networking has been extensively used not only for promoting products and services through digital advertisement, webinars, and experience sharing on micro-blogs but also in selling products through the social media channels. The mobile applications have also been contributed extensively in propagating the use of online platforms to manage the business-to-consumer and business-to-business activities during the COVID-19 pandemic situation. The social e-commerce customers' purchasing behavior game model integrates

[45] Cajaiba-Santana, G. (2014). Social innovation: moving the field forward. A conceptual framework. *Technology Forecasting and Social Change*, *82*(1), 42–51.

[46] Hajipour, V., Aminian, M., Gharaei, A., & Jalali, S. (2021). A business retrieval model using scenario planning and analytics for life during and after the pandemic crisis. *Healthcare Analytics*, 1, (*in press*).
https://doi.org/10.1016/j.health.2021.100004

different e-commerce social networks, calculates the internal interaction between web and customer exchange, and estimates the buying rate in various social e-commerce networks.[47]

The change in the product designs with value enhancements has also affected the conventional businesses during the economic turbulence as observed using the COVID-19 pandemic. Due to incidental unemployment and diminishing household income, most companies have switch to low-cost production to provide products at the low price to customers. Consequently, the scope of frugal innovation (FI) has gained significant importance during the turbulent trade and economy situations. The use of FI has emerged as a novel way to serve low-income consumers in developing countries and encouraged niche businesses models. The FI-led products significantly support the consumers of lower purchasing power and their distinct buying preferences. Consequently, the use of FIs has become a new frontier for multinational companies.[48] However, many local many enterprises find it difficult to adopt existing technological platforms that best serve their needs, as their needs differ from already established firms in the marketplace. Hence, the need to find and adopt new technological platforms designed to offer strategic services arises for the start-up enterprises in emerging markets.[49]

[47] Lv, J, Wang, T, Wang, H, Yu, J, & Wang, Y. (2020). A SECPG model for purchase behavior analysis in social e-commerce environment. *International Journal of Communication System, 33*,e4149.
https://doi.org/10.1002/dac.4149

[48] Hossain, M. (2021). Frugal innovation and sustainable business models. *Technology in society*, 64, (*in press*). https://doi.org/10.1016/j.techsoc.2020.101508

[49] Ferneley, E. & Bell, F. (2006). Using bricolage to integrate business and information technology innovation in SMEs. *Technovation*, *26*(2), 232–241.

Index

A. Molina and Rajagopal, *Challenge-Based Learning, Research, and Innovation*, Palgrave Studies of Entrepreneurship and Social Challenges in Developing Economies,
https://doi.org/10.1007/978-3-031-29156-2

The manufacturer's authorised representative in the EU is Springer Nature Customer Service Centre GmbH, Europaplatz 3, 69115 Heidelberg, Germany. If you have any concerns regarding our products, please contact ProductSafety@springernature.com

Printed and bound by CPI Group (UK) Ltd, Croydon, CR0 4YY
28/09/2026
02224072-0003